What do the colleagues say?

...I have been working at a primary school for 23 years and have been teaching with these non-verbal techniques for the last four years. I had a very difficult class last year and was close to throwing in the towel. With the help of these tools I was able to work with the class as I imagined it. It is unbelievable how well this approach works!

Lisi R., Elementary school

...I would like to thank you very much for two great seminar days. It was an entertaining, useful, amusing and very informative seminar. I went home on Saturday with a real feeling of elation, because it gave me confirmation for a lot of my teaching techniques. I also experienced many new and proven suggestions. That did me good and motivated me to bring new energy into the classroom.

Brigitte F., Vocational School

...I learned so much. Now I can save my voice and teaching has become much less stressful. The students themselves are the main characters. They are always busy so they don't have time to act up. I love my job and what I learned here contributed significantly to making it even more enjoyable. Thank you so much.

Andreas S., Middle school

...I remember my first encounter with Pearl. The topic 'Nonverbal Communication' interested me, but I was not sure if I wanted to do the entire seminar series. There was the possibility to take a taster afternoon. I signed up for it. Many teachers, principals and even the district school inspector were present that afternoon. A woman came in, who immediately started with a story, sat down on the table, whipped off her shoes and captivated me with her positive expression and winning smile. This carefree attitude, her cheerfulness and her ability to create a good group dynamic were absolutely fascinating.

Before I started writing this letter, I was rereading some of Pearl's books. I am touched by the respect and love with which she describes the students. It warms my heart to read the descriptions of the different behavior and learning types. I am happy to be a teacher and with the help of her books and her knowledge I now have the tools to better understand my students and to work with them more successfully.

Gerhild V., High School

Table of Contents

Table Leg No. 3: Structure! Structure! Structure!

Table Leg No. 4: Setting boundaries - Giving support!

Talk less. Teach more!

Pearl Nitsche

THE SELF-DISCIPLINING CLASSROOM

Win-Win Strategies

Illustrations by

Andrew Wright

1st edition

Illustrations by Andrew Wright

978-3-9504384-3-7 Paperback
978-3-9504384-4-4 Hardcover
978-3-9504384-5-1 E-Book

pearls of learning
PRESS

Florianigasse 55/25
1080 Vienna, Austria

http://www.pearls-of-learning.com / e-mail: pearl.nitsche@chello.at

"he" and "she"

For reasons of better readability I have refrained from using the double-gender form of address – „he and she“. I have tried to distribute the female and male forms equally.

Thank you!

I have done my best to give credit for the ideas I have collected over the last three decades in the appropriate places in this book. Especially my two most important mentors, Dr. Charles Schmid (Suggestopedia) and Michael Grinder (NLP for teachers), have given me a tremendous amount of knowledge and insight. I would like to take this opportunity to express my heartfelt thanks for their support and the wealth of ideas and input they have given me.

I would also like to thank my son and colleague, Derrick Nitsche, for his inspiration in writing this book and also for the many wonderful hours we have spent together in the seminars. Without you, Derrick, it would only be half as much fun!

And a HUGE THANK YOU to all the teachers who participated in the courses and contributed their experiences to this book. I am grateful and also very, very proud of you. You are excellent teachers who, just like me, are looking for ever better ways to reach and teach our youth. You are the carriers of these positive messages that will inspire our children and shape our future.

Introduction

Welcome to "The Self-Disciplining Classroom. Win- Win strategies.", a book in the series: „Talk less. Teach more!" written by an enthusiastic teacher and teacher trainer.

Perhaps you already know me?

Either from the seminars that my son and colleague, Derrick Nitsche, and I hold for the Pedagogical Universities throughout Austria.

"Do what you love and love what you do. and you will never work another day in your life." **Mark Twain**

Or maybe you have been to one of the workshops in the 25 countries where we have held courses on nonverbal classroom management and brain-friendly learning techniques,

Top left: Mae Sot, Thailand
Top right: Mallorca
Bottom left: Novosibirsk, Russia

or perhaps you know us from our book series,
"Talk less. Teach more!":

If we have already met, I am very pleased that you have returned for new input. And if you're here for the first time, welcome!

A quick word about me:
I was born in the U.S.A. and have lived in Vienna, Austria for more than four decades. I am a teacher, teacher trainer, language and communication trainer as well as an international conference speaker. In 1984 I founded the **Pearls of Learning Institute** (formerly SLL Institute), where we specialize in communication techniques and learning with (w)holistic teaching methods such as Superlearning, Suggestopedia, Neurolinguistic Programming (NLP). I have worked with learners of all ages, from kindergarten children to university students and adults. I was a teacher for eleven years at a middle school, high school and commercial academy in Vienna and have trained thousands of teachers in Austria and worldwide over the last 25 years.

I love my work

I look forward to guiding you through the contents of this book with a little theory and a great number of practical examples, tips, techniques, activities and tools that you can use one on one in your classroom tomorrow.

Some of you will be familiar with some of the stories and examples from our books or seminars. They will present the basic concepts for the new readers, who are entering the world of non-verbal classroom management through this book. As we educators know, review is good. I have tried to keep repetition to a minimum, and I would like to take this opportunity to warmly recommend your reading the other books in this series if you want to delve deeper into this topic. The nonverbal techniques presented in our seminars are described in the books in detail. And of course, the more you know about the topic, the better it will work in your classroom.

My approach to writing the books has remained the same: I write down everything I say in the seminars - and much more besides! Writing these books is very liberating for me. Sometimes I have mixed feelings at the end of a seminar: I am happy about the teachers who enthusiastically take in the contents; on the other hand, there is still so much that I would like to include in our courses. The time is always too short. This book series offers the possibility to deal with the topics in more detail.

It is also important to me that you are able to learn from the experiences of teachers who use these techniques daily in their teaching. I am happy about every email you send me. Thank you for your contributions! I have included some of them here. Your successful use of these techniques is wonderful feedback for me and points me in the right direction for further books.

This book also gives me the opportunity to get my message across. I use the word "message" intentionally, because its contents also represent my philosophy of life and teaching: The techniques presented here offer our students the opportunity to learn with joy, and they enable us to teach with joy as well. The approach is humane, efficient and brain-friendly. It results in successful learning and respectful interaction between teacher and student. It saves our nerves and voices and creates a sense of harmony in the classroom. We are educating the citizens of the future and I am convinced that the atmosphere in our classrooms today will determine the world of tomorrow. The responsibility we bear is great - and the contributions we make will change the world.

A buffet with a wide choice of delicacies

The focus of this book is on the process level and dynamics in the classroom, in other words: on the foundation and framework upon which learning takes place. This is not about WHAT you teach, but about HOW you teach it. The contents of this book are suitable for any subject, school level and age group.

It was important to me to offer you a wide range of tips, techniques and tools. Different situations, different classes, different age groups, school levels and in this case different school systems in different parts of the world require approaches tailored to those special needs. But there are also common denominators which tie teachers the world over together.

Most of the examples given here are from teachers in Austrian schools. The terminology and traditions are sometimes different, from those I was accustomed to in the U.S.A. – but the students, the challenges and the joys are the same the world over. It is from our differences that we can learn the most.

For your orientation, children in Austria go to school for 12 years. The first four years are elementary school. Usually, but not always, they have the same teacher for all four years. Then come four years of middle school followed by four years of high school or vocational school. In middle school and high school the subject teachers generally go from one classroom to the next and the pupils stay in the same classroom.

Some techniques will be suitable for your current situation, others are different but will, in any case, give you valuable food for thought. Therefore I would like to invite all of the readers here to a "classroom management buffet". Help yourselves, and fill up your plate with exactly those delicacies and techniques, which you need at this moment. Enjoy them, and use them for more effective and enjoyable lessons! And what about those you don't need? I would like to suggest that you wrap up the buffet leftovers that you do not need at this moment and store them in the freezer. You might need them later, so take good care of them for another day and another situation!

I wish you bon appetit!

We can change the world!

May I tell you a story?

Those of you, who know me, know that I love stories and metaphors. Stories are powerful. With stories we can reach our listeners more easily. In the classroom, they can serve as a vehicle for ideas and suggestions that we want to convey indirectly. With a story, we can overcome resistance. They show us solutions that might otherwise remain hidden from us. They awaken our dreams and make them possible. They are a gift that comes from the heart - and that is exactly why I would like to start with a story now:

The man who changed the world

Once upon a time, there was a man who wanted to change the world.
But within a short time he discovered that the world was much too big to be changed by one single person.

So he decided to change his country.
Unfortunately, dishonest politicians and lobby groups prevented his efforts.

So he decided to change his neighborhood.
But the neighbors just locked their doors and closed their windows.

So he decided to change his family.
But his children rebelled and his wife threatened him with divorce. Things only got worse.

Finally, the man decided to change himself.
And when he did so, everyone around him changed. And so did the world.

We too can change the world. The good thing is that everything you need to do this is already inside you. This book should serve as a guide. It should help you to recognize and use your immense potential of abilities, resources and strengths. Reading this book is a sign of your personal commitment and dedication to our noble profession, one that will determine how the world will look tomorrow. It is my wish and goal that these pages will help you to tap into your inner potential. So that together we can make a contribution to a better world!

In order to achieve this, I would like to give you a few tips in this section on how you can successfully implement the contents of this book.

- Try something new!
- Take action!
- Act consciously!
- Concentrate on solutions rather than problems!
- Remember: The class is your mirror!

Try something new!

Some years ago, when I was still a teacher in a Viennese middle school, I flew to America to visit my family during the Christmas holidays.

One evening my brother said to me: "Guess whom I met on the street today: your former math professor! First he asked me how you were doing in Austria and then he asked if you had already learned which direction to sit on a chair!" He went on to explain to my brother: "You know, every time I have to tell a student in my class: 'Turn around!' I think of your sister."

We laughed a lot about that. I was a real chatterbox in school and was constantly being admonished for chatting with the students behind me, to the right and left of me and sometimes even on the other side of the classroom!

When the holidays were over, I returned to Austria and to secondary school. The very first day at school, I found myself saying to a student, "Turn around!" I was surprised. Things had not changed! I asked myself: "How many centuries have teachers been saying that?" All over the world! Teachers in America say, "Turn around!" in German-speaking countries we say: "Dreh' dich um", in Argentina the teachers say it in Spanish, in Novosibirsk they say it in Russian and so on!

And what good has it done so far?
Apparently none.
Otherwise we wouldn't have to repeat it again and again.

The message of this story is very simple:

If I keep doing the same thing over and over,
I'll get exactly the same results over and over again.
If I want a new result, I must change my behavior!
I must do something different.

Take Action!

That's the most important thing. Don't be satisfied with theory! In order for changes to actually take place, you need to put what you read here into practice and take action.

In my seminars it occasionally happens that some teachers like to listen to the explanations and also to the suggestions - but then they become lost in theory and sometimes ask the question: "Yes, that sounds good. But what happens if it doesn't work? What should I do then?"

My answer is: "First you try it. Act as if you expect it to work. And most of the time it will. But if it doesn't work, send me an email and describe the situation. Then we will consider the next step together."

Very often in life I have postponed decisions for days or weeks because I have been going back and forth in my mind and could not come to a decision. Should I or should I not? Then I started using a very simple technique. I just ask myself, "What's the worst thing that could happen if I actually take this step?" I was amazed. The answer to my question was almost always, "Nothing."

If you don't try it, nothing will change - and you will also miss the chance to see if it works or not!

Therefore: Be courageous and act!

Act consciously!

You are holding this book in your hands because you are looking for new ways, alternatives and solutions that make our classrooms more harmonious places; where learning is fun; where students and teachers treat each other with respect. You sense that this book will bring you closer to those goals. You are right. Hundreds of teachers have already tried it and can confirm that it works. But the best thing is: the techniques presented here are also very easy to implement.

You're probably asking yourself, *"How can it be so simple?"*

Basically, the ideas presented here are nothing new. They are simply good common sense. Many of them you will already be familiar with. You may have used them in your classroom for a long time. On an intuitive level you are doing it right – that is the level of the so-called **unconscious competence**.

The goal is: These unconscious intuitive acts should become conscious to us. This creates **conscious competence** that we can then use systematically and reliably.

What you used to do intuitively, has become a conscious and a reliable tool.

First identify the problem!

School and our students are different today than when many of us started teaching or went to school ourselves. Nowadays, children and young people are exposed to an enormous number of - sometimes very negative – external influences. We are constantly and continuously bombarded by the media with impressions and news. These impressions are often anything but empathetic. Children and adolescents routinely experience brutality, swear words and disrespect on television, in newspapers, on the internet, in the cinema and - occasionally - sadly also at home with their parents and their families. Our existing social values are changing, and the simplest rituals are often missing in our students' lives. The structures that gave us a firm foundation to stand on no longer exist.

By defining the problem, we have taken the first and most important step. Many teachers stop here and take the easy way out. Does this sound familiar? „Parents don't care about their children nowadays. They leave all the work to us; They have no manners. No social skills, etc. The media accuses us and makes it difficult for us to work with parents and children; students behave disrespectfully towards each other and towards us; the school system underpins our efforts, etc."

The list of complaints could go on endlessly.
And the sad thing is that many of these statements are correct.

But if we want to change our everyday life in a positive way, we may not stop there. Complaining alone does not solve the problem. The problems are reality. They exist. If we want to achieve change, we have to recognize and assess this reality and then actively seek solutions to change it.

The topics of self-discipline and self-responsibility will often be dealt with in the following chapters. These are the qualities that our students urgently need to make their lives full and happy. They are also the qualities that create a self-disciplining classroom - the theme of this book – and make such a classroom possible. To achieve these goals, we must start with ourselves!

Think solution-oriented!

I have two citizenships: I am Austrian and American. This enriches my life in many ways - among other things because it gives me different ways of looking at things and varying perspectives on everyday situations.

Shortly after her return from vacation in the United States, an Austrian friend of mine, who is also a psychologist, told me

> *"I have noticed a marked difference between European and American thought patterns. Here in Europe we have a long history behind us and a rich culture. I think that this is transferred to the way we deal with problems in everyday life. We look for the origins of problems and have a tendency to dwell in the past. We concentrate on the problem.*
>
> *America is a young country and Americans do not have such a long history. They do not linger as long as we do with their thoughts in the past. They identify a problem, and then they look ahead and search for solutions for the future."*

If we can combine these two ways of thinking, we are strong.

I must first face reality. I can only act meaningfully if I understand the problem. Understanding makes me strong. To bring about change, however, I must act. This makes the feeling of powerlessness disappear, because I can consciously and purposefully steer towards solutions.

The class is my mirror!

Mahatma Gandhi said, *"You yourself must be the change you want to see in the world"* and told the following story:

> *Gandhi was busy with the preparations for a large political assembly.*
> *A farmer came to him and said, "Mahatma, I am a simple man, and there are many things I do not understand. I know that you are a great man and you speak the truth, but could you please tell me, in very simple language so that I can understand, "What is your message?*
>
> *Gandhi looked at him, thought for a few seconds and then said, "That's easy. I am my message."*

That's how it is - for Gandhi and for us too. We are our message, and our class will in turn reflect the message we send.

The Recipe:
The Self-Disciplining Classroom

The Recipe for Success:
Teaching with Structure & Love.

A classroom that disciplines itself? Is this possible?

The words above: „Teaching with Structure & Caring", contain the keys to the self-disciplining classroom.

Every person on this earth wants to be accepted as the person he or she is. This is true for you, for me, for our students, their parents and every person who crosses our path in life. Our students want to be liked - even if they do not always show it. If they feel that you like them, you can pick them up where they are and then lead them to the point where good learning and a trusting atmosphere in the classroom are possible.

The aim is to satisfy both the need for acceptance and the need for structure that our children and young people long for. If we can implement our concept of positive classroom management in a systematic, reliable and fair way while at the same time showing our students that we like them, everyone wins - and we can do what we actually became teachers to do - we can teach!

There are recipes

Teachers have often told me that while they were studying to become teachers, they asked their professors how they should deal with behavioral problems in the classroom. They usually got one standard answer, namely: *"You must deal with each problem individually. There are no recipes*!" With all due respect to your former professors, I say: *"That's not true."* There are recipes, and the recipe for the self-disciplining classroom is what we will look at in this book.

Naturally, there is no single recipe that fits every situation. As in everyday life, the recipes have to be adapted to the respective occasion. If you enjoy cooking, you will also have several cookbooks at home with a variety of recipes. You choose exactly the right recipe according to the occasion and the personal taste of your guests. For Christmas, you might have a stuffed turkey on the table and for a birthday, the birthday boy or girl's favorite cake. You look it up and carefully select the right recipe for the occasion. Maybe you change the recipe a little. The recipe in the cookbook gives you the guidelines. It's up to you how you use them. It's the same in the classroom.

The ingredients of a self-disciplining classroom

Each recipe begins with a list of ingredients, from which - correctly combined - a delicious dish can be conjured up.

The basic ingredients for a perfect cake are food products. The basic ingredients for the self-disciplining classroom recipe are concepts. On the following pages we will look at the following concepts:

- My reality is not your reality
- Everyone is unique and has the right to success
- Motivation is the basis for success

And then in the following chapters we will look at the other ingredients of the self-disciplining classroom:

- Brain-friendly, engaging learning techniques
- Positive, trusting and respectful group dynamics
- Cooperation instead of competition
- Structure! Structure! Structure!
- Setting limits - giving support!

When these ingredients are present, the need to discipline students is eliminated. The atmosphere in the classroom is harmonious, learner-centered and productive. The group works successfully as a team toward common goals. Learning and teaching are fun. There are no or fewer disturbances and there is no need to discipline.

Now let's take a closer look at the first three concepts.

My reality is not your reality

We all have different needs, talents and preferences. Our realities are different. Just as we strive for differentiated teaching based on the learning needs and potential of our individual students, so too should we aim for this in other classroom management skills. If we can pick our students up in their behavioral and communication styles, it is much easier to connect with them. Reach them to teach them. Once we have reached them, we can guide them to where good learning and adaptation to the group as a team is possible.

But when we adapt to the needs of individual students, other students often say, *"That's not fair!" „Why is he allowed to do that and I can't?", "It should be the same for everyone."*

No, it's not like that. Of course we have rules and boundaries that apply to everyone. But at the same time there are situations in the classroom where not everyone can or should be treated equally. Therefore I would suggest that you eliminate these students' objections immediately at the beginning of the school year, if possible during the first week of school. The guiding principle used here is:

"Each person is unique and has a right to success! "

Laminate a sign with this sentence on it. Discuss it and hang the sign in the classroom. If a situation arises where the sentence fits, point to the sign without saying a word. Do exercises, activities, and role-plays that illustrate these concepts. You can find some of these activities in the chapter "The 10 Commandments of Group Dynamics", and I am happy to include a very effective activity recently described to me by a teacher here:

> In the first week of school we sit in a circle of chairs. Each pupil has to think of an imaginative injury, e.g. a finger that has been hurt, a broken leg, a nosebleed, etc. I ask each pupil individually how and where he or she was injured. I commiserate with him and then stick a band-aid on his or her left upper arm. Then I ask the next person. She too - no matter where she is injured - gets a band-aid on her left upper arm. And I continue this way with the rest of the students.
>
> When a student asks why I put the band-aid on his arm when he actually has an injury on his foot, I look surprised and say: "Yes, but I want to be fair. That's why each of you will get the band-aid in the same place." If they say again that they want it where they're hurt, I look surprised and ask, "You mean you want the band-aid where YOU need it?" And then I keep insisting that it would be unfair. Everyone gets the band-aid in the same place.
>
> After everyone has been given a band-aid, we look at this picture

and discuss what "fair" actually means. "Fair" doesn't mean that everyone gets the same thing. Each of us is unique and our needs differ. We all want to be successful in school, and if someone needs something different to make him or her successful, we will give it to them whenever possible. That is fair.

If someone says the sentence "That's not fair" during the school year, I simply point to the upper left arm where everyone's patch was stuck in the first week of school, smile at the student - and the matter is settled.

Susanne B., secondary school

Motivation is the basis

The acronym WIIFM consists of the first letters of the words: *"What's in it for me?"* This acronym is a central principle in advertising and is also the basis of motivation in every area of life. The aim of every ad or commercial is to make the viewer or reader aware of the advantages of this product and to motivate them to buy it.

It's the same at school.
If our students feel that the school/subject/task etc. benefits them personally, they will participate without resistance. When it comes to the material we teach, it is the question of relevance. How can I apply this information to my life? And with behavior - our topic here - it is about the fulfilment of needs.

Our society is constantly changing. Technology is advancing faster than we can keep up. It is said that every student who goes to school today will change professions at least three times in a lifetime. The vast growth of knowledge in everyday life makes it increasingly difficult to predict the demands of the future. The same applies to the curriculum.

It's easier when it comes to behavior. We all share the same needs, and by addressing and meeting those needs in our students, we can reach and motivate them.

Let us teach with structure and caring

Let us meet our students' two basic needs. Let's pick them up exactly where they are. Accept them as they are. Let them feel that we care about them and at the same time give them the structure in the classroom that they long for. If we give the students structure, if we set reasonable and thoughtful boundaries for them, and if, above all we treat them and others with respect and fairness, they will be happy and will join in. This result is a "win-win" situation for classrooms, students and teachers. The advantages are manifold - for the students, for you, for our society, and for the world.

The Rug

To ensure that our classroom management table is completely stable, there is a **RUG** under the table. This rug is the foundation that gives us and our students firm footing in the classroom.

The carpet consists of two parts:

- Part 1: Professional competence in our subject matter and
- Part 2: Our aura of positive, natural authority

If these two ingredients are present, the prerequisites for success in the classroom have been met. We have mastered the subject content while studying. Universities and teacher training colleges concentrate mainly on content. It is the second quality, the aura and a sense of positive, natural authority that is often missing. This is easy to learn. And it is the subject of this book.

In the following chapters we will take a closer look at various aspects that lead to this aura of positive, natural authority in the classroom:

- Chapter 1: The easy path up to the summits of "Teachers‘ Mountain"
- Chapter 2: Developing teachers‘ positive and natural charisma

1

The easy path up "Teachers' Mountain"

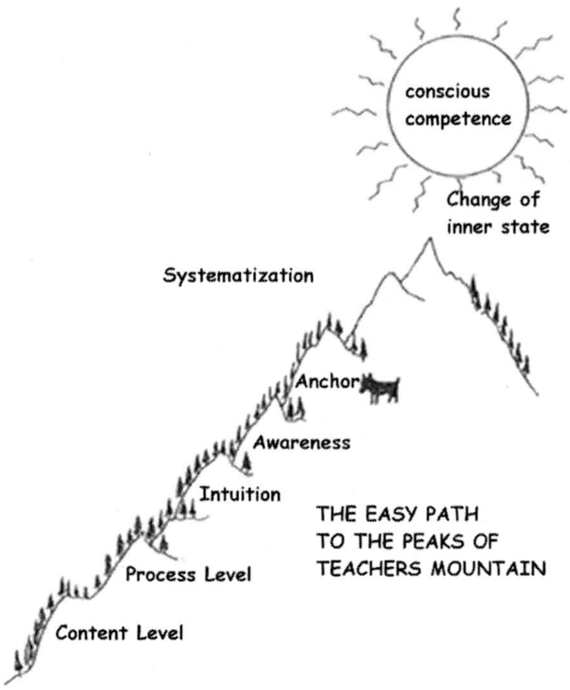

First steps

I did my teacher certification in America. But I had never actually taught before coming to Austria so many years ago.

I can remember my first day of school here as a teacher very well. I was so scared. I stood outside the classroom door. My mouth was dry and my heart was pounding. Then I gathered all my courage and bravely entered the classroom.

The school is a beautiful art nouveau building in the center of Vienna and the classrooms are huge! At that time, in the mid-1970s, it was a school for boys aged 14 to 19 and there were about 43 boys per class! Upon entering the classroom the first thing I saw at the front of the room was a high, stage-like podium, as was customary in Austria in the old days. And because there are no such podiums in the classroom in America, I had no idea what it was!

Despite my nervousness, my brain turned on and told me, *"I probably belong up there!"* So I climbed up on the podium and as soon as I got to the top, all the students stood up. My confusion was great. In America, students don't stand up at the beginning of class. I thought I had done something totally wrong and my students were going home. Fortunately, however, everyone stayed standing in front of their desks and stared at me in expectation. Somehow I managed to say, *"Good morning, class. Please sit down."*

I'm sure you realize that my students immediately figured out that I was a fledgling and had no idea whatsoever what was going on.

That day I took my first steps on my way up the path of „Teachers' Mountain". And – as it has been the case for so many of us – it would prove to be a very strenuous beginning.

We teachers are all somewhere on this path up the mountain. Some have progressed further than others. There are times when we move quickly, but there are also days when we slip or fall back a few steps. In order to reach our goal, we occasionally need signposts. And that's why I would like to take on the role of your guide on these pages, and together with you, step by step, take a look at the different levels we will cross on our way up "Teacher's Mountain".

First plateau: The content level

As young teachers in our first year of teaching, we are often overwhelmed. It starts the very first day of school as we are simultaneously confronted with the first two levels of the mountain - **the content level** AND **the process level**.

The content level is our mastery of the subject matter – math, language skills, etc. Luckily our teacher training studies have given us a very solid base concerning WHAT we will need to teach. Nevertheless, it is a challenge at the beginning to recognize immediately what exactly is essential and what is over and beyond that. The more experience we have though, the faster we learn to simply shake the content out of our sleeves. It becomes automatic.

Second plateau: The process level

Here the air is already much thinner; the challenges are greater. At this level, it's not a question of **WHAT** to teach, but **HOW** to teach it; that includes managing the class. Radiating an aura of positive, natural authority is the basis we build upon for the process level. Some teachers have this talent by nature. Those who do not have it need to acquire it as quickly as possible – and, thankfully, it can be easily learned!

At the beginning of my career, this aura of positive, natural authority was clearly lacking. I was at a loss and in need of help. At times my classes were out of control. An offer of help came promptly in the form of a collegial tip: *"Make strict rules and don't smile until Christmas."* The tip was well meant but quite impossible for me to follow seeing as I love to smile and laugh. (And after I learned how to manage my classes, my students and I could laugh and smile together.)

On the one hand, I understand what my colleague meant by this. If we are too loose at the beginning of the school year, it can be difficult to tighten the reins later. On the other hand, the first impression is very important, and a teacher who greets the class in a friendly way with a confident smile wins the class over much more easily because of her positive charisma.

Smiling or not smiling - the first year of service was the hardest for me, and in spring I had to decide whether to apply for an extension of my contract. I thought: *"Okay. It can hardly get any worse than this. If I survived one year, I'll surely survive a second one! If not, I'll just get a different job.*

Third plateau: The level of intuition

And lo and behold, it actually got better and better. Intuitively I (more and more often) did the right thing. I had no idea why it was working, but the "why" was not so important to me at that moment. What counted was: *It worked!*

In fact, it worked so well, that after that first introductory year at the commercial academy my principal always assigned me to the classes with behavioral problems.

"The class is acting up? OK. We'll give that class to Mrs. Nitsche, she'll manage!"

And I did too. For the next five years. But if someone had asked me exactly WHAT I did to make it happen - I couldn't have explained it. I didn't really know why. I simply acted intuitively and was happy that I was having more and more success!

When we act intuitively, we act from the gut. Often it works, but it can also happen that it does not work. Our success is left up to chance. This intuitive action is also called **'the unconscious competency'.** I am competent, I do it because it feels right - but I cannot say exactly why I succeed.

Many of you, dear readers, will be at this level right now. You've already come a long way, and now the next step is rapidly approaching. If, in addition to dealing intuitively, you want to personally take control of classroom situations, then please accompany me to the next level, the level of cognition.

Fourth plateau: The knowledge level

In 1984 I left the teaching profession and opened a language school, the SLL Institute (now named Pearls of Learning). Our focus was on brain-friendly learning techniques such as Modern Suggestopedia and Superlearning and our students were mainly adults in business. The courses were very popular. I trained my own teachers in these methodologies; this was also the beginning of my career as a teacher trainer.

In order to successfully teach these brain friendly techniques and methods to other teachers, I had to leave the intuitive level and focus on the cognitive level. I took a step back, observed what I and others were doing. And suddenly I understood what was happening here. This level of cognitive knowledge is the content of this book.

An example that we all know:
The lesson is well-planned. I think I know exactly how the students will react during the lesson. And surprisingly, they react quite differently than I expected!

Whether positive or negative, the important thing is to take a step back and ask yourself: *"Why did the students react the way they did?*

Only when we understand WHY something works - i.e. when the **'unconscious competence'** becomes **'conscious competence'** - do we have a tool that we can use systematically, successfully and reliably in the classroom.

This technique is called **"dissociation"**. Dissociation is the ability to mentally view a situation as an outsider. We „step outside"and gain more distance as well as a different perspective. This helps us to observe and analyze the students, ourselves, and the situation objectively. When we change our perspective in emotionally difficult situations, we can often see solutions to problems that would otherwise remain hidden. We observe the situation from a different angle. The unconscious becomes conscious. Intuitive coincidences become conscious behaviors.

The first summit: The systematization of non-verbal behavior

Now we are rapidly approaching our goals, the lofty peaks of "Teachers' Mountain". In order to achieve good classroom management, systematic behavior in the classroom is indispensable. Through this systematization the inner state of the student or the teacher changes automatically, mostly without using words, and classroom management suddenly runs like clockwork without effort or excitement.

We often do this by means of anchors, a very important teaching tool. We will discuss anchors in more detail in the chapter "Structure! Structure! Structure!" In short: An anchor is a stimulus - be it a visual or auditory signal, a ritual, a recurring behavior - that automatically results in the same reaction over and over again.

For example, if I always discipline on the same spot in the classroom, if I always play the same music at the beginning of the English lesson, if we have the same daily ritual for collecting the homework, etc., our students know - usually unconsciously and without words - what is going to happen next.

The second summit: Changing inner state

This systematic behavior leads to a change in the inner state of the students - respectfully, without words and without emotions. For example, upon hearing a certain piece of music, they know it is time to clean up their desks and pack their schoolbags. The result: an atmosphere of trust, harmony and togetherness is created. And, without using (or raising) our voices, we are able to do what we became teachers to do: To teach.

But can we use the same techniques on ourselves?
Can we strengthen our own inner state, for example, so that we feel good?
The answer is: "Yes. We can."

"If Mama ain't happy, ain't nobody happy! "

A magnet with this saying was hung on our refrigerator door while my children were still at home.

These words are so true!
This applies not only to mothers of small children, but also to us as teachers. If we are doing well, our students are doing well. Therefore it is very important that we take care of ourselves and our own inner state. It is similar to what we do on an airplane. If the oxygen masks are needed, the adults should put them on first and only then help the children. It's the same in the classroom.

The inner state

There are days when I get up in the morning with a smile on my face! I jump out of bed, get dressed and look forward to the day ahead. I go happily toward the events of the day. There are no problems. I joyfully anticipate every task. And I succeed at everything I undertake!

Then there are those other days.
The alarm clock is ringing. I open one eye, switch off the alarm clock and quickly close my eye again! I don't want to get up. I'm still tired. Today I have to do all kinds of things I don't like doing. I don't feel like doing them. I want to stay in bed! But I have no choice. I must get up. I drag myself out of bed and get dressed. That day, I am confronted by one problem after another. Mountains of problems!

Each of us knows both situations.
The question is: What is the factor that makes the difference?

I'm the same person on both days. I have the same skills and resources. The events on the 'good' day are no different from those on the 'bad' day. So what is different?

The decisive factor is my inner state.
When I am in a good inner state, all challenges come easily to me. If my inner state is not in order, what is otherwise a challenge becomes a huge and tedious problem.

The good news is that you can determine your inner state yourself.
You can do various things to make yourself feel better. It starts with very simple - and very effective - procedures.

In the next chapter you will find a variety of ways to consciously change your own inner state and thereby strengthen your radiant aura of positive, natural authority.

2

Positive, natural authority

What is authority?

This radiance of positive, natural authority is the epitome of good classroom management. EVERYTHING we do in the classroom should support this impression! And especially during the first seconds - or at most minutes - of the first lesson on the first day, the teacher's charisma is crucial.

> SCENE
>
> I am about to meet my new class for the first time. I hesitantly walk through the door. My posture is stooped and I avoid making any eye contact with the class. I stand in front of the class and look at my hands, which I am wringing nervously. My voice is soft and barely audible:
>
> *"Good morning... my name is Mrs. Nitsche ... and I have been assigned... as your teacher. I don't know exactly what we'll do this year...*

Sorry – but I missed the boat!
It wasn't only the words I used but my non-verbal signals also doomed my introduction – and possibly the entire school year! - to failure.

Soon we will rewind this film and watch the same scene with different nonverbal signals, but first I would like to tell you a true, short story:

Your personal attitude to authority

Once when I held a seminar abroad, a teacher couple, who had organized the seminar, picked me up from the train station. In the car on the way to the hotel we talked about all kinds of things. In a completely different context than school, the woman suddenly said: "I hate anything that has to do with authority!"

Suddenly a light bulb came on in my head!

The source of many of the problems teachers have with classroom discipline is, in my opinion, due to their personal attitude to authority. Each of us - some stronger, some less strong - goes through a phase in puberty where we rebel against authority. By the time we grow up, most of us have overcome this phase. We have a healthy attitude towards authority and can easily distinguish between positive authority and imposed authoritarian behavior.

However, some teachers remain in this phase. Since they still feel strong resistance within themselves against authority, they do not want to slip into the "teacher role". They do not want to make rules, which students need to follow. This attitude leads to many problems in the classroom.

We are in charge in the classroom! You are the boss. It's the only way. Students need and want boundaries, and it's our duty to set them. Students need limits. They demand those boundaries - through negative behavior: *"How far can I go until I cross the line?"* We must be prepared to assume the role of authority in the classroom, otherwise chaos will reign.

There are two forms of authority: The authoritarian approach or as we mentioned before, the preferable aura of natural positive authority. To clarify what I mean by this, let us look at our scene in the classroom again, but this time I will be sending different nonverbal messages.

This time, imagine that I step into the room smiling. My posture is upright and open. I stand in front of the class and make eye contact with the entire class. I maintain this open posture, and while I am smiling and speaking in a clear and warm voice, I also occasionally show the palms of my hands:

> *Good morning!*
> Pause for a moment so that the class can greet me.
>
> *"My name is Mrs. Nitsche, and I'm your English teacher. I am happy to be here with you. We will learn a lot this year! By the end of the year, you will be able to speak English very well. And we're going to have fun, too..."*

It's the difference between day and night. The foundation for the coming school year has been laid.

Self-confidence is obvious!

The common definition of a self-confident person is one who assumes that everything he does will be positive. In my opinion, there is much more to it than that: For me a self-confident person knows that if something should go wrong, he will be flexible enough to deal with the situation. This confident demeanor and behavior is the definition of **self-confidence** or **self-assurance**.

Recognize your strengths

Our sense of self-confidence determines how easily we can access our own strengths and resources. The first step is to be aware of our resources so that we can call on them in a stressful situation. This is also a kind of **"conscious competence"**. For this you have to be able to change your perspective, i.e. to take a step back and observe yourself - or the situation. You look for the strengths and techniques in your repertoire that you might need at a particular moment and then use them consciously.

Here are some ideas on how to identify and analyze your own strengths.

Keep a journal

Take the time to write down a list of your strengths - on paper or on your computer. It is important that you actually write the list down. Start small. A strength or resource does not have to be earth-shaking! If you have a beautiful smile, write it down. If you can make good pork chops, write it down. Can you listen well? And so on. This is your private list - you do not need to show it to anyone. Writing this list feels good. I guarantee you, the more you write, the better you will feel! And if there's a day when you don't feel very confident, read through your list. Maybe it will give you some innovative ideas on how to use your existing strengths.

Start and end the day on a positive note

When you wake up in the morning, think briefly about what you can be thankful for today. What situations will you be facing where you can use some of the resources you listed in your journal?

At the end of the day, write down three situations that went well and three qualities or resources that you used to get those positive results.

Speak less in classroom management!

Our goal is to go home with more energy than we had at the beginning of the school day. When I say this sentence in teacher training seminars, there are always some teachers who laugh and say: *"That's not possible!"* Believe it or not, it is possible and I know many teachers who can confirm that statement! That is what this book is all about!

Think about it:

Which days are particularly stressful for you?
What happened on the days when you go home exhausted?

I dare to assume that this happens on school days when you talk a lot. You may get upset or scold students who behave in an impossible way. Very often this behavior makes our students feel that we want to exercise power over them. But is a teacher who talks all the time, complains, scolds and sometimes jumps up and down in front of the class like a Rumpelstiltskin really powerful? Can her students look up to her? Does this behavior promote respect among our students?

No. I maintain that if we behave like this (and what teacher hasn't lost her temper on occasion!), we do so because we feel powerless. We would like to behave differently, but we just don't know how else to get students to do what we want them to do. Out of sheer frustration we act this way - and it costs us a lot of energy.

Deliberately speak less. Use the non-verbal techniques you have learned here and in my other books. Take a step back and observe yourself and also the situation - if possible, without emotion.

If you speak less and use non-verbal techniques, you are taking concrete action. You are actively seeking solutions - but emotionally you are less involved. When you are calm, you have better control of the situation and can act more objectively. The tendency to overreact decreases. You are using your charisma and your aura of positive natural authority to manage the class and are putting your feeling of powerlessness behind you.

Pay attention to your inner dialogue

Do you talk to yourself?
If you say *"yes",* you're not alone. Supposedly about 70 percent of the population has internal conversations or dialogues with themselves.

And now another - much more important – question: While conversing with yourself:
Are you always saying nice things? Or are you being critical of yourself and making statements like:
"I did it wrong again!", "Only I could have done something so stupid!", "Am I silly?!?!", "Typical!", etc.?

If so, then it is high time that you stop doing this!

We often look for excuses and scapegoats when something goes wrong in our lives. *"I can't speak Spanish well because I had a bad teacher!" "It was my parents!", "It's my mother's fault!", "Society,"* etc., etc.

But here is the most important question:
"With whom do you spend most of your time?"

Yes. You spend it with yourself. Day in, day out, year after year. And if you keep telling yourself in your inner dialogue that you aren't able to do something, that everyone else is better than you are, etc., then that will be the case. These are self-fulfilling prophecies! Therefore I would like to suggest: Be nice to yourself. Build yourself up. Praise yourself (even if you don't do it out loud), when you do something well. Don't hide your talents! In other words: Dare to be proud of yourself!

And - very important - during these conversations with yourself, focus your attention on positive expectations. What you expect, is what you will also get. Look for the positive. Because if you focus your thoughts or your words on everything that could go wrong, that is what you will surely get!

Self-confidence is a behavior and not a feeling

That's exactly how it is: In order to have a self-confident charisma and feel its positive effects, you first have to DO something. There are many different techniques for this. The three most simple and effective ones to raise your mood and energy level within the shortest time are

- Adopt **an upright and open posture**
- Do **cross-over movements** like walking or aerobics
- And use the most powerful nonverbal technique: **Music**

The combination of these three ingredients automatically changes your inner state, and the effect borders on magic.

Until a few years ago I sang in a gospel choir in Vienna. That was a pure "positive mood maker"! The choir rehearsals always took place Monday evening at 8.30. Often I was so exhausted in the evenings that the temptation to stay at home was strong. But then I always pulled myself together and went to sing despite my lethargy. Fortunately! All three ingredients needed to lift my spirits: upright posture, crossover movements to match the choreography and lively music were there! After two and a half hours of singing, I gained enough energy for a week!

Your mood and your physiology - how you sit or stand - are directly connected. You only need to change one or the other, and the second will change with it. This means that you yourself can determine your own mood and thus your charismatic aura simply by changing your physiology!

First analyze, and then act as if ...

NLP is sometimes also called **"A Model of Excellence"**. This means that if we want to learn something new, we do not need to reinvent the wheel over and over again. Instead, let's find someone who already has an excellent command of this skill and follow or model him or her exactly. Or look for a situation in which you yourself have the quality you need in a certain challenging situation. And then consider how you can transport this ability to the situation where you need it.

A teacher once told me that she lacked self-confidence standing in front of a class. I asked her, *"Can you tell me about another situation where you do feel confident?"* She told me that in her free time, she was an amateur actress in musicals. She enjoyed it very much, and she thought she had a real talent for it.

So I said, *"Interesting. So imagine that you're on the stage, performing for strangers. You dance and sing and wear imaginative costumes. That's a challenge, isn't it? Please tell me how you do it!"*

She thought about it and then said, *"I rehearse. And I have a script. That gives me a sense of security, and it makes me feel experienced and saddle-fast. I can feel the audience responding, and that gives me strength."*

"Well," I said, *"these are certainly resources you could put to good use in school. If you can do it on stage, you can do it in the classroom. You just have to transfer those resources from the stage to the classroom."*

The resources that each of us needs are already within us. We just have to recognize them so that we are aware of them, and then learn: how can I transport this resource from situation A to situation B so that I can cope well with this new situation?

What does "self-confidence" look like?

Now we will search for nonverbal resources. Do it like the amateur dramatist did. What can you do well? Think about: How do you behave when you feel confident? What do you look like? How do you sound? How do you feel?

- How do you move?
- How do you enter a room?
- What does your posture look like?
- Where do you stand or sit?
- How is your eye contact with the class?
- Are you smiling?
- How is your breathing? Is it shallow? Deep?
- Are you speaking? And if so, what are you saying?

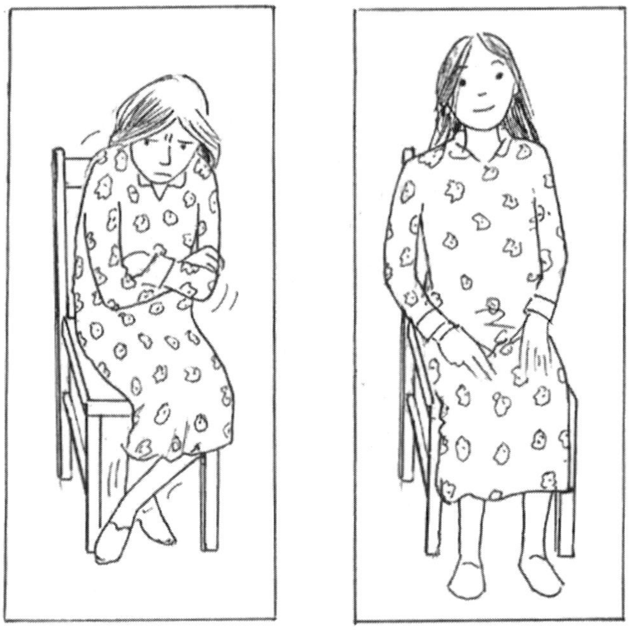

New perspectives through dissociation

Look at this optical illusion:

What do you see here?
Do you see the word "optical" at first glance?
Or do you look "between the letters" and see the word "illusions"?

Now look again at the optical illusion so that you see what you did not perceive the first time. How did you have to adjust your eyes in order to see the second image?

Yes, right! You changed your perspective. You had to take a different perspective so that you saw something completely different the second time around.

In other words, you had to dissociate. **Dissociation** is the key to dealing effectively with stressful situations in class. It is the ability to consciously take a step back and view the situation, ourselves and others objectively - with logic, distance and fairness. Dissociation gives you a different perspective. It's like looking at a photograph of yourself and your surroundings. You see yourself and the situation but you are detached without emotions

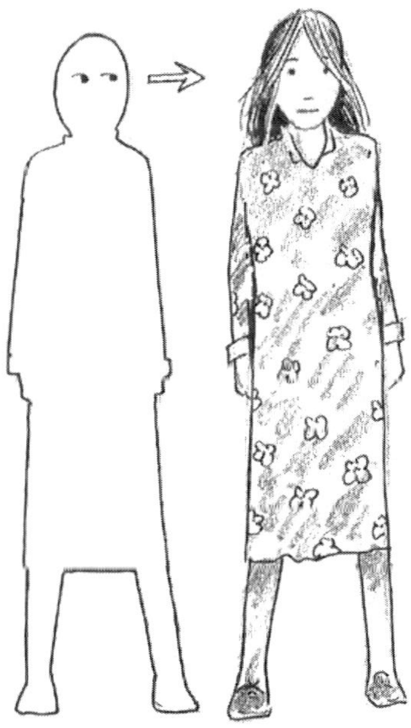

Dissociation

Dealing with emotions

My son and colleague in teacher training, Derrick, went to acting school. He often tells us how important it is that an actor doesn't get lost in the emotions he's playing. For example, if an actor plays Romeo and dies twice per performance on the stage, six evenings a week plus a Saturday matinee, he dies passionately fourteen times a week. If emotions were really involved, he would not be an actor for long!

The same applies to doctors. They cannot totally empathize with every patient who suffers or dies, because otherwise they would be an emotional wreck in no time!

And how does that apply to us as teachers?
Dissociation is a skill that we urgently need to learn.
It is above all important for us to be able to distinguish: When should I empathize? And when not?

Sometimes it is better not to get emotionally involved. For example, if you are disciplining a student, it is important that you remain objective. You should be confident and view the situation more from an outsider's perspective. This is the only way you can be fair to the student. And staying calm is also good for you.

This is exactly how we should react in sensitive situations in the classroom. **I cannot always control everything that comes my way. But I can very well decide for myself how I react to it.** Every unpleasant situation in the classroom offers us the opportunity to either react automatically or to act consciously. If I react spontaneously, the matter is settled. I have no further options. But the more conscious and calm I am in the situation, the more choices I have. The feeling of powerlessness disappears. I have options and I can choose the best solution. My self-confidence rises, new solutions appear - I have the situation under control.

Is it a threat or a challenge?

When something happens and you need to act, the first thing you should ask yourself is, *"Is this situation a threat to me, or is it a challenge?* How you act is determined by your answer to that question.

If a situation is threatening for you, your brain will switch to the so-called "fight-or-flight" reaction. There are two possibilities here: you counter your "opponent" with full force, or you run away.

A challenge provokes a different reaction in you. With a challenge we bring out all our strengths and take action with power and enthusiasm.

Threat or challenge? It's all a matter of perspective.
And how you assess the situation will determine the outcome.

Whose problem is it?

Teaching is a caring profession. Most of us genuinely like the students who sit in our classes. We want the best for them. We want them to reach their full potential. That's our job and that is our nature. When they are hurt or, as is so often the case, ignored or abused at home, our hearts bleed. In other words, we are emotionally involved. Empathy is good to a certain extent - but sometimes we feel too much! Then we go home at the end of the school day and are exhausted - physically and mentally. We take it too personally.

For example, how many teachers are there who get extremely upset because a student doesn't do his homework: *"It's the same old story. He doesn't have his homework! I'm sure, he does it on purpose just to annoy me!"*

No. He's not doing it to annoy you. There can be many reasons. Maybe he doesn't want to do it. Maybe he's forgotten. Or maybe there's some other reason. But he certainly isn't acting this way to provoke you. If you take it personally, you are wasting your energy. Thinking this way also arouses emotions that complicate the situation.

In such a situation - or in ANY situation, be it school or private – when you get upset, ask yourself the question: *"To whom does this problem actually belong?"* I'll bet that most of the time, the problem doesn't belong to you, but rather to the student or at most to his parents. You're not responsible for him for not doing his homework. And you're not responsible for most of the situations you might get upset about. This realization is liberating. You as a teacher are relieved of this responsibility. It is **not** your fault. You can show the student the way, but he has to go it alone.

The effect is amazing. The moment you discover who is actually responsible, the weight on your shoulders disappears. You have strength again. And the bonus: Since you have gained a bit of emotional distance, you will have the energy to actually be of more help to the student. Once again this is a "win-win" situation, where student and teacher both have advantages!

We can choose

These behavioral tips are powerful tools. When you use them you are no longer at mercy's fate. You have the basis to make neutral decisions. You and you alone determine your own mood. You are independent and not ruled by your own emotions. Of course, if you want, you can wallow in your negative feelings. Or you can choose to become stronger and make your day and life easier. If you choose to focus on the positive feelings, the challenges of the school day will be much easier to overcome. You will become powerful instead of powerless. If you feel good on the inside, you will communicate this to others and your aura of positive, natural authority and success in the classroom will be guaranteed.

Table Leg Number 1:
Brain-friendly Learning Techniques

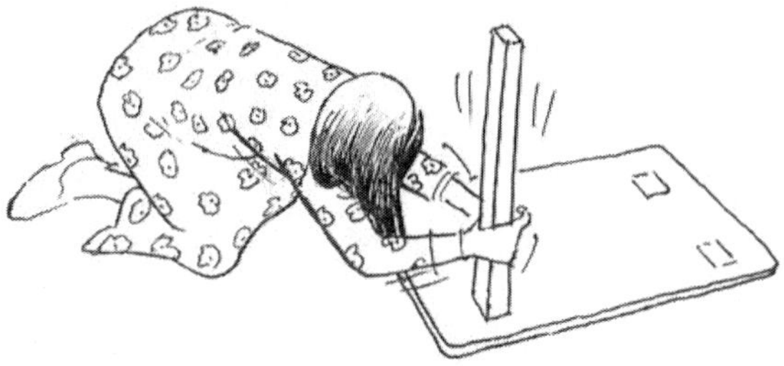

The first leg of the table is called "Brain-Friendly Learning Techniques". Some of these are "Modern Suggestopedia", "Superlearning" or Howard Gardner's "Theory of Multiple Intelligences". We will touch on these and further methodologies in

- Chapter 3: What is brain-friendly learning?

Brain-friendly learning is also called **Suggestopedia**, **Superlearning** or, sometimes in English-speaking countries, **Accelerated Learning**. It consists of four factors or pillars that contribute to the efficiency of this method. Three of these four factors, i.e. the rhythm of our lessons, the role of suggestion in the form of a positive learning atmosphere in the classroom and the use of music will be dealt with in the following chapters:

- Chapter 4: The learning environment and the learning atmosphere
- Chapter 5: Welcome! Arriving in class
- Chapter 6: We've got rhythm! Making your lessons flow.
- Chapter 7: The power of music

The fourth factor, group dynamics, is the subject of the next chapter.

These five factors enable the teacher to guide the class inconspicuously and effectively without being in the center of attention herself. They enable student-centered rather than teacher-centered learning.

3

What is Brain-Friendly Learning?

Left AND right
The Magical Word of Suggestopedia

When I sat down at the computer and asked myself this question, the ideas shot back and forth in my head like fireworks. Brain-friendly learning, also known as Suggestopedia and Superlearning, is ...

- learning with all the senses
- learning that utilizes both brain hemispheres, i.e. the logical and analytical on the left as well as creative, holistic and with the emotions on the right. This is done by means of, for example, playful, creative learning techniques, drama, music, guided fantasy, visualization and mnemonics
- learning with joy, laughter and curiosity
- learning that is sustainable, accelerated, effective and entertaining
- learning by doing!

Learning by doing!

The best way to teach brain friendly learning is by using creative learning techniques, which we will do below in the form of a suggestopedic text i.e. a short skit which contains all of the most important information.

But first a bit of background information: I would like to share with you the short play which I have been using for many years in teacher training courses. All the essential information is included in this dialogue. Thus you will be experiencing the theory in practice – This is the so-called presentation phase. You will then find ways to implement the second part of Suggestopedia, the activation phase, which consists of interactive, communicative and playful activities, advice, tips, techniques and tools, in the coming chapters.

What is Suggestopedia?

Suggestopedia is a (w)holistic teaching and learning method that enables people to learn faster and retain what they have learned. Above all, they realize that learning can be very pleasurable. The approach was developed by a Bulgarian doctor, Dr. Georgi Lozanov, at the University of Sofia in Bulgaria in the 1960s. Nowadays there are many brain-friendly approaches to learning, but at that time Suggestopedia was the very first holistic learning and teaching method. Over the years it has developed further and today it is known under different names - **Modern Suggestopedia, Brain Friendly Learning, Superlearning** or **Accelerated Learning**.

Modern Suggestopedia is a combination of a variety of methods. All of these methodologies aim at optimizing learning processes and exploiting our enormous potential of unused mental reserves. Lozanov's method is considered to be the core of Modern Suggestopedia. In addition, the approach includes the latest findings from brain research, stress reduction, multiple intelligence approaches, and humanistic psychology theories such as NLP and kinesiology, etc. Modern Suggestopedia can be applied successfully to every subject and for all age groups and is very motivating.

The magical world of Suggestopedia

What are the benefits of Suggestopedia?

Learning takes place more quickly, successfully and efficiently. Creativity, social behavior and physical well-being are increased. Learning is enjoyable and therefore both the learner and the teacher become more motivated.

In Suggestopedia, for example, new material is often presented in the form of short plays or fantasy journeys, underscored with classical or baroque music. By means of this presentation, the material is learned three to five times faster than with conventional learning methods. However, this newly acquired knowledge is only stored passively in the brain. In order for it to enter active long-term memory, the passively learned material is activated with creative, playful learning techniques.

In this book I have included several suggestopedic texts. The advantage for you as a reader is twofold: You are dealing with the topic of this book - "The Self-disciplining Classroom", and at the same time you are becoming acquainted with the suggestopedic process.

What is a suggestopedic text?

One of the cornerstones of suggestopedic teaching is texts or skits in dialogue form, which contain the subject material presented in an entertaining way. As you can see on the following pages, the dialogue is located on the left side of the page and on the right side the most important facts, tables, illustrations and other important information are listed again.

The text is read and acted out dramatically by the teacher to specially selected **classical or baroque music** (See the chapter on using music in the classroom). Playing several roles is often a challenge for the teacher. The students, on the other hand, have no problem following the teacher playing the various roles (perhaps wearing a scarf or a hat, etc. to represent each role). The students love these presentations and later on, during the activation stage, they can act them out themselves.

The text below - as well as the other suggestopedic texts in this book - are examples to help you become acquainted with this form of presentation.

On my website (www.pearls-of-learning.com - Materialien & Listen - suggestopedic texts) there are about two hundred such texts, written by teachers of all levels and all subjects who attended our suggestopedic teacher training courses. Most of the texts are in German but some are in English. They can also be easily translated into other languages either with Google Translate or with my favorite translation program Deepl. The texts are Word files and can be downloaded for free. So you can easily make changes and adapt texts to a higher level simply by adding a few lines. If you have questions, you can, of course, write to me: pearl.nitsche@chello.at.

Use the dialogues in class. Of course, if you are trained in Suggestopedia, you will achieve even better results with them. But even without training, these texts are great teaching aids that you can use, for example, as role-plays in the classroom.

Before we look at our text about brain-friendly learning (unfortunately I can't present it here with music and drama), I'd like to show you some e-mails I have received from teachers who use Suggestopedia in their classrooms:

Pythagorean Theorem
Last week, I introduced the Pythagorean Theorem in a brain-friendly and suggestopedic way with a text from your website. My teammate was thrilled. The children were happy and didn't even notice how much and how hard they worked during that lesson. They were so surprised by the "theatrical performance" and followed our reading of the text to music with their eyes wide open. These looks and their cooperation should have been filmed. Our principal was also present. He was quite impressed and also surprised at the amount of enthusiasm and joy the children showed.

I hope that many more teachers will be trained in Suggestopedia. The students will thank you,

Burgi S., secondary school

The multiplication tables – something different!
Today I did the suggestopedic text on the multiplication tables with a very weak class. It was a hot day. The atmosphere was charged and the kids were restless due to the heat. The teachers were also quite irritable. I usually only work with individual students in this class, but offered to do this lesson with the whole class that day. The class teachers were pleased about a "break" and let me do the lesson while they listened from the back of the room.

At the end of the story about the multiplication tables, which I acted out and read with classical music playing in the background, everyone was like a different person! The atmosphere was great despite the heat. Even the teachers were "rested" and more patient. The children worked on the story with great concentration

It was a wonderful experience and has confirmed and strengthened my conviction of brain-friendly and suggestopedic learning techniques!

Sylvia O., elementary school

What do you remember?
...what surprised me most was the long-term effect of suggestopedic texts. Today, my children are in the 3rd grade. In the 2nd grade we learned the multiplication tables. I wrote several texts to add to the series on your website. In 3rd grade I asked my students which of the multiplication table chapters from 2nd grade they remembered best. I had forgotten my little experiment and it was only when my students retold me parts of the story that I remembered our Suggestopedia lesson. Months had passed in the meantime, but the children still knew exactly what had happened in this lesson.

Rotraud L., Elementary school

Teachers become actors!!

And now for our suggestopedic story about Suggestopedia:

Radio EU Reports

An educational adventure in the Land of Brain Friendly Learning by
Judith Hazdra and Pearl Nitsche

Today Yesbut was knighted by the EU
Commission for Education and Learning.
He was also awarded the coveted
"European Union Teacher of the Year Medal".

Why?
Yesbut recently returned
from the land of "Brain Friendly Learning",
where, during an exciting chase,
he literally saved a person's life
at the very last second.

And whom did he save?
His student. A real princess, Apple White.
One day - in the middle of class - Apple fell into a deep coma.

But how did he save her?
He took up the fight with the dreaded "Demotivation Monster"
that has plagued our schools for centuries.

And how did that happen?
Let's listen to what the media has to say about it:

....

There is a big crowd in front of the Education Ministry.
Many reporters from home and abroad
are holding out microphones toward Yesbut.
Of course Radio EU is on the scene.
The reporter is giving details in a special broadcast
of the exciting events of the last few days.

Reporter: *Yesbut! Yesbut!*
Is it true, that you
have changed your name?

Jaber: *Yes, that's right.*
Everyone used to call me "Yesbut",
because I started almost
every sentence with the words,
"Yes, but..." !

Then I defeated the Wicked Witch of
Negativity on my adventurous journey,
So, I changed my name to Positive Thinking.

Reporters: *Interesting.*
That attitude will make life a lot easier
for you and for your students.

Can you tell our listeners how it all began?

Positive Thinking: *I remember the day very well...*
I was teaching in the same way as
I have taught for the past 50 years..
Suddenly the princess fell into a coma.
Her parents, the king and queen, were
very worried and sent me
on a mission to revive her.

At first I was at a total loss.
But – it was like a miracle –
a rabbit suddenly appeared
and saved me!
He led me to

THE LAND OF
BRAIN FRIENDLY LEARNING

There he showed me a magic sword.
To save the princess, I'd have to pluck
the sword from a rock.
But I couldn't move it a millimeter!

Reporters: *Did the rabbit help you?*

Positive Thinking: *The rabbit told me that only*
a chosen one would be able to
bring Apple White out of her coma.
It would be a teacher and
he would need to know everything
about

BRAIN-FRIENDLY LEARNING

He said: It increases students'
MOTIVATION

They learn (w)holistically with the

LEFT & RIGHT CEREBRAL HEMISPHERES

They then remember the material and learn
it much easier and faster than in the traditional way.

That was the first time I ever heard
that learning can be so much fun!

Positive Thinking: *This was a real breakthrough for me!*
Because if learning is fun,
then the students are motivated.
If the students are motivated,
then the teachers are motivated too.
Now I look at teaching differently!

Reporters: *Unbelievable!*
Right AND left?
How does the ministry feel about that?

Positive Thinking: *(laughing)*
This has nothing to do with politics!

The right and left brain hemisphere
want to work together harmoniously.
And that's easily possibör through the use of

RELAXATION TECHNIQUES,
MUSIC** and **PLAYING,
***INTERACTIVE** and*
COMMUNICATIVE ACTIVITIES

The left hemisphere is
logical and analytical.
This hemisphere is the one
traditionally used in school.

The right hemisphere is different.
It's global.
Colorful, musical, creative,
And it can remember
so MUCH for a very l....o....n....g time.

When the left and right sides work together,
they can't be beat!

Reporter: *Interesting.*
What happened next?

Positive Thinking: *I still had to go through the Province of*

LEARNING STYLES.

SUGGESTOPEDIA:
Dr Georgi Lozanov,
Sophia University, Bulgaria The
first holistic learning method

SUPERLEARNING or
MODERN SUGGESTOPÄDIE
= Suggestopedia as a focus,
combined with other brain-friendly
learning methods

Learning barrier wall

***Roger Sperry** Nobel*
Prize for his work on left and
right cerebral hemispheres
(We know now that his theory is only
partially correct. Nevertheless, the two
hemispheres of the brain hemispheres are a
good metaphor to explain the learning
processes :-)

http://de.wikipedia.org/
wiki/Roger_Sperry

Positive Thinking: *That's where I realized for the first time that each of us has a different*

MAP OF REALITY

My reality is not yours:
Each of us filters our world
according to our individual

PREFERRED SENSORY
***PERCEPTION** or **MODALITY**:*
visual, auditory, kinesthetic,
olfactory or gustatory

http://de.wikipedia.org/wiki/Neurolinguistic_Programming
www.nlpaed.de - NLP for Educators
Figure 7a - NLPaed Logo

*This is called **VAKOG** for short*

Each of us also has our own idea of "reality"
that we have constructed over the years.

John Grinder** **Richard Bandler
NLP
NEURO-LINGUISTIC
PROGRAMMING

Then, using a technique from NLP,
I learned how to establish

RAPPORT

Rapport means to get on
the same wavelength as the person
you are talking to.

That is the key to good communication..

VAKOG

RAPPORT,
if the chemistry is right!

Reporters: *Well done!*
Did you do that all by yourself?

Positive Thinking: *No. Not all alone. The nine*

MULTIPLE INTELLIGENCE

dwarfs helped me.
Each dwarf stands for a special kind of intelligence:

http://de.wikipedia.org/wiki/Theorie_of_multiple_intelligences

- *Dwarf **INTERPERSONAL** is a great team player and performs well within groups*
- ***INTRAPERSONAL** is the philosopher among the dwarfs. His ideas come when he is quiet and looks inside himself*
- *Dwarf **SPIRITUAL** thinks a lot about the life's meaning*

itive thinking: ***MUSICAL-RHYTHMICAL*** *has his strengths in the field of music and rhythm*

- *Dwarf* ***LOGICAL-MATHEMATICAL*** *gets straight to the point*
- *Dwarf* ***VERBAL-LINGUISTIC*** *is the poet and writer*
- *Dwarf* ***VISUELL-RÄUMLICH*** *is the architect among them*
- *Dwarf* ***BODY-KINESTHETIC*** *is constantly in motion and very often the center of attention*
- *and Dwarf* ***NATURALISTIC*** *is the gardener of the house*

The dwarfs showed me the different approaches I needed to reach my students.

As we say:

REACH THEM TO TEACH THEM!

Howard Gardner
Harvard University

THEORY OF MULTIPLE INTELLIGENCES

http://de.wikipedia.org/wiki/Daniel_Goleman

Reporters: *And what about emotions? Doesn't what is learned remain in the memory longer when it is associated with one or more emotions?*

Positive Thinking: *Exactly! That is a very good question! That's why I'm very interested in learning about my students'*

EMOTIONAL INTELLIGENCE

Reporters: *And then?*

Positive Thinking: *At the end of my journey, after I had mastered all these techniques, I suddenly found myself back in front of the magical sword.*

This time I could pull it out very easily. I woke the princess out of her coma by tapping her shoulders with the magic sword.

DANIEL GOLEMANN
Harvard University

THEORY OF EMOTIONAL INTELLIGENCE

Reporter: *That was quite an achievement! And has your teaching changed?*

Positive Thinking: *Oh, yes! I'm motivated. And my students are too.*

MOTIVATION *is a major factor.*

LEARNING & COMMUNICATIONAL STYLE

and I can also more easily
recognize the learning styles of my
students.

I use

DIVERSE TEACHING STYLES,

I design my lessons so that various

SENSES *and also the* ***EMOTIONS*** *are represented.*

In my lessons there is
something for everyone!
This way I can reach ***ALL*** *the students.*
And what they learn goes into long-term memory!

Reporters: *It sounds like*

BRAIN FRIENDLY LEARNING

appeals to the whole person and all of his needs.
Is that right, Positive Thinking?

Positive Thinking: *Yes, that's right.*
Brain-friendly learning is

LEARNER-CENTERED,

and that means

LEARNING WITH BODY, HEART *AND* ***BRAIN!***

Reporters: *Mr. Positive Thinking, congratulations.*
and thank you for the very informative conversation!

pearl.nitsche@chello.at;
Website: www.pearls-of-learning.com

4

A Positive Learning Environment

Where would you rather study?

In the waiting hall at the bus station or in a nicely decorated classroom?

> SCENE
> Just imagine ...
>
> ...today is Martin's first day at a new school. Upon entering the school, he looks around. Everything is new and different. He has mixed feelings. On the one hand, he's excited about the new adventure awaiting him. But at the same time he is afraid.
> What will it be like in this unfamiliar school and with the new teachers?

As soon as Martin enters the classroom, he has the answers to his questions.

Without even having seen you, he sees in the classroom what your attitude toward learning and school is. The classroom is full of clues, and our students, consciously or unconsciously, perceive these clues. They affect their expectations, their future school experience as well as their attitude towards learning on the subconscious level. The learning atmosphere that my classroom and I create in the first few minutes, hours and days is decisive.

So it is essential that I ask myself what impression I want to make with my classroom at our first meeting. This is the message I would like to convey:

"Here is a place where you can feel comfortable and learn well.
It is inviting and you feel that you can listen, participate and grow here.
Your emotions will be respected here."

The classroom should be a place where students can develop confidence, take responsibility, exercise self-discipline and learn without limits.

The learning environment

When I enter a school for an afternoon in-service teacher training course, I usually pass the students in the hall who have just been dismissed. That's when I get my first clue about the atmosphere in this school and the teachers I will be dealing with in the workshop. Experience has shown me that the smiling faces of pupils are the most reliable sign of a school with a positive learning atmosphere.

The second sign is the learning environment, the corridors, the classrooms, the cafeteria, etc. Recently, fire safety regulations have been tightened up considerably. Many teachers have complained that it is now difficult to make the rooms look nice, as no flammable objects such as drawings on paper may be hung up and nothing may be placed along the corridor that could block the escape routes. But if the sense of aesthetics and, above all, the desire for it are there, schools and teachers will find ways to create a positive environment. I have seen many school corridors that contained tiles made by the students or hand-painted wall decorations that looked as if they were made by the Austrian artist, Hundertwasser. I have also seen many classrooms beautifully designed by parents, children and teachers. Colors, plants and flowers, a well ventilated and tempered room, scented lamps, beautiful things like sand pictures, fresh drinking water and fireproof curtains all contribute to the atmosphere of well-being. Theme corners for reading, painting and handicrafts, English Corner and exercise areas or corridors enhance the appearance and feeling of being comfortable in the available space.

Comfortable - but not distracting

Pupils, especially the liveliest ones and also pupils with ADHD, can easily be distracted from their lessons. Therefore, a nice and colorful learning atmosphere, which does not distract from the lessons, is important. I have taken the following tips from a newsletter by a teaching consultant, Angela Watson (if you want to subscribe to her free newsletter, here is the link: http://thecornerstoneforteachers.com/).

Distractions can be reduced to a minimum with these rules:

- No additional learning materials, posters, pictures etc. in the front of the classroom. These learning aids should hang on the side or back walls
- Colorful, patterned carpets or curtains can also distract ADHD children
- Tables where easily distracted students sit should not face the window, door or a computer monitor.
- If you have an area or table where you work individually or in small groups with students, this area should be in the back of the classroom
- Turn the tables around so that the desk opening is on the outside of the table. This eliminates a student's temptation to play with the contents inside the desk compartment.
- There should be as few school materials as possible on students' desktops. Store utensils such as scissors, paste, rulers, protractors, etc. in boxes or other containers on shelves in the classroom. If necessary, pupils should fetch them when they need them and then put them back when finished

Students with an attention deficit often need something to hold in their hands to improve their concentration. We adults usually only do one thing at a time. But the liveliest children in our classes learn quite differently than we do. In order to be able to concentrate well, they often have the need to do two things at once. They cannot just sit still and listen. They also need a second activity, preferably something tactile.

Let them do that - as long as the lesson itself is not disturbed. For example, we can put a soft, squishy ball in their hands. Under no circumstances may the ball fall to the floor or fly through the room. Otherwise you will take it away. Or we can give them a small piece of plasticine (it is important that it is not a big piece - otherwise the snake production crossing three tables will begin!) Or we distribute mandalas which can be colored while listening to the teacher.

"Yes, but won't everyone want something like that? "

I get that question a lot. My answer: *"Probably not. But if that should be the case, there is a very simple solution: If the students want it, they need it. We simply have to provide more balls."*

"Yes, but doesn't it bother the other students? "

And here's the answer: *"The others may not, under any circumstances, be disturbed by this, or the ball will be confiscated by the teacher."* It is better if the pupil holds a ball in his hand than if he bothers others or bumps into and disturbs them. Most of the time, the other students do not even notice what that child is doing. This is a win-win solution that is good for everyone.

Some ideas

A feel-good classroom

I make sure that we always sit in a nicely decorated classroom in which we feel comfortable. In first grade we celebrate the children's birthdays by giving them a small gift. In the following grades, the pupils bring sweets or a cake to celebrate their birthday with their classmates.

From time to time we eat a potluck breakfast, to which each student contributes something. Once or twice a year, there are class or school parties where students bring food from their countries. And we celebrate festivities such as carnival, Halloween or the Advent season with an Advent calendar filled with little inexpensive items.

We have a large empty vase in the classroom. If the pupils are particularly well-behaved, helpful, or if they peacefully settle disputes, I put reward stones into the glass. When the jar is full, the students may wish for a special outing or an event.

In our classroom there is an oversized thermometer on which the children hang their names depending on how they feel that day. In our school we have special lessons where the class learns social skills. Board games on this topic are played. Topics that have led to conflict are discussed - partly in cooperation with the guidance counselor or the school social worker. During recess we make sure that the kids have the opportunity to either be active or, if they prefer, to pull back. The girls especially like having their own table or cushions where they can sit and talk to one another during the breaks.

We do various activities to ensure that the students are integrated into the class team. The emphasis is put on the positive qualities and the strengths of each individual.

Our students have also learned mediation techniques. They can discuss disagreements or problems with each other.

Margit W., Secondary School

"Choose a comfortable place to sit"

When students read or do dialogue work, learn roles or do pronunciation exercises in my language lessons, they are allowed to find a comfortable place to sit in the classroom. They "have to" leave their seat and find another "place" to learn. Students love to sit on the sofa, lie on the floor, sit in front of the closet or even under the sink!

Elfie K., middle school

Your attitude sets the tone!

SCENE

Imagine this situation ..
You want to learn French. You have registered for a French course, and today is the first lesson. I am your teacher. You and the other students sit in a semicircle in the classroom, and I come in.

"Bonjour!" I say. And then I enthusiastically tell the participants what to expect in this course ...

Then I look around the semicircle and enthusiastically say to the first pupil sitting there: *"Yes, Susi, you will be very successful in French. I can see that when I look at you! And you too! Martin and Roxy! You'll be great - you even look French!"* Then I keep looking around the circle. And suddenly the smile on my face disappears, and my enthusiasm fades as I look at Peter: *"Well, you, Peter...I don't know. Well, somehow you'll make it... we'll support you..."*.

Imagine you are Peter. How would you feel at this moment?

Definitely bad. And your chances of success in mastering French have been reduced to a minimum through my words and my nonverbal message. My personal attitude concerning my students' chances of success or failure are decisive.

„We get what we expect"

If I believe in my students, they will succeed!
Therefore it is very important to understand that your attitude and expectations have a tremendous influence on the behavior and success of your students. It is clearly a self-fulfilling prophecy.

Hence my advice:
Expect a lot from your students. Set the bar high. Express your high expectations and let them know that you believe in them and in their capability to fulfill those expectations. Set short term and long term goals and discuss with the class how these goals can be achieved - step by step.

Let your students see, hear and feel that you yourself are enthusiastic about learning and school. Often teachers say to me with a laugh: *"But if I use these techniques in class tomorrow, my students will ask me: "Mrs. Smith did you attend another seminar?"* My answer to this objection is: *"Yes! And I learned a lot! You need to learn and I do too!"* We don't need to be embarrassed if they realize that we like learning! When the students feel that you enjoy learning, they will too. Enthusiasm is contagious!

Almost all of my colleagues at the secondary school were very motivated and enjoyed the teaching profession. You could literally feel that in our school and in their classes. It was a real pleasure to work with them. But there are always a few teachers on almost every teaching staff who have a negative aura. Fortunately, there were fewer of them in our school than you could count on one hand! But still they were there, and their negative influence was detrimental to the learning atmosphere and to our enjoyment of working as a team.

I once taught together with a teacher in a first middle school class of 10 year olds. One day we had a visit from a supervisor who took over part of the lesson and did a fun unit with the students. At the end of the lesson he asked the class: *"Who likes going to school?"* The whole class shouted out loud: *"I do!"* Only my colleague, their homeroom teacher, said loudly and cynically: *"Well, not me!"* For a few seconds there was total silence while the pupils digested what their homeroom teacher had said about her attitude toward school. Four years later, when this class finished at our school, the students had just as little motivation as their teacher did. Your attitude - be it positive or negative - transfers automatically to your class.

Are you here?
Arriving and getting into the right state of mind.

Very often our students are physically present, but their thoughts are elsewhere. Everywhere else - except with us! We often forget that. We have put a lot of work into preparing the lesson and sometimes we overlook the fact that our material is not as important to our students as it is to us.
Once again, we are looking here at two very different realities.

What can you do here? If we want the students to transition from, for example, recess to math class smoothly, you need to first pick them up where they are at that moment and then lead them to where you want them to be - where they will be fully concentrated and ready for math. "Arriving" is very important. In chapter 8 I will show you some arrival exercises to help your students transition.

Greetings

Greeting is an important social skill that establishes contact between people and also provides a positive basis for communication. When I greet another person, I convey the feeling that they are important to me. But many of our students don't know this anymore. If the parents do not greet, if the others in their circle of friends and acquaintances do not do it either, if the advantages of greeting are not known to the students, or if they do not know exactly how it is done, they simply do not understand what it is good for. So they don't do it.

Felt wall paintings made by pupils
Polytechnic School in Aigen-Schlägel / Upper Austria

Be a good example and set the tone. Greet your students personally - in the classroom or in the corridor and on the street. Exchange a few words with them. Show personal interest and ask them how they feel. Perceive them personally - with eye contact, open posture and a smile on your face (see Chapter 20). Talk to them about the importance of greeting. This is guaranteed to improve the atmosphere in the classroom.

Giving structure and support

A new situation or environment often creates stress. Students are afraid to embarrass themselves. Rules and structures make them feel comfortable in the classroom. Structures provide security. Introduce rituals and guidelines: *"Our goals for today are..." "When I'm thirsty, I may refill my water bottle at recess."* Date and schedule are always in the same place on the board. Do a school and classroom tour with your students, or have them draw a "school map", etc.

Structures reduce stress. A structured classroom, in which events are predictable, creates a harmonious and calm atmosphere. Read more in the chapter "Table Leg No.3: Structure! Structure! Structure!"

Reflection time

Lively and quieter periods of instruction should alternate in the daily routine. The quieter parts of the lessons should also offer time for reflection. Here are some ideas:

- If something went particularly well or badly in the lesson, give the students time to think about it: *"Now close your eyes for a moment and think about what happened. How could we do it differently the next time?"*.

- Or let the students write their thoughts on this in their journals

- At a later date when emotions have cooled down, the events, ideas and suggestions can be discussed during circle time.

If we give students the opportunity to reflect, this is time during which newly learned material or behavior patterns „mature" in their brains. Reflection helps students learn to think independently, to strive for responsible action and to discover solutions to problems on their own. It is especially advisable if a child has been disciplined and is experiencing emotional turmoil.

Make sure that there are time slots as well as guided activities to promote reflection. Create the possibility for students to withdraw shortly. This could be to a corner of the room, a place in the hall. One teacher told me when she was cleaning out her garage she wanted to discard a beach umbrella but took it to school instead. She opened it and placed it in a corner at the back of the classroom. Students could have some time out sitting underneath the umbrella. Give students time to work quietly on their own. Depending on the type of task you choose, your students can draw, write, work on the computer, or start with their homework.

I once substituted in a very lively and noisy class. The class was notorious and it was not a class that I normally taught in. I was assigned to substitute there for the last two periods before the Easter holidays! Luckily, I found out a day earlier that I would be substituting there and was able to prepare myself well for these last two lessons before the Easter holidays began. The day before I bought some puzzles in the toy store.

I entered the classroom. Needless to say the kids were worked up and not too interested in learning that day. I quickly got their attention and immediately announced: *"In two years, you will be finished with school and moving into the working community. I would like to play a game with you today that is often played in companies during management training. It's about teamwork."*

This announcement surprised them and took the wind out of their sails, at least briefly.

I then quickly formed teams and let each team sit around a table. Then I explained that I would give each team a puzzle - without a template showing them what the finished puzzle should look like. It was their task as a team to put the puzzle together as quickly as possible.

The most important rule, however, was that they might not under any circumstances talk. They had to put the puzzle together in complete silence.

If someone did talk (it happened twice in the course of the two lessons), I pressed a stopwatch into his hand. He had to leave the group for five minutes and silently watch. While waiting to return to his team, he should think about what effect his absence had on the task and his team.

We played different versions - all non-verbally without words.
The last one was that the whole class tried to put together a bigger puzzle.
Silently and without a template.

Then I had each student write five sentences on the topic *"What did I learn about teamwork while playing this game*? One of the most interesting contributions was: *"I've learned not to hit someone when working in a team."* (A very valuable lesson!).

At the end I thanked them and said how nice it had been working with them. This thank you is very important. That's how you win the whole class - especially if it's a class that gets scolded a lot – for now and in the future.

It was a very valuable lesson – for them and for me.
One of them even suggested that I should ask the principal if I could come to them more often as a substitute teacher. I didn't take him up on that. But after these lessons, they were my "best friends" until the end of their school days. Whenever they saw me in the hall, they waved at me and asked me when I would come again. And actually I was there a second time – which was much easier because I had won them over.

Some practical ideas:

Assessing your own work

If the students work in teams on a project or other work, they can then jointly assess the quality of their cooperation. What has worked? What hasn't? Why?

Ernst S., elementary school

Help anchor

...I have a velvet box in class with a slit in the lid (like a money box), which I empty once a week. The students can put all their worries, problems and questions anonymously or with their name on it in this box. We talk about these contributions in circle time.

In my current class, the students also know that they can ask me to go outside the classroom with them so we can talk privately in front of the door. The students come to me during a break or sometimes during quiet work. This helps us solve many small problems early on before they become big ones!

Daniela G., secondary school

Class Council

Once a week the students sit in a circle. Clear rules are followed: only one person speaks at a time, and each pupil is allowed to speak. Tolerant behavior is a must. At the beginning of each class council meeting, we go around the circle giving one round of positive feedback. This creates a pleasant working atmosphere. If conflicts are on the agenda, first those involved speak and then others can express their opinions. In the end, solutions should always be proposed. These are recorded in the minutes taken by one of the students and are discussed again at the next class council. We can then decide together if the solution was a good one and what further possibilities could look like.

I hold class council meetings every Friday at the end of the school day. In the beginning the pupils were sometimes at a loss for words. In the meantime they have gotten used to this kind of emotional communication and have become very open.

Andrea W., Middle school

A classroom full of little mediators

Mediation is a "win-win" method of conflict resolution and creates a feeling of harmony in the classroom. With the support of a neutral mediator or a team of mediators, the parties involved in the conflict work out a fair, future-oriented and binding solution to their problems. The goal is a so-called "win-win" solution, i.e. a creative solution that is acceptable to all and therefore sustainable. The mediators create a constructive atmosphere and are responsible for the course of the discussion. The responsibility of the conflicting parties is to contribute the content and to find a solution to the problem. The mediators are there to simply guide them to the solution.

If there is no official mediation program at the school, the class teacher can work through the principles of dispute resolution with the entire class and train an entire classroom of mediators. Teachers, who have completed mediator training, train their students to become conflict helpers, so-called peer mediators. If a problem arises, the disputants choose two mediators. They all go into the mediation room and usually a solution is found shortly afterwards. This works for every age group - from first grade children to adults. The results are amazing. Conflicts within the classroom are solved and life skills are learned which can be used in every conflict situation, be it at school or outside of the classroom.

Renate Schertler (e-mail: mediationsteam@gmx.at), a mediator and teacher, attended my Suggestopedia course and wrote the following text as an introduction to school mediation for pupils. I invite you to present this text in your classroom either with Suggestopedia (more information on this in Chapter 4), or simply as a role play with your students. Then do various activities with this information and practice with the mediation techniques presented in the text.

Your students will be grateful to you. And you will have passed on a very valuable tool for them to use inside and outside the classroom.

Streita, Zorno and Mediation

by Renate Schertler, mediator and mediator trainer

Streita and Zorno attend the 7th grade in a middle school in a big city. Even while they were in elementary school they could not stand each other and were constantly arguing. To this day nothing has changed! During gym class today they got into another argument.

Zorno: *Well, there is no way that we will allow*
girls to be on our team!

Streita: *What do you mean?*
You're not the only one
who decides who gets to play.

Zorno: *You have no idea!*
Don't forget, I'm the captain of our team.
So I get to choose the players!
Let me repeat that:
I choose who gets to play!

Streita: *That's not true!.*
There isn't only one team!
You don't know what you're talking about!

Stupid moron!
It doesn't make sense to argue with you.
We want to practice for the tournament.
We're losing time with these discussions.

Streita: *You conceited ape!*
Listen to me for once:
Without girls on the team,
you don't stand a chance anyway!

Zorno: *Stupid women's libber!*

Streita: *Really? Well, tell me about it,*
which one of us has been playing
in this club for four years?

The new teacher, Mrs. Solva, approaches the two.

Mrs. Solva: *Well, that's enough!*
You obviously don't agree.
Without agreement, you can't be a good team.

Mrs. Solva: *But I'll tell you how you can solve your problems.*

Try: **MEDIATION**

Constructive conflict resolution

Streita & Zorno: *Medi-what?*

Mrs. Solva: *That is a way to resolve conflicts together*
You work together until you both are satisfied.
This is a so-called:

WIN-WIN SOLUTION!

Streita: *I've never heard of that before.*
Is that really possible?

Zorno: *I can't imagine that either.*
How does it work?

Mrs. Solva: *Two pupils in my class learned to be*

CONFLICT SOLVERS

Their names are Media and Tion.
Go and talk to them.
You will soon find out
if this would be good for you.

Streita: *Well, it's worth a try.*

Zorno: *Whatever.*
The main thing is we win the tournament!

So the two of them go to the conflict solvers the next afternoon.
Media and Tion go with them to a room in the school
they use for mediation meetings.

Phase #1:
The introduction

a. the presentation

Media: *Welcome!!*

Please take a seat.
This is Tion and I am Media.
We are trained mediators.

Zorna: *And we are Zorna and Streita.*
Mrs. Solva sent us to you.

Tion: *Yes, she told us..*
Are you here
of your* own free will?**, ***b. the requirements
Do you really want to
find a solution together*?*

Streita: *I want to,*
I just don't know how yet.

Media: *We will teach you that.*
We are **non-biased**. ***c. Non-biased***

So we will help not just one of you,
but both of you equally and we will
guide you to find solutions.

Zorna: *Only if my friends don't find out!*

Media: *It's good you brought that up.* ***d. Confidential***
We will not tell anyone what is discussed here.
We also ask you for confidentiality.

Tion: *We also want to agree on some rules.* ***e. The Rules***

Zorno: *All right.*

Tion gets up and walks to a poster that says ***The Rules of Mediation****.*
He points to the individual sentences, and reads them out loud:

Tion: ***Rule number one:***
We listen to each other.

Rule number two:
We let each other finish speaking.

Rule number three:
Everyone speaks for themselves and

Rule number four:
We do our best to find a solution.

Media: *Are you both okay with this*

Media: *If you have understood*
everything and you agree
with it, we will draw up a

MEDIATION CONTRACT

Streita: *Do we put it in writing?*

Media: *Yes. It's all there,*
We write down what we have said.

Zorno: *That's good.*
Then you can't say later,
it was different.

Tion: *Well, Media, please explain the further procedure.*

Media: *Yes. In Phase Two, Streita,*
you will present your problem
from your own perspective.
I will repeat what I have understood.
We write all the topics you name on a
chart and agree on the order to discuss them.

Tion: *In the 3rd Phase we will clarify the points one by one*
and try to find out your motives and feelings.

Media: *In the 4th Phase we will work out different solutions,*
discuss them and look for a solution you **both** *are satisfied with.*

Tion: *Yes, and the fifth and final Phase*
is then our written agreement.
We write down everything you agreed upon
and everybody signs it.

Zorno: *How long will it take us to get there?*

Media: *That depends, of course,*
on how committed you are to the process.
I think that about four or five sessions will be necessary.

Tion: *What do you think now?*

Streita: *Well, I agree and I definitely want to try.*

Zorna: *Yeah, me too.*

Tion: *Then we will draw up*
the mediation contract.
After everyone has agreed on
the content of the contract,
each of us signs it.
Then we make an appointment
for our next meeting.

They say good-bye and leave the house.

Streita: *Funny - although we*
have actually not even started yet,
I feel really confident
that we will find a solution!

Zorno: *Yes, I'm looking forward to*
our next meeting.

For the first time in a long while the two of them walk together to the bus stop - without arguing.

5

Attunement: Arrival and centering

Let's start again with a story:

> *The Mohawks, a Native American tribe, is known for the fact that its construction workers are free from vertigo at great heights. Therefore, they are in great demand for building skyscrapers such as the Empire State Building and the World Trade Center.*
>
> *Once a construction company had a number of Mohawks flown into New York to help build a skyscraper. Shortly after their arrival at the construction site, a foreman discovered them sitting on the ground in a circle meditating with closed eyes. He asked them what they were doing there. It had cost a lot of money to bring them to New York, and they were supposed to be working and not meditating.*
>
> *They replied: "Our bodies have already arrived by plane. We're waiting now for our souls to arrive."*

This also applies to the classroom. You may have noticed: Very often our students are physically in the classroom, but their thoughts are everywhere else and not with us. If you have the feeling that the students are very restless or that their minds are elsewhere, you can pick them up with various activities right at the beginning of the lesson after you have initially gained their attention.

The rapport principle applies here:

**Pick the students up
where they are now.**

**Then lead them to an inner state,
where optimal learning can take place.**

If they are lively, pick them up briefly with an activity involving movement, and if they are completely lethargic, as is often the case on Monday mornings, start slowly with less intense activities and build up the intensity. With some practice, it will take only a minute or so until your students are mentally present in your classroom.

Establishing group rapport

One of the most important factors when creating a self-disciplining classroom is establishing group rapport. There are many ways that this can be done and we will discuss group dynamics in more detail in the next chapter. At the moment, it is enough to say that group rapport results in a feeling of togetherness and harmony within the group. One very effective technique is to have everyone in the group do something simultaneously – such as singing, speaking in chorus, movements and – most effectively – breathing together. Many of the following activities contain such elements. So the benefit is twofold: you pick the students up where they are at that moment and, at the same time, you create the feeling of group rapport.

To stand up or not to stand up?

When I started teaching in Vienna in the mid 1970's, I was not familiar with the customs, rituals and traditions in the Austrian school system. Initially, standing up at the beginning of the lesson seemed a bit authoritarian to me. In the meantime, I find it one of the best inventions since the introduction of the school bell! When the pupils stand up, they consciously come to rest. They are switching gears. Recess has finished. They concentrate. Standing up at the beginning of the lesson is a clear anchor. It signals the transition from recess or break to lesson.

I am aware that not everyone likes this ritual. However, if it suits you, adapt it to help students become centered. You can practice "energetic standing" at the beginning of the school year, which ensures that they are grounded. To let the energy flow, they can stand like a tree, for example.

I am a tree.

"Stand up. Close your eyes for a moment and imagine that you are a tree. Feel your roots reaching deep into the earth. Your feet are parallel to each other and placed shoulder width firmly on the ground. Your knees are slight bent. Breathe deeply. Feel your breath going deep into your belly. Feel the power that the earth gives you. It flows through your whole body, down your arms ... your branches and into your fingers and toes ..."

One day the students are a tree, another day a rosebush, a flower seed that slowly begins to grow, a campfire, a babbling brook, etc.

Activities with movement

Kinesiological exercises - Brain Gym

Brain Gym, a method developed by Dr. Paul Dennison in the 70's, is gymnastics or mental exercise for the brain. Cross-over movements activate both halves of the brain. Blocked energy begins to flow. Learning, concentration and brain performance are activated and improved. It supports not only learning at school, but also health and emotional balance. We feel well. And we become more open to new solutions to (old) problems.

Fit for the day!

Morning aerobics, gymnastics on the spot, yoga for children etc.

Body Canon

All students sit in a circle. The teacher makes the following movements and sounds. The students imitate them:

4 x stomp your feet
4 x clap your hands
4 x clap your thighs
4 x snap with thumb and ring finger, stand up, turn around and count to 4
4 x shouting "Ha-ha-ha-ha" etc.

Once the sequence has been memorized and practiced, the class is divided into two groups and the sequence is performed in the form of a canon. This means that after the first group has finished stomping, the second group starts stomping. Three or four groups can then be formed.

MEDITATIVE - TIME TO REFLECT

Student journals

Another means of encouraging reflection and encouraging students to arrive in the here and now is to have the students keep journals. They have five minutes at the beginning of the lesson to write in their journals. They can write down everything that comes into their minds. The journals are their private property and are not looked at by anyone else. (If necessary keep them in a locked cupboard) This exercise is particularly suitable for Monday, as the students are often still thinking about their weekend, and writing helps them to "arrive" and be present at school. This exercise can also be a daily anchor or whenever you feel your students need to become centered.

Circle Time

In elementary school, circle time is a common and very powerful ritual. There is much to be said for implementing this ritual in secondary school as well at least once a week. If done on Monday, for example, it can represent a new beginning. And, if possible, do it again on Friday to summarize the events of the week.

During circle time the students are „attuned"to the here and now and being in the classroom. The teacher gives the students information about the week's activities and responsibilities. The circle ends with a gong and the students return quietly to their seats.

Guided Fantasy - I feel

- I make myself comfortable in my chair.
- I keep my back loose and upright.
- I place both feet firmly on the floor.
- And I close my eyes.

- I feel my feet where they touch the floor.
- I move my attention up my legs and feel my thighs and buttocks touching the chair. I let the tension go and notice how my body relaxes.
- Now I move my attention further up my body, into my spine. I imagine that it extends downwards, through the chair and deep into the earth. I let go and relax. I am held and supported.
- Now I turn my attention to my belly. I feel it rising with each breath I take and falling again as I release that breath. I let go and relax.
- I move further up into my chest - I feel it rising and falling. With each breath I take my lungs expand and take up more space within my chest.
- I feel myself into my shoulders and imagine all the tension and responsibility slipping away. My shoulders become lighter and lighter and relax.
- Now I turn my attention to my head. I imagine that I can open a small window here in my head. Fresh thoughts and ideas can flow in through this window. And all the thoughts that are old and unnecessary simply float away. I open my mind to learn new things.
- I'm connected :
    - with my feelings
    - with my physical perception
    - with my mind and my inner wisdom"

  And now I open my eyes.

"Enter your quiet house"

Put your head in your arms and relax. This is your quiet house. I will play soft music for you for a few minutes. Simply relax and feel your body and your mind tanking energy.

I tell younger students: "I am the magician. I have enchanted you all. You will now rest for a few minutes. When you feel my wand (a wand filled with glittering stars) touch your back, sit up quietly and open your eyes again.

Breathing consciously

The students sit down comfortably. The teacher initiates the breathing rhythm:
"Close your eyes and inhale slowly and calmly through your nose. Exhale. And inhale again. Draw the breath deep into your stomach. Feel your breath spreading out throughout your body. Every cell of your body fills with your breath. Hold your breath for a bit. And now breathe out through your mouth. A calm and steady stream of air flows through you."

"Now, inhale for five seconds. Hold it. Exhale eight seconds..."

MASSAGE

The students stand in a circle. Each one massages the back of the person standing in front of him. There can also be a second "massage round" in which everyone turns around and has a new partner in front of them. The theme of the massage can be adapted to the theme of the lesson.

Painting Massage

1. Imagine placing a sheet of paper or canvas on the back of your massage partner
2. Stretch the canvas tight and attach it firmly to your partner's back.
3. Mix/blend colors
4. Choose a landscape motif. It is better to choose large motifs like mountains, river, field, meadow, clouds, sun, etc.
5. Describe to your partner in detail what you are „painting" on his back.
6. Decorate the frame

Gardening Massage – Planting peas

1. Till the soil.
2. Pull out the weeds.
3. Work the fertilizer into the soil
4. Spread the soil until the surface is even
5. Create flower beds.
6. Make long and even furrows.
7. Water the soil.
8. Place the peas, spaced evenly, in the furrows.
9. Cover with earth.
10. Cover with foil.
11. Let the sunshine come.
12. Sometimes it rains.
13. And sometimes the sun shines.
14. First shoots are sprouting.
15. Remove the foil.
16. Plant the shoots in the earth
17. Plant keeps growing
18. Pick the pea pods
19. Shuck the peas.
20. ...or go to the supermarket and rummage in the freezer!

Weather Massage

1. The rays of the sun break through the fog. They touch us lightly.
   - Palms stroke gently over the back (outwards), sunrays (fingertips) gently touch the back.
2. Clouds are gathering.
   Palms form clouds, push themselves together.
3. Wind's coming up. Leaves fly around. Tree tops bend left and right.
4. Drops start to fall sporadically. Stronger and stronger. Lightning flashes. Hail patters down.
5. Suddenly absolute silence.
6. The clouds are clearing.
7. Rays of sunshine come through and warm your body (rub hands and lay on back).

Baking cookie massage

1. Put the pastry board up.
2. Make a pile of flour in the middle of the board.
3. Sprinkle in salt, sugar, vanilla sugar and baking powder.
4. Spread pieces of butter on the flour,
5. Chop with a knife and then crumble with your fingers.
6. Press a hollow in the middle of the mixture.
7. Gently break open the egg and spread it inside.
8. Knead the dough, form a ball, let it rest (lay hands on the ball).
9. Roll out the dough.
10. Form cookies and put them on the baking sheet.
11. Brush with egg.
12. Decorate with a nut on each cookie.
13. Put it in the oven.

Or how about a **"pizza massage"** at the beginning of your Italian lesson or a **"Baguette massage"** in French class?

The internal clock or How long is a minute?

"Can we feel how long a minute is? Let's all get up and close our eyes. I'm going to count the first few seconds for you, and then you keep counting inside. When 60 seconds have passed for you, open your eyes and sit down quietly."

I count up to eight out loud and keep looking at the clock. When 60 seconds have passed, I quietly write (or hold up a sign) "1 minute".

Do this exercise more often and see if the students develop a feeling for time.

HOW ARE YOU?

Finding out your students' inner state or mood can be a very short exercise - with a very large effect. When we do this, we are showing that the well-being of our students is important to us. They appreciate this.

Sentiment Barometer

For this purpose I write a "mood scale" from 10 to 1 on the blackboard. Then I ask the students to look inside themselves and find out where they are currently on the scale. The feedback can take place in different ways:

"Who is between one and three?
who's between 4 and 6?" etc.

or

"Turn to your neighbor. Ask him where he is on the scale and how he's doing." If the group is small, we can talk about it in the group. (on a voluntary basis, of course).

or

Put stickers on a poster

Each student is given a sticky dot and sticks it to the barometer where her inner state is at this moment. This way the teacher can determine the class's mood in general, and the sense of community is strengthened.

Thumbs up (or down)

There are many types of mood barometers that can be used. One of the simplest is "the showing of thumbs".

"If you feel really good, point your thumb up at the ceiling. If you're doing moderately well, hold your thumb parallel to the floor. And if you're miserable, point your thumb at the floor."

Or show or point at the correct smiley on the board.

Or hold up a green, red or yellow card.

Writing an internal weather report.

Sentiment Barometer

Emotions Cube

There are large cubes made of foam on which the sides of the cube can be labeled differently. Each side stands for a different location. Place on the table. Discuss the different sides or the emotions that are written on them. Where are you today

A show of hands

Sun = spread fingers, cloud = move fist up and down etc. When the teacher asks how the students feel, they show the corresponding hand signals.

The Feelings Mountain

Students mark the spot on the mountain where they are at this moment. At the top it is sunny and positive. In the middle it is neutral and at the bottom it is cold and gloomy.

What did you do this weekend?

- Whoever was at home stands in the middle of the classroom
- Whoever went to the country stands next to the door
- Whoever went to the movies,
  stands next to a window ...

We do this exercise after the Monday morning sitting circle, because usually one or two students don't say anything and then we know exactly what questions we can ask). The aim is to find and highlight commonalities. Outsiders are brought into the group in this way.

Martin R., elementary school, Vienna

Letting hand puppets talk:

Distribute hand puppets or put some in the middle of the room/circle. What is important to me today? If you want to talk, take a hand puppet and let the puppet talk for you.

If I were an apple

Draw a basket on the board or on a piece of wrapping paper.

Discuss different varieties and types of apples - yellow/green/red/ shriveled/ crunchy/ small/big etc.

If you were an apple, what would you look like?

Have them draw their own apple or choose one from the apple cards you have prepared. They put the apple in the basket and explain why they chose this apple and why it is in this particular place in the basket.

Maria D., Graz, middle school

Pick a card

Lay out pictures or postcards as a mandala on the floor. The pictures can belong to a certain theme. For example, in a teacher training seminar on the topic of "goal setting" I lay out postcards showing different paths (roads, paths, rivers, forest paths, etc.). When it comes to communication for conflict resolution, I lay out pictures of different bridges. Each student should choose a card that represents how she feels at that moment. How can communication be established? Why did she choose this card?

Mood pictures

Hang up different pictures expressing moods throughout the room. The pupils stand in front of the mood picture that best corresponds to their current mood. They talk to the others who are also standing by this picture, or when a student is standing there alone, he takes his feelings with him and joins another group and discussion.

Wailing Wall and Pleasure Garden

On one wall in the classroom there is a surface called the "Wailing Wall". At another place is the so-called "Pleasure Garden". When entering the room, the students can write down their current emotional state on the appropriate wall. They can also paint or stick on pictures and symbols. The statements are anonymous and are not discussed.

PICKING THEM UP WITH SUBJECT MATTER

Playful queries

All students stand up. Give them problems to solve. Let them do calculations in their heads or sets of irregular verbs. The teacher says „Go"and the student says „went - gone". Or go around the circle counting. A student who says a prime number sits down.

Form Italian sentences

I start every Italian lesson with an activity that involves movement. I distribute, for example, wordlessly and - if necessary - with a finger on the lips, so that the students know that they should not talk, one or two pieces of paper with an Italian word on each. Without speaking, the pupils form sentences by placing themselves in the correct order.

Peter F., secondary school

How I start the lesson depends on the students' mood

If they are excited, I start with brain gym exercises (cross-over exercises - elephant, thinking cap, writing exercises with the nose, breathe deeply in and out).

In English I like to start with repetitions for pronunciation or review questions while the students are standing. I throw a ball or a small stuffed animal. If they answer correctly, they sit down. But usually they get so into this, that after a few further tosses, I let them stand up again to stay in the game!

Sometime during the first lesson, I cannot expect any active cooperation or discussions, because some of them are still in deep sleep. So I start with quiet activities and slowly increase the amount of movement toward the middle of the lesson.

The resting phases also work well, where I put an hourglass on the table to determine the resting time.

Margit W., middle school

On the road with my backpack

At our school in Tirol, it is not the custom for students to stand up at the beginning of the lesson. I think this is a pity because standing up and becoming quiet at the beginning of the lesson automatically results in a quiet and peaceful beginning of the lesson. It's also a sign that something new is beginning. But I didn't want to be the only teacher who insisted on this. I was afraid to come across as too authoritarian.

When I have a lesson in the first period, they are often still half asleep. So I do a meditation activity with them while standing. I often use the guided fantasy exercises I learned with you. This helps them to concentrate and pay attention. They become centered and a peaceful start to the school day is guaranteed.

One of our favorites is „Hiking with my backpack". I tell the students to imagine that we are going hiking. Everyone carries a small backpack with a sandwich and a cold drink. On the way we find lots of beautiful stones, roots, flowers - and everything we find goes into the backpack. Even before you reach the first ascent, the backpack is heavy, you are tired and you feel like you can't go on. What can we do?

The students knew the answer: Take out everything you don't need. That's exactly what I wanted to hear from them. I told them that the same thing could happen in class - especially if the class was later in the day. The whole morning they were busy filling their backpacks. A lot happens at school: nice and sometimes not so nice experiences in other lessons, maybe something happened at home in the morning before coming to school. And in order to be able to really start afresh, it is sometimes necessary to free your mind from everything that is a burden for you, that annoys or simply occupies your mind either positively or negatively.

The students do the following with enthusiasm.
We all stand up, shake our arms and legs and wipe our body down with our hands to get rid of everything we don't need or want to have. It is amazing. It is absolutely silent in the room as they do this. Then I told them that it is not good if the backpack is completely empty, because we need strength to be able to learn well. So a little something to eat and drink has to stay in it. And then we stoke up on energy by breathing calmly with the fingertips of our hands touching each other. Then we calmly sit down and start the lesson. It works so well that my students have even asked other teachers if they could do the same in their lessons.

Claudia M., Secondary School

Arriving is important!

Teachers often tell me: *"I don't have time to do such exercises at the beginning of the lesson. We only have 50 minutes to work, and there's so much material to cover!"*

Believe me, the few minutes it takes to pick the students up are worth their weight in gold! If the students are concentrated and really present, they can do many times the usual amount of work in the remaining 47 minutes.

Do it like the Mohawks.
Allow the souls and spirits of your students to arrive!

6

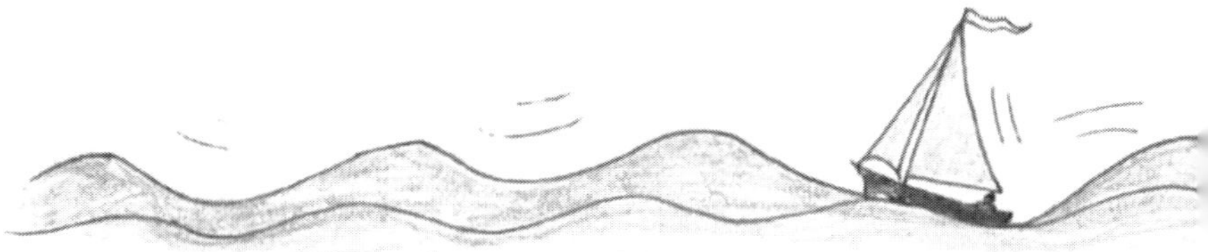

"To teach gracefully and beautifully, flow with the energy of your students" James Asher

"We've got rhythm! " Lessons that flow.

Rhythm is everywhere, and everything in life has rhythm.

The seasons, the weather, low tide and high tide, bodily functions, day and night, tension and relaxation, being active and resting, the rhythm of your heartbeat or the rise and fall of your rib cage when inhaling and exhaling. And there are also wave-like rhythms in the classroom. The noise level during group work, for example, is not uniform, but always goes up and down in a wave. Chatting or restlessness in the classroom also spreads in waves. Activities and games and also the moods of the pupils and the teacher are rhythmical.

If we are aware of these rhythms, we can use them. We can save ourselves a lot of energy and annoyance if we flow with the rhythm and energy in the classroom. We can then add new rhythms that make the lessons more engaging and effective. If active and reflective teaching phases, moods, social forms such as pair, small group, large group and individual work, guided and free work are consciously alternated by the teacher, students can work in a much longer and more concentrated way. They are integrated, fully involved, and the additional advantage is that the teacher can steer the group well by consciously determining the energy level. Extreme reactions are avoided and the lesson flows.

The rhythm of an activity

A very good question that I often hear is: When should I stop an activity?

Good timing is very important, because if you finish an activity at the right time, it is very motivating for the group.

Every activity, every game is also like a wave. The wave can of course have several crests and troughs, but to simplify our explanation, let's take an activity that has only one crest.

For example, I would like the students to play **signature bingo.**

> In this game each student gets a sheet of paper with nine squares and a question on each square. The pupils walk around the room and ask their classmates questions such as "Do you like pizza?", "Who won yesterday's football match?", "The capital of France is...", "9 x 8 is the same as..." etc. If a classmate can answer the question, he writes his name in the box. Now the second pupil may also ask the first one a question and, if he knows the answer, his name is written in the appropriate field. Then they say goodbye and look for a new partner to ask. The first person, who has a signature in all nine fields, shouts "Bingo!" and sits down. The students who are still standing look for more signatures until I say, "Done!"

If I sketch the rhythm of this activity, it would perhaps look like the one shown below. During the explanation, the students are quiet and listen to me with concentration - therefore there is a flat line leading to the wave. The activity begins quietly and becomes increasingly lively. At some point the wave will reach its peak. Everyone is excited, looking for new signatures and it automatically becomes louder. Shortly after the climax is passed, the group becomes calmer and calmer.

Now the question is, when should I end this activity?

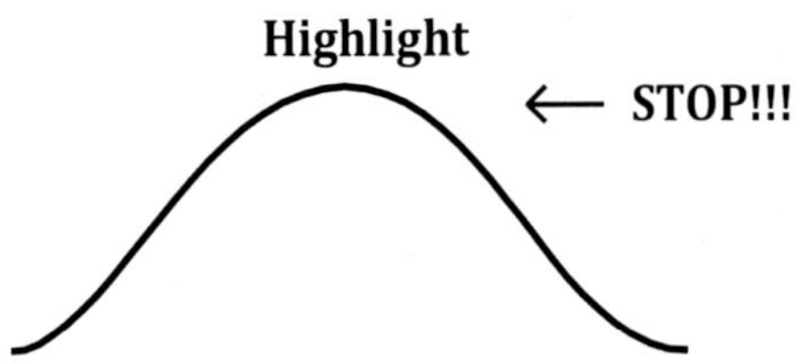

GOOD TIMING RESULTS IN HIGH MOTIVATION !!

If I wait until the wave goes back down into the trough, the students become lethargic. It was a lot of fun in the beginning, but now they are becoming bored. And, as we all know, bored students get into mischief!

One alternative would be to finish the game before it reaches its climax. But if I do that, they will miss out on the fun part of the game.

Good timing would be to end the activity shortly after the climax. The students are still fully engaged and would like to continue. They groan when they hear that they have to stop now and are happy when you say that they will soon have the opportunity to enjoy similar activities again.

The goal is that at the end of the lesson, your students will walk out the door saying to each other or to themselves: *"Today, the class was really fun. I'm looking forward to the next one!"* If that is the case - bingo! Then you and your students have won!

The ingredients for this success are a good sense of the timing or rhythm of the lesson and also the choice of activities that match your students' preferred modalities. Find something that your class really enjoys and do it during the last few minutes of the lesson or school day. If you use engaging, brain-friendly learning techniques, students will be totally engaged.

An example: When I was teaching at the middle school, it bothered me when the pupils read aloud. Their reading was often halted and monotonous. There was no color to their voice. No melody. So I told them: *"I have an idea. Today we will read the text the way the actors in the famous Vienna Burgtheater practice their lines. I will read you a sentence or phrase dramatically, and you will read the words in chorus exactly as I read them to you. That means the emphasis, emotion, volume, etc. should be exactly the same."* Then I whispered the first sentence dramatically. I also made dramatic gestures and facial expressions. They imitated me in chorus. Then I read the next sentence perhaps loudly and with a sad expression on my face, the following angrily and so on. It is very important that the students imitate your volume exactly - otherwise the exercise could get out of control.

My students loved doing these exercises. They did them with total enthusiasm and kept asking if we could please do this every lesson. And they indeed learned to read much more fluently. It even happened quite often that when the bell rang, they said they didn't want recess today and would rather continue reading!

The noise level is also rhythmic

The next time your class is involved in group work, consciously take a step back, dissociate and listen carefully to the level of noise. You will notice that the volume of noise in the classroom goes up and down, sometimes louder and sometimes a bit softer like a wave. If I want to get the group's attention and I interrupt the wave on its way up, I am swimming against the current. That means to get the group's attention I must become louder than they are. First of all that is bad for my vocal chords and the danger also exists that I will pick the group up at their volume and then move them to an even louder level.

The trick is to intervene when the wave is going down and not up. It is only a matter of waiting a few seconds - and our chances of success are much higher! However, it requires a fine ear, a lot of practice and a sense of timing.

In my book "Nonverbal Classroom Management" some techniques to get the attention of the group at the beginning of the lesson or in between are explained in detail. Here you will find a short summary:

If the students see you when you enter the classroom, you should not say anything. Assume a frozen posture and make eye contact with the students. Do not say anything. You lead the students to be still by being still yourself. Many teachers say, *"Well, I might end up standing there for the whole lesson, and they won't get quiet."* It won't be like that, although it may take them a while to get quiet the first few times. In a situation like this, a minute seems like half an hour to a teacher! But hang in there. It will be worth it.

It is also important that you do not scold the class after they have become quiet. This is a mistake I often made at the beginning of my teaching career at the commercial academy. Later when I mentioned this in a professional development course, a teacher asked me: *"But Pearl, why did you scold them? They were already quiet. You should have praised them instead!"* That statement was a major turning point in my career. How right he was! And how often do we complain or scold about a negative behavior that has ended and been replaced by a more positive one!

The next week when I was back at school in Vienna, I tried this. I came into the class, the students were all excited. They had had a test the lesson before this one, there was a fight during the break, and they were excited and loud. I came into the class, they stood up but were still very restless. I used an anchor that I often use: *"One, two, three - FREEZE!"* They froze like statues in place, and then I said in a whisper. *"Very nice. Now please sit down very quietly." After they had sat down,* I praised them and said, *"Great. You got quiet so fast! I have rarely had a class that could calm down as quickly as you can."* The expressions on their faces were wonderful. They were surprised because I did not criticize their loud behavior and happy about the praise (which was true and has to be meant honestly). They literally grew by a few centimeters right before my eyes! And the next time I came into the class, they settled down very quickly.

However, if the students do not notice that you have entered the room or that you want their attention, you must first briefly raise your voice above the volume of the class. Pause for a few seconds before continuing in a whisper. Then gradually increase the volume until you have reached your normal volume again.

This technique also works very well with music, which you can use for noise level control instead of the voice. Read more about this in Chapter 7: The Power of Music.

The „rhythmitization" or flow of the lessons

Your lesson plan should also ideally be wavelike. When designing your lesson plan, it is important to pay attention to the rhythm of the activities. The structure of the lesson should take the form of an infinite wave, i.e. at the highest point of the wave you will have active games and in the trough you will have energy-giving, reflective activities. In this way, the concentration and energy level can be kept at its highest level for a longer period of time AND you will always have the group under control. In this way, you can direct the energy level so that the students are attentive and active, but never become too lively or overexcited. And if your timing is sometimes a bit off, no problem. You can use the non-verbal tools which you are learning in this book to effortlessly get their attention again.

The wave sequences

The rule of thumb is: The older the group, the longer the sequences. In a group of teenagers or adults, they can stay concentrated and usually work for fifteen to twenty minutes. Then the attention span decreases and if I do not change the type of activity, my students get bored, frustrated or stressed.

But how do I do that with a class that is excited or unfocused?

First of all, I have to perceive where the group is at the moment. Many of our students are physically in the classroom, but in spirit they are somewhere else. As discussed in the last chapter, you can save yourself and your students a lot of time and energy in the classroom if you don't simply impose your lesson plan upon the students.

Pick them up where they are at the moment and then lead them to where optimal learning can take place. That is, when they are excited and unfocused, start with short sequences, and then gradually introduce longer sequences.

When they are restless, NOT like this:

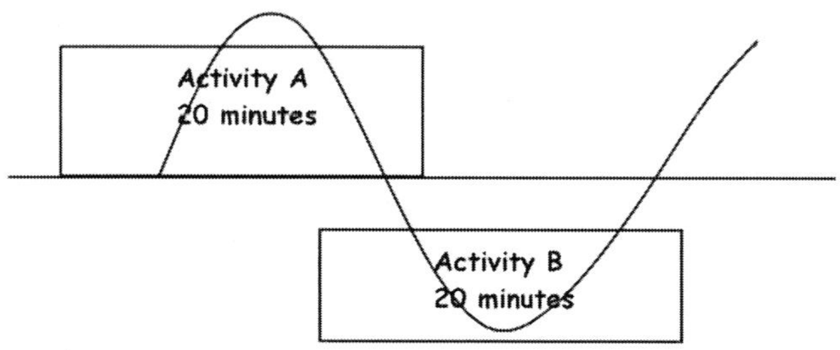

BUT SO:

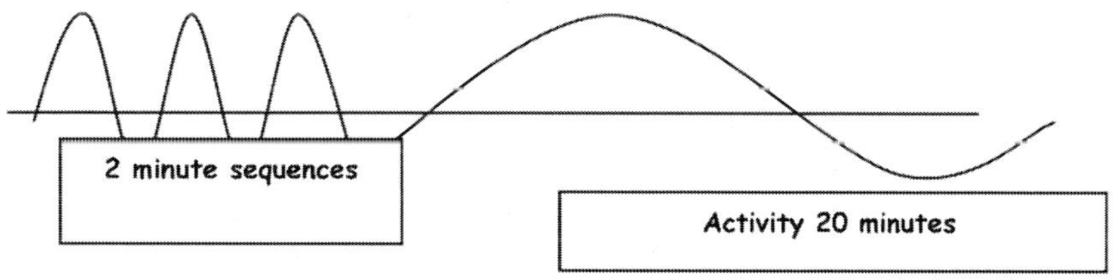

Or pick them up in the lively state they are currently in and bring them down step by step.

An example:
I enter the classroom. The students are all excited and unfocused. I have them stand up and I say, *"1 - 2 - 3 - FREEZE!"* They freeze their posture and they are quiet. Then I lead them through the following activities while standing behind their chairs. At the beginning, the activities are lively and gradually become more and more calm, for example:

Imagine,

- you are running (in place behind their chairs) in a marathon,
- you're getting faster and faster... and faster... you want to win!
- but now you're getting tired. You're slowing down... and getting even slower...
- the marathon is now over, and you're strolling home along a shopping street...
- you occasionally stop at a store window and look in...
- and now you are home ...
- you go into the living room and sit down, exhausted...
- there's a visitor at your house. They have a baby. The baby is sleeping and you're holding him in your arms. You rock the baby gently back and forth.
- You get more and more tired and carefully give the baby back to its mother.
- You put your head on your arms and close your eyes for a minute.
- You breathe in and out deeply and enjoy this minute.
- And now you open your eyes again. You feel completely concentrated and awake and you are looking forward to our lesson.

„Work with the learners, not against them!"
Jim Wingate

Use the class's energy - and not your own!

In martial sports such as Judo the goal is to use your opponent's energy rather than depleting your own strength. The same should apply to the classroom. Pick them up at their energy level and gently lead them to a more acceptable one. This is another situation where the ability to dissociate is so important. If I take a step back in a metaphorical or in a literal sense, and can see, hear and assess where the class is, it is then a simple task to pick them up at that moment. I can then steer the class's energy in such a way that I have the events in the classroom under control - without excitement or raising my voice. Simply go with the flow and then peacefully lead them where you need them to be. Use the class's energy rather than your own. It's good for them. And it's good for you!

A teacher recently wrote to me:

> *"It's genius. Now I understand why I used to be so exhausted at the end of the school day. When the energy level in the class was low, I tried to lift it up with my own energy. And when the students were too lively, I would use all my strength to try to reduce their energy level and avoid chaos in the classroom. Today I do it differently. First I determine where the class is at this moment, and then I direct the energy of the class instead of wasting my own.*

The ideal lesson is like a wave. Activities with a low energy flow, such as storytelling, visualization and fantasy journeys, painting, reading, writing, drawing and meditative dancing are followed by activities with a high energy flow, such as pair and group work, ball games, drama and role play, movement exercises, etc. In this way you achieve a high level of concentration. And because you alternate the energy levels, you can easily control the energy level of the class.

Change the mood or the inner state

If you notice that the students are becoming lethargic or, conversely, restless, you can change this mood, or - as it is also called - the "Inner State", by consciously raising or lowering the energy level by choosing another activity.

If you want to lead the class from being lively to calm

- Students automatically become calm - externally and internally - as soon as they start to write or read or perform a visual activity such as drawing
- Guided fantasy and visualization activities

Or do a short **concentration exercise** such as

- Distribute finding mistake pictures, mazes, Sudoku or puzzles.
- Close your eyes and stay completely still for one to two minutes.
- Close your eyes. Open the windows. Recognize five sounds from outside and then write them down.
- Yoga exercises, Kinesiology/Brain Gym.
- Breathe together - either the entire class or with your neighbor.

- The students close their eyes and are each given ten paper clips. The aim is to make a chain with their eyes closed. Talking is prohibited.
- Stretch, stretch and collective yawn.
- A wooden bowl with a glass marble inside is silently passed around the circle. The marble must always remain in circular motion. Do this with up to three marbles!
- Silently pass a bowl of water with a burning candle around the circle.
- Writing or drawing on the back of another child. The other child has to guess what has been written or drawn.
- Laying a mandala (silent exercise according to M. Montessori). You need a round, space or cloth and different objects - possibly according to the season - with which you can lay a mandala and quiet music. The teacher starts by placing an object in the middle. The students follow one after the other - always without speaking! Together they create a beautiful picture. This exercise requires a great deal of concentration and promotes the feeling of group. The students love it!
- A basket with different stones in it is passed around the circle. Each student takes a stone, feels it and looks at it. The stone is then passed on to the person sitting on the right. Continue passing the stones on until the students receive the original stone again.
- A gong is struck by the teacher. The students should keep their eyes closed and listen as long as they can still hear the gong vibrating.
- A cloth with various bells arranged in a circle is placed in the middle of the student circle. Each child may ring a bell of their choice.
- Building a stone castle. Material: Basket with different stones (it also works with building blocks - but stones are more natural and beautiful). Music in the background.
  Each student takes one stone. He should memorize what it looks like. The students take turns building a castle. The stones must be placed so that the castle is solid.
  After the castle is built, each student takes his stone away again without knocking the others over.

A preschool class creates a mandala

Gabriele S., elementary school

If you and the class have done a lot of mental work, bring a little **life and movement** into the classroom with the following activities, which can be adapted to the learning material:

- shake hands
- tongue twisters
- ball games
- guessing games, riddles, puzzles and quizzes
- facial expressions and role plays, pantomime
- boardgames and card games
- structuring, categorizing and pairing
- interactive information exchange through pair and group work
- movement songs and dances, rhythmic exercises
- relays and other team games
- open learning and work stations around the classroom

7

The Power of Music

Music affects our emotions. It makes us happy or thoughtful. It sets us in motion and fills us with energy. It can lead us into a relaxed state and increase our concentration. It evokes powerful memories and associations. Music can heal. Babies who listen to classical music in their mothers' wombs can be calmed after birth when the same music is played. If Alzheimer's patients are aggressive reduce their aggressions with music. Mozart is played in dairy barns so that the cows give more milk. Music and singing or playing instruments together binds groups together.

Since the beginning of time, music has played a central role for people of all cultures and in all parts of the world. But when you go to work or get "serious" about a topic, the music is turned off! Why?

In this chapter, I would like to present some valuable guidelines and suggestions which, through the targeted use of music, can support

the self-disciplining classroom
as well as **the joy of learning**

for all age groups and school types.

"Music is one of the most powerful means of suggestion we can use in the classroom!"
Dr. Charles Schmid

When using music in the classroom, you are the conductor. Your class is the orchestra. You lead, and together with the class you can achieve great performances and successes. In the classroom, the orchestra, and not the conductor, should be the focus of success. Brain-friendly learning is learner-centered. The students take responsibility. The teacher moves out of the spotlight. Sometimes she even seems to "disappear". At the same time she has everything under control and conducts inconspicuously in the background.

When using music in brain-friendly lessons, YOU - without it being obvious – are in charge. You choose the music that is used. The music sets the tone and determines the mood in your classroom. The result, which we will discuss on the following pages: An atmosphere of resonance, energy, harmony and relaxation. A group dynamic is created which promotes learning and cooperation.

Music can be used both for content and material mediation and as an instrument for classroom management.

Teaching content with music

In the brain-friendly classroom, the use of music is indispensable. Individual musical elements can be used, and there are teaching approaches such as Suggestopedia, where music is an essential component for learning.

The Theory of Multiple Intelligences

In 1983 Howard Gardner, professor of psychology at Harvard University, presented his **Theory of Multiple Intelligences** after many years of research. He considered measuring intelligence with traditional IQ tests to be much too narrow. These IQ tests only take verbal-linguistic and logical-mathematical abilities into consideration. A student could have low scores on a traditional IQ test but be a genius in some other area. Gardner's theory has resulted in a learning revolution. He divides intelligence into eight or nine categories: verbal-linguistic, logical-mathematical, spatial, auditory, bodily kinesthetic, naturalistic, interpersonal, intrapersonal and musical-rhythmic. The 9th intelligence which he is still in the process of developing is spiritual. Gardner believes that classroom learning should address multiple areas of intelligence. This makes it easier for us not only to reach our students' preferred „intelligences", but also to strengthen and expand the others.

The musical-rhythmic intelligence is particularly pronounced in the age groups represented in our classes. How often have parents come to me and said: *"We don't understand this. Our son is almost failing English and does not bring you any homework. "But he sits at home every afternoon and translates pop songs from English to German."* Such statements opened my eyes. When I went through English song lyrics in class, when we worked on selected English music videos in class, when my students gave presentations on pop musical groups, I could reach my pupils who were learning English as a foreign language. The rest was child's play. Use music in class - Reach them to teach them!

The use of music in Suggestopedia / Superlearning

Dr. Georgi Lozanov and Dr. Evelyna Gateva, who developed the brain-friendly learning method Suggestopedia, focused part of their research on memory enhancement through the use of music. Suggestopedia uses classical largos and adagios as background music to present the subject material. This results in an atmosphere of mental alertness and a relaxed learning atmosphere. In Suggestopedia the amount of material learned is much larger, and it is learned three to five times faster than in conventional learning. The next stage is activating this material which has been passively stored in the brain with communicative, interactive learning techniques.

I am a certified Suggestopedia trainer and have also taught together with my colleagues from the middle school and high school with techniques from modern Suggestopedia and Superlearning. Our students achieved very high results and, most important, learning in this manner was very motivating for them.

I tell the students at the very beginning that this is a special music that benefits our bodies as well as our brains - the heart and our breathing are slowed down by the music, and after we have listened to it for a while we feel calm, fresh and rested. The music also turns on our brain so that we can learn better and easier.

I am often asked if the children do not rebel and say they want to listen to more modern music. So far, this has not been the case. They like the music, and since I have told them about its benefits, they often ask: *"Could you please turn on the music that helps us learn better?"*

Creative activation of material learned with music

There are countless ways in which music can be used to activate the teaching material. Here are just a few of them:

- Music can be used as an **introduction** to a topic. If we are discussing the baroque period in history class, I can play baroque music at the beginning of the lesson. If the topic in the geography lesson is Africa, I can play African drum music for a warm-up exercise and so on.
- **Songs, poems** and **raps** help pupils to remember facts and details better. There are such teaching materials for sale, e.g. "Young Poets and Thinkers", which is a children's group that rhythmically and musically deals with topics such as the multiplication tables, classical poems such as Sorcerer's Apprentice and also modern poems. (See also: http://www. youtube.com/watch?v=FJw2LsXHrzY)
- Another way of learning foreign languages is presented by "The Grooves". English, French, Turkish, etc. A special combination of music and language ensures that the vocabulary is stored in the memory. The music, which matches the cultural area, creates an authentic atmosphere and you will experience the first language course you want to dance in. Highly recommended! (See also: http://www.thegrooves.de/site/about.html)
- A creative challenge for the learners is to create new lyrics containing the newly learned facts to the tune of a familiar melody such as „Happy Birthday“ or „She'll be coming round the mountain.
- Guided fantasy or visualizations of the material learned with relaxing music in the background.

Music as a classroom management tool

You're the conductor. You choose the music, and by selecting, timing and adjusting the volume, you determine the atmosphere in the classroom.

Music as a mood enhancer

Arriving

What influences have your students been exposed to during the break or in the lessons before yours? School activities, arguments during the recess, other excitement, perhaps problems at home. It was often the case that a hectic, sometimes aggressive atmosphere was in the air when I came into class. So I picked them up where they were by showing understanding and saying: *"I know you are tense now. It was very busy today. What do you think about the idea that you just spend two minutes relaxing? Put your heads on your arms, close your eyes, and I will play beautiful music for you."*

They felt understood, and the short break was very welcome. I turned on a quietly flowing music. Sometimes I would say at the end of the two minutes: *"If you like, you can just keep listening to the music while I read you the short story about Pedro in Chile from our geography book."* By the time I finished reading, the atmosphere in the room was completely different and we were able to spend the hour productively.

In my language institute the participants were mainly adults. Many of those who took evening courses came to us exhausted after work. When they arrived and sat down in the classroom, music was usually playing in the background. We choose this music very carefully! If we played slow, meditative music, they would fall asleep! But if we put on more lively music, they would also get lively. They weren't so drowsy anymore and we could work and learn better.

In other words: we can use music to regulate the students' energy. Tired groups can be refreshed by movement and rhythm. Groups that are overly excited and very lively can be put into the right mood by using soft and calming music. It is all done without talking. You set the tone. Without admonitions. Gently.

Ending the lesson

You can also use music to round off your lessons or the school day. Just as you welcomed the students with music at the beginning of the lesson, you can also bid them farewell with lively and fast music. You know: First and last impressions are the most lasting! Therefore choose "catchy tunes" for these phases if possible, so that the lesson and your subject will be remembered positively!

Breaks

It depends on your school situation whether you can use music during the breaks. Some of the schools I have worked with also have a quiet room with meditative music for the breaks and those who want to, including the teachers, can use it. The teacher can signal the end of recess with a piece of music she always uses for this purpose: signaling that the break is over. She plays it once and signals nonverbally toward the classroom. The pupils hear the music and head toward their seats without a word.

Music as an anchor

The definition of an anchor is: A stimulus that causes the same reaction over and over again. When a teacher repeatedly and systematically uses a non-verbal signal in connection with an event, concept or idea in the classroom, the signal and the concept become anchored together - words become superfluous (more about anchors in the chapter "Table leg no. 3: Structure! Structure! Structure!").

Think, for example, of signature tunes on radio and television. We all recognize the theme tunes for the news, the weather or "The Dream Boat". We can consciously use this knowledge in the classroom. For example, if you always play the same music at the beginning of the math lesson, the students will automatically know that the lesson is about to begin.
Or how about James Brown's "I feel good!" as a welcome song in the morning? Each student greets and shakes hands with three other students before the music fades out. Or Madonna's "We are living in a material world" as a theme song for chemistry class. Positive group work results are celebrated with Queens "We are the champions!"

Music as a noise curtain

We as teachers can make learning easier for our students in many ways. One of many ways to reduce the fear of making mistakes is to use music as a background „curtain“.

As a seasoned foreign language teacher, I know that the biggest obstacle to learning a foreign language is fear of making mistakes or sounding silly. Suppose I ask a group a question for discussion in the foreign language. I briefly leave the room and suddenly I notice that there is total silence in the classroom. I look inside and see that the group is working hard, but instead of talking at a normal volume, they are whispering to each other.

The cause is immediately clear to me – fear of making mistakes!
This is the number 1 enemy in foreign language learning as well as for other subjects. It is only when our students overcome this fear that learning will take off.

It is embarrassing for all of us - whether in language classes or otherwise - to make mistakes. And when we find ourselves in a new, unfamiliar situation where we don't know anyone and feel insecure - like at the beginning of a new school year, for example - we have the tendency to speak more quietly. So no one hears our mistakes. It is quite natural. And at the same time a huge obstacle to learning.

In learning situations, making mistakes is inevitable. And it is also good. Otherwise nothing is learned. Learning, just like change and growth, means taking risks. If I don't take risks, I will feel very comfortable in my familiar world, but everything remains the same - until I am ready to risk making mistakes!

If I see that a group for some reason is not loosening up, I can use music as a protective "curtain". I play music in the background during group work. This takes their inhibitions away because they have the feeling that no one outside of their group can hear their mistakes. And slowly I increase the volume. As the music gets louder, the students also speak louder and their inhibitions disappear.

Music as volume control

As mentioned in the chapter "We've got rhythm!" the volume of a group automatically adjusts to the volume of the music.

There are only a few exceptions to this rule, e.g. if the members of a group perform a very interactive - and therefore loud - activity, then they do not notice the music anymore. But for the most part, you can control the volume of the group with the volume of the music.

The sounds in the classroom are not linear, but wavelike. They constantly go up and down, getting louder and quieter. If we try to interrupt while the sound wave is getting louder, we are swimming against the current. Of course, then we have to become even louder, and there is a great danger that we will lead the group to an even higher volume.
The trick is to catch the group's attention with your voice as the wave and the volume are going down. It's only a matter of seconds - and as a result our chances of success are much higher.
We can pick the group by matching their volume and then guide the volume with our voices. However, this requires a fine ear and practice. You can do this with your voice – or you can adapt the volume of the music to achieve the same result.

During group work, for example, I play music softly in the background. The group unconsciously adapts to the volume of the music. This means that if I turn the music up, the group gets louder, and conversely, if I fade the music out, the group gets quieter. So I stand next to the CD player when I want to end the group work and slowly turn the music up. The group adapts itself unconsciously and gets louder and louder as I create an artificial wave with the volume of the music. Then I slowly turn the music down more and more - and the group also becomes quieter. Then I simply start with my normal voice volume - a little louder than the music and the group - and continue with the lesson without any effort.

The faster the music, the faster the group's work tempo

Set the working tempo

Recently, in a learning techniques seminar for adults, I tried out your tips on how to guide a group's working speed with slow/quiet or fast/loud music. It worked perfectly. I could calm the group down with slow music and get them to work faster with loud and fast music!

Based on this experience, I now use music much more consciously in class and also in tutoring lessons! The results are great!

Ruth L., elementary & middle school

Group dynamics

Music is a great way to create a beautiful group dynamic atmosphere. Music helps a group experience a sense of belonging; music binds different cultures and people together; class rituals such as greetings or goodbyes, performed with music in the background, help students identify with the class or the school.

Some more suggestions:

The music sets the tone

The first thing I do in the morning upon crossing our welcome doormat to enter the classroom is to turn on the music.

Today we had our art lesson. Each child received an A3 sheet of drawing paper and prepared their paints. I played a total of six different pieces of music. First a calm piece. I invited them to paint something to the music. I played the piece twice, for a total of about six minutes. At first the children found it difficult to paint something to it. Then I collected all the sheets of paper, passed out new ones and played the next piece of music. This was a fast piece. We did a total of six rounds (slow music, sad, pop, a march, a love song, etc.) It was interesting to see how the children's moods changed with the music and also how their pictures changed. It was very difficult to bring the children down again after a very pop and fast music piece. I was amazed at the effect that music had on their art!

Harald S., secondary school

Music is powerful

It makes our hearts cry and laugh. Music sets the tone. And since you choose the music, you set the tone! You have complete control over the atmosphere in your classroom. Choose the music according to the mood you want to create - sometimes lively, sometimes quiet, sometimes exciting, etc. The effect is like magic!

Table Leg Number 2:
The 10 commandments of group dynamics

If we believe that our students come to school only to learn, we are wrong! The real reason students come to school is for relationships and friendships. Relationships with each other and also with their teachers are important to them. If your students feel that you like them, and if the relationship between the individual students in your classroom is also harmonious, discipline problems disappear.

In this part we will discuss the 10 commandments of group dynamics. Follow these so that your students are motivated and enjoy coming to school. We will look at the theory and especially the practice. How did other teachers do it? And what games and activities can you try out 1:1 in class tomorrow to create a group that works as a team.

The 10 Commandments of Group Dynamics

The First Commandment

Establish **RAPPORT**!

The Second Commandment

RELATIONSHIPS are everything!

The Third Commandment

Create an atmosphere of **TRUST**!

The Fourth Commandment

Emphasize both their **UNIQUENESS** and
also what your students have in **COMMON**!

The Fifth Commandment

Promote team building through **COMMON GOALS**
and **ELIMINATING COMPETITION!**

The Sixth Commandment

Let the students do something **SIMULTANEOUSLY**!

The Seventh Commandment

Tell **METAPHORICAL STORIES!**

The Eighth Commandment

Pick them up: **PHYSICALLY** and also **MENTALLY**!

The Ninth Commandment

INVOLVE them!

The Tenth Commandment:

INTEGRATE THE **OUTSIDERS!**

The first commandment

Create RAPPORT:
the prerequisite for good communication!

Let's start with a story:

Once upon a time there was a man who died. He stood before the Pearly Gates to heaven and waited patiently while St. Peter looked him up in his book.

"So" said St. Peter. "I see that you were very well-behaved on earth. So I'm going to give you a choice: Do you want to go to heaven or do you prefer hell?"

The man pondered for a moment and then asked, "I find it difficult to decide, sir, since I have never been to heaven and I have never been to hell. May I please look at these two places before I make a decision?"

St. Peter agreed, and they left right away on the road to hell.
They walked down a long corridor and came to a large bright room at the end of the corridor. In that room a group of people sat in a circle. In front of each person there was a spoon with a long handle, and in the middle of the circle a large pot of fragrant and tasty looking goulash was steaming. The people all looked sad.

The man asked St. Peter why the people were so sad. Peter answered, "They are sad because they are hungry. They cannot eat the goulash because the handle of the spoon is so long that they cannot put the spoon into their mouths."

The man replied that he did not really want to be hungry for all eternity. He wondered if he could take a look at heaven?

St. Peter agreed and they walked down another long corridor and came into a large bright room, similar to the first room. In this room there was also a group of people sitting in a circle. In front of each person there was a spoon with a long handle, and in the middle of the circle stood a large pot of fragrant and tasty looking steaming goulash. The only difference was: these people looked quite happy.

The man asked Peter, "I don't understand. Everything here is exactly the same as in the other room. But these people are happy and satisfied. What's different here?"

Peter replied, "It is very simple. These people have learned to use their spoons to feed each other."

This metaphorical story represents our goal in the self-disciplining classroom: We want to achieve a class that works together as a team, a group that strives for common goals, a community where members cooperate rather than compete, a class where outsiders are integrated into the group as valuable members. If we can achieve this, the class will function as a self-regulating and humane community where discipline measures becomes unnecessary.

Rapport: the key to good communication

One of the important prerequisites for the self-disciplining classroom is rapport. There are two different types of rapport: **Individual Rapport** and **Group Rapport**. Both types are necessary. They differ only in the way they are produced.

Let us first look at rapport with an individual.

Rapport

SCENE

Imagine ...

...you're at a seminar and you sit down next to another participant you have never met before. During the break you start chatting with each other. You get along right away and are amazed at how much you have in common! It's as if you've known each other all your lives!

It simply clicked between you...

But you will also be familiar with situations like the following one ....

...you have an aunt you have to visit every two or three months. Actually, the aunt is a very nice woman, but for some reason you don't feel good going to see her. You don't quite understand why. You may even feel a little guilty. There's nothing wrong with the aunt. But every time the visit is over, you breathe a sigh of relief.

It didn't click here like it did at the seminar. But why? What is the difference?

The answer is rapport.

Rapport means to be on the same wavelength with another person. We feel in harmony, in rapport, with people or groups that are similar to us. Rapport is an important prerequisite for good communication.

Each of us has our own style of communication, which is shaped by our preferred main mode of communication - visual, auditory or kinesthetic. This style of communication is expressed - usually on an unconscious level – nonverbally through our gestures, facial expressions, posture, movement, voice and choice of words. If both conversation partners share the same main modality – visual, auditory or kinesthetic - the result is spontaneous rapport. In other words you are both on the same wavelength and enjoy being together.

With the aunt there is no rapport. You do not share the same modality and have little in common.

When two people share the same modality, rapport occurs by itself:

Two visual personalities watch a beautiful sunset. They don't have to talk at all. The fact alone that they are allowed to experience this beautiful sight together is enough to give them a great feeling of togetherness. Two kinesthetics are jogging into the sunset - and they experience that same feeling of harmony and rapport. And two auditories watch the beautiful sunset - and talk the whole night about every sunset they have ever experienced. They enjoy each other's company, and they are in rapport!

In these examples, rapport arises by itself because the modalities coincide by chance. But what does it look like if you have a conversation with a person who has a different preferred modality? How can you make good communication work when there you have varying modalities?

The first step is to determine the communication style of your counterpart. After I have identified the visual, auditory or kinesthetic communication style on the basis of her verbal and non-verbal messages, I can briefly step into her reality by mirroring her communication style. We are then on the same wave length, the prerequisite for good communication has been fulfilled.

First comes rapport. Then pacing and leading

After rapport has been established, use "pacing", i.e. walking in step with the person you are talking to for a while before you take the lead. Pacing can be compared to jumping onto a bus that is already moving. If you jump directly onto it, you will injure yourself. First you walk or run alongside the bus for a while until you are equally fast and then you jump on. When a teacher "paces" a student she listens and watches to determine where he is at the moment; she acknowledges him. She perceives his reality and may even step into that reality for a short time. She goes with him for a while before taking the next step to lead him to where he can actually learn more easily and better.

Rapport takes place for the most part on a non-verbal level. You do not have to agree with someone to be in rapport with him. It is not even necessary to like the person you are talking to. Rapport is simply a respectful interaction on both sides. You and your dialogue partner can have completely different opinions and still be in rapport. Just because you have different opinions, you can still be in rapport. A person is - fortunately - more than what he does or believes.

In this first type of rapport, rapport with the individual, you mirror your conversation partner to establish rapport.

Group rapport

With **group rapport** it is different: the group is your reflection!
That means if you're quiet, the group is quiet. If you talk a lot, your students will talk a lot, etc.
In other words: YOU SET THE TONE.

The class reflects the teacher

I work with my girlfriend in a buddy project at our school. During a meeting with the students we planned several games in a "relaxed atmosphere".

My friend has a very loud voice. As soon as she started to say or explain something, the noise level in the classroom automatically became louder. I, on the other hand, talked a lot, and when I took the lead, the group suddenly talked a lot too.

This was really very interesting for me to observe. My girlfriend and I talked about this phenomenon afterwards, and this reflection did us both good.

Andrea W., middle school

Group rapport is a kind of "chemistry" between you and your class. It is like a dance where you lead and the others follow. When you are in rapport with your class, you can control what happens in the classroom gently and without resorting to power tactics. Therefore, the relationship you establish with your students is one of your most important tools for creating a learner-friendly atmosphere.

Rapport opens the door to their world. And where rapport reigns, a lot of the stress and the time required for classroom management is greatly reduced. The tone - also on the part of the students - and the atmosphere are very respectful and therefore much quite efficient. Power struggles disappear and are replaced by productive discussions. Through the use of influence instead of power and through your charisma and aura of positive, natural authority, a harmonious cooperation is created. You and the class have common goals. The "I" has become a "we".

And how do you do that?
The other nine commandments will tell us that.

Group Rapport

The second commandment

RELATIONSHIPS ARE EVERYTHING!

Have you watched the movie "Dangerous Minds" with Michelle Pfeiffer?
It describes the experiences of Lou Anne Johnson, an ex-marine and English teacher in the run-down Parkmont High School in California. She was given the task of teaching English literature to a bunch of disinterested and violent kids at this ghetto high school. Hate, drugs and violence dominated the difficult daily life at this school. She was fighting against a myriad of behavioral problems with these students. But slowly and surely she began to win their trust. Her superiors, colleagues and sometimes the parents questioned the unconventional methods she was using. But she asserted herself and by doing so changed lives.

In the meantime, Lou Anne Johnson is active in teacher training and I recently attended one of her online seminars.

How did she do it? How did she win over this difficult and sometimes dangerous class? The answer is simple: on the relationship level.

Her – as well as my – advice is:

Show your students you like them.
Like them as students - but like them even more as people.
Talk to them like adults.
Treat them with respect. And expect or demand, if necessary, respect from them.

What does everyone need and want?

Each of us wants to be accepted as the person we are. We don't want anyone to "tinker" with us and try to change us. If you can accept and like your fellow human beings, your students, your colleagues, your friends and family members as they are, resistance will disappear. By accepting them they become open for change. They offer less resistance and are more willing to listen to and consider your suggestions, ideas and impulses. Because you accept them, you have opened the door to building a positive relationship with them. Let them know that you like them. This is the way to reach even the most difficult students.

It's not always easy – especially at the beginning. Sometimes a student is suspicious. They're not used to the fact - as sad as it is - that others like them. Maybe they think you're trying to trick them. Or that they'll get hurt if they open up. There may be some you won't reach at all. But when and where it works, you'll see a big change in behavior.

It is very important that you distinguish between the person and her behavior. If a student breaks the rules, if she does something that is not acceptable to you or the class, it does not mean that she is a bad person. It just means that this behavior was not appropriate at that time and place. She's still a good person. You still like her. For (most) teachers this distinction between behavior and person is clear. It's not like that though for the kids.

For most students friendships at school and their relationship to you are more important than learning. Elementary school teachers notice this more than teachers who deal with older students. Young children love their teacher and they want to be loved by the teacher. Everything is clear and obvious. Then they reach puberty. Their behavior changes. The pupils, who a few months ago were so lively, appear to become lifeless zombies who only loll around in their chairs. It costs them far too much strength to even raise their hands.

In addition, at this age it is no longer "in" to like the teacher. Otherwise, the students might think... -that the student is a brownnoser. Outwardly the youngsters are "cool" - but inwardly they are still very insecure. Their needs are the same. Teenagers also want you to like them. But they don't show it. This difficult age group can also be won over by clearly showing that you accept and like them.

I hear some of you saying, *"Yes, but I have a student in class I just can't stand!"* I understand that feeling - I've experienced it myself. But, I guarantee you, if we actively search, we will find something positive in every person we meet in life. It doesn't have to be something big. A small thing is enough to change the whole situation for the better.

I had a student called "Happy" (Yes, that was really his name.). He was a refugee from Africa and had a difficult history behind him. At the same time - and maybe because of that - he was a very difficult student. He was at least three or four years older than the others in the class (as with many refugees, his actual age was not known), and outside of school he moved in circles that did not exercise a good influence on him and consequently on the other children in the class. I was sympathetic to his situation. But I simply did not like him. I think that's okay. We don't have to like everybody, be it at school or anywhere else. So I decided to take my own advice (it's not always so easy) and find something positive about Happy. After some thought I came up with something I could honestly praise, and the next day I told him in passing: *"You know, Happy, I like it so much when you smile. Your smile really matches your name."* The effect was stunning. He was radiant. And I had finally reached him!

I don't mean to say that all the problems were solved. That was not the case. But I did find a way to make a connection with him. It was now possible to talk to him and the door for change was open. By openly showing empathy you achieve much more than by criticizing, ranting, raving, ignoring, getting excited etc.

The ability to build honest relationships with problem students is the most important tool a teacher can have in her toolbox. If you succeed, you will gain the respect of your students. And if your students like you and trust you, they will cooperate and behave better. A process is set in motion. If you like them, the students will start to like themselves. If they like themselves, learning and their future become important to them. And everyone is a winner.

There are no problem students, There are only students with problems

The difficult students who sit in our classes were not born like that. They have learned this behavior. They are problematic because they themselves have problems. They do not lead an easy life and often come from a milieu that does not support them and does not convey values and empathy. But although they do not enjoy the same benefits that other, more docile classmates who behave positively enjoy, they have exactly the same needs. The teachers who can meet these needs will be able to deal with them more easily.

As Rob Plevins, teacher trainer from the British organization "Behavior Management" writes:

"These are the very students we need to reach: the behaviorally challenged; the students who are difficult and challenge us; the vulnerable and confused; the angry, the bad and the sad. These are the students who cause problems in class: the silly ones who want to draw attention to themselves, the mischievous ones who play pranks and fool around, the sneaky ones who make other people's lives miserable and the absent ones who don't care.

To solve the problem we need to identify the need. Very often the discipline problem solves itself as soon as the need is met. Let us now look at some of the needs that we want to address in our students in order to reach them more effectively.

The need to be autonomous

Students want choices. They need a feeling of recognition as well as freedom. We can give them that while teaching them, at the same time, to be responsible and self-disciplined.

Let go! - Hand over responsibility

The most important step is that we ourselves give up control. Very often we teachers take on the problems of our students as if they were our own problems.

The essential question you should ask yourself in such a case and in all such situations in life is: *"Whom does the problem belong to?"* In most cases, you will find that the problems you are upset about are usually not yours at all, but the problems of your students or their parents. It is HIS responsibility, not yours, to do the homework.

We are not responsible for everything. We're always supposed to do our best. That's our responsibility, and it's a very big one. But I'm sure you do or you wouldn't be reading this book. But the student and his parents also have responsibilities. And if the student has not yet learned to take on responsibility and be self-disciplined, then I am doing him, the class and myself something very positive by teaching him this.

Labels

Another obstacle is "labels" such as "ADHD" or "behavioral problems", which are "officially" imposed on our students. When you give a label to a student, he or she can choose to give you or the world the responsibility. *"I can't control my behavior because I have......."* And then the responsibility is yours again.

There is a wonderful (and very amusing) short lecture on You Tube by Sir Ken Robinson entitled, "Do schools kill creativity?" (http://www. youtube.com/watch?v=iG9CE55wbtY). He tells the story of Gillian Lynne, a woman who was a dancer, theatre director and choreographer of the musicals "Cats" and "Phantom of the Opera".

When Gillian was about eight years old, her teachers complained that she was unfocused and could not sit still. So her mother took her to the doctor. The doctor listened to her entire medical history and then told Gillian that he wanted to talk to her mother alone in the other room for a moment. When the doctor and the mother left the room, while passing by his desk, he turned on the radio. Outside the door he stopped with the mother and asked her to watch Gillian. When Gillian heard the music, she jumped up and started dancing spontaneously. They watched with fascination and then the doctor told the mother: "Mrs. Lynn, Gillian is not ill. She is a dancer. Enroll her in a dance school."

If this had happened today, Gillian would probably have been diagnosed and "labeled" with ADHD and the world would have missed out on an artist.

Distribute class jobs

Very often the students who cause the most problems are the ones who have the most leadership potential. Offer them responsible tasks. This shows them that we have confidence in them, gives them something meaningful to do and builds their self-confidence.

I had one student in my English class, Richard, who was notorious for being a problem student. He was no angel with me either - until I appointed him to be my "cassette expert". We had CDs to accompany our English lessons, but I always took the old-fashioned cassettes for the lessons in Richard's class. Of course it was cumbersome to find the right place for the current exercise on the cassette. That's why I always let Richard, my "cassette expert", sit at the teacher's desk and quietly search for the correct exercises on the cassette. He was very busy - forwards, backwards, forwards - and there was peace and quiet in the class. It didn't bother me that he was sitting at my desk. I didn't sit there during the lesson. While Richard was searching for the right place on the tape, he was still listening to the lesson. And afterwards I always praised him. It worked wonders. He became the best behaved student I ever had.

Once he came to me during the break and told me that his father had visited him at the weekend and given him a music cassette. He had brought it with him to play as background music in English class. I thought *to* myself: *"What kind of music will this be? And how do I tell him if it's not suitable?"* It was Chopin, and I'll never forget his proud face when we played his cassette in class.

It is incredible how much a bit of individual attention and a sense of achievement can motivate these students. Richard was the cassette expert, and there were a number of other jobs for the students.

For example:

- the gymnastics master for warm ups at the beginning of the lesson and in between
- the homework student, who summarizes the task at the end of the lesson and informs the class again of what they should do
- the bookcase inspector
- the paper filer
- the table group leader
- the message carrier
- the lighting director
- the controller of teaching materials
- the conflict manager
- Head of the helper team
- Noise level controller
- Buddy helper

The tasks can be changed weekly. And please do not forget the praise!

Some more ideas

The class technician

Since my CD player is on the windowsill, but my teacher's desk is opposite the windows on the wall, I asked Niklas, who sits next to the device, to operate it. Niklas has become our "technician". He is also responsible for connecting the beamer to the DVD player. This works perfectly - he even reacts to eye contact...

Petra F., elementary school

The exercise helper

Our 10 year old Jan is a very lively child and needs movement even during the lessons. Since he works very fast and is usually finished sooner than the others, he goes to his classmates as soon as his own work is done and helps them with the exercises. This way he gets his movement and is proud to be able to help the others.

Hannes L., elementary school

Facebook friends

I teach fifth grade religion and have a difficult student in that class. So I started to give him special tasks (list missing students in the class register etc.). I gave him a lot of praise and his behavior has improved. Of course he still occasionally wanders around the classroom like a cowboy and throws his classmates' pens on the floor. But he responds to my admonitions, and these excursions have become more and more seldom.

We are friends on Facebook, and I sent him a message. I asked him to help a student who was being bullied in the classroom. He took this task to heart. In fact, he let this student sit next to him during the lessons, and made sure that no one bothered him. I did not mention anything in front of the other students, but instead I wrote to him again, praising him and asking him to help other children.

His behavior is rapidly changing for the better. It seems that his secret "kindness" is doing him good.

Christine L., religion teacher

Our class is like a "family"

The following tasks contribute to a sense of responsibility and also to students' identification with the class. Strengthen this feeling of togetherness wherever possible. Ask your students for their opinions or some good advice. When I was designing my website, I had my middle school and high school students vote between two background images. They were proud to be able to help me and made a lot of really helpful suggestions.

Some more ideas that contribute to the sense of community:

- Set up a "box of ideas" in the classroom. This is where students can post their suggestions and other ideas for improving the class community.
- Each of them pulls a piece of paper with the name of a classmate out of a hat labeled "Good Deeds." "This is your secret friend. During the next week, each of you should do something kind for this person."
- Praise on sticky notes. If you have something positive to say to another student, For example, *"Thank you for helping me with the school exercise,"* or *"I'm glad you got a good grade for your school work,"* the students should write this on a sticky note and wordlessly stick the note on his desk.

Promote emotional and communicative intelligence

And, last but not least, strengthen the emotional intelligence of your students by teaching them how to deal with their emotions. Set up a place in the classroom or, if possible, in the corridor close to the classroom door where they can withdraw if upset to "cool down". Train the whole class to become mediators, and - if it is possible in your school introduce a group of student-mediators (see chapter 4) Teach your students communication skills, for example, to communicate grief, anger and frustration with words rather than force.

Student mediators

Beginning the first week of school, my students learn that I am not an arbitrator of disputes because I see only last moments of the incident. So I train the kids to be mediators. The students learn to talk about the incident in a one-on-one conversation, to admit their own mistakes, to apologize, but also how to accept an apology. Although this is always time-consuming at the beginning, it is very worthwhile and contributes to a very relaxed and pleasant atmosphere in the class.

Elfriede H., elementary school

There are two other very important needs that must be met, these are:

The need to be involved

If the lessons make them curious, arouse their interest, are fun, contain surprises and diversity, the students are fully involved. More about this in the ninth commandment of group dynamics.

The need to be part of the group

This sense of belonging is extremely important. Otherwise individual students become outsiders and may form groups or gangs. See the tenth commandment of group dynamics.

How do the students know that we like them?

It's a lot easier than it sounds. Our students learn more from the example we set for them than from the lectures we give them. What should you see, hear and feel in our classroom?

It's nice when our students...

...see:

- a proud look
- a smile
- adults as role models
- us living our values
- joy, laughter and fun while learning
- People who like each other

...listen:

- "You're doing good."
- "You try."
- "You can be proud of yourself."
- "I'm glad you're in my class."
- "You're a great kid."
- "I like you."

...feel:

- "I'm all right."
- "I fit in this group."
- "The others like me and are there for me."
- "I am an important member of this group."
- "The others listen to me."

Treating each other with respect

My son Derrick taught for a while in an alternative middle school near Vienna. When he got home after the first day at school, he called me and said: *"You can't imagine how disrespectfully the students talk to each other. But not for long!"*

In Chapter 21, "The Respectful Classroom," you can read about how he changed the way students interact with each other. Most importantly, he picked them up where they were. It is important that we don't just assume that they know what, for example, respect is. We say again and again: *"We treat each other with respect,"* but many of them don't know what that means. Especially if the tone and the words used at home are not respectful.

The first step is to teach them the meaning of the word. After they understand **WHAT** it is, we need to show them **HOW** to do it.

Have high expectations!

You surely know the musical "My Fair Lady". The play is an adaptation of George Bernard Shaw's comedy "Pygmalion", which in turn is based on the ancient Greek myth of Pygmalion. The original Pygmalion was a king who was also a sculptor and who immortalized his ideal image of a woman in stone. He fell in love with his work and then asked Aphrodite, the goddess of love and beauty, to bring the statue to life. Aphrodite fulfilled his most fervent wish, and the image became reality. The same motif is taken up again in Shaw's Pygmalion and in "My Fair Lady".

Self-fulfilling prophecies: The Pygmalion Effect

The metaphor of Pygmalion, the sculptor, fits very well with our role in school. We are the sculptors, and our tools are the expectations with which we - consciously or unconsciously - form and shape the image of our students. Our students reflect our thoughts, ideas and expectations - both positive and negative. What teachers think of their students is transferred to the achievements that the students will attain.

The Rosenthal-Jacobson Experiment

In the mid-1960s an American professor of psychology, Dr. Robert Rosenthal, began his famous experiments on the way our expectations affect our students' success. He started the experiment with albino rats. He wanted to see how well they could find the right path to their feeding place by traversing a simple labyrinth. Twelve psychology students were told that half of the rats were particularly capable of learning because of breeding choices, the other half were only "street rats". This was not true and the rats were assigned at random. However, six experimenters were told that their animals belonged to the "clever" rats. The other six believed that they had been given the "stupid" rats. The experimenters' task was to carry out ten "training procedures" in the labyrinth with his group of five rats on five days and to note whether the animals chose the right exit. At the end of the experiment, the supposed "smart" rats were three or four times faster than the "stupid" rats. The students filled out a questionnaire after the experiment was finished. They discovered that the "smart" rats had had more positive and caring treatment than the "dumb" rats.

The experiment was continued in collaboration with a second psychologist, Lenore Jacobson, in two Californian schools. Students were randomly assigned to different classes. Some teachers were told that their class was highly gifted, others were told nothing at all. The "Rosenthal Effect", also called "Pygmalion Effect", i.e. the influence of the teacher's expectations on a result, was even more pronounced in school than in animal experiments.

Rosenthal and Jacobson believe that teachers can subtly convey their expectations to students by seeing how long the teacher is willing to wait for a student to respond, how often and how strongly the student is praised or rebuked, how much attention is paid to the student, and the level of achievement expected of the student.

What does that tell us?

Have high expectations - both in terms of performance and behavior. Let learners know that you believe in them and that you are convinced your high expectations will be fulfilled.

If you emphasize the positive events in the class and tell your class how great they all are, they will be great. And if you tell a class that it is the worst class you've ever had, the students will not disappoint you! Emphasize the positive. It pays off.

An example:

I underestimated them.

Despite a serious ear infection, I went to school - it was flu season and our staff was so limited that there were no colleagues to replace me if I called in sick. But there is a positive side to this story.

I was able to lie down in the back of the class for two hours after explaining to the children how bad I felt and asking them to help plan the lesson for Friday, when they give their reports for what had happened during that school year. The children are always allowed to bring guests with them (parents, family, etc.) for these occasions. They worked and discussed for two hours - without asking me anything (except whether I was feeling better or whether they should ask the principal to get a doctor).

Today - healthier again - I looked at their ideas with very low expectations regarding the results. The results are fantastic! I am still completely speechless!

They had independently structured the whole school year in terms of time and also worked out scenes, poems, songs, a rap, pantomime presentations for the parents to guess the answers, a posed mediation of a problem, a well-known English song with previous vocabulary training for the parents so that they can sing along. I am simply amazed.

Renée T., elementary school

Some more ideas

- Show them that you care about them: Greet them with a smile at the door.
- Exchange a few words with individual students in the corridor before the lesson begins.
- Ask your principal to invite individual students and praise them for the progress they have made.
- Write a positive message to the parents.
- Stay up to date so that you know what your students like and what interests them. Use these preferences - movies, music, websites, books, magazines - in your lessons where appropriate.
- Talk to them, and most importantly, listen to them!
- At the end of the lesson, thank them for their cooperation, the nice lesson, etc.

Emphasize the positive!

We all know it:

It is precisely the students who cause us the most difficulties that seek – and crave - recognition and attention.

Of course, they would prefer to receive attention for what they do right. But if that doesn't work, they are satisfied with negative attention. They act according to the motto: *"Better any attention than none at all!"* And unfortunately, the more we focus on bad behavior, the more of it we will see.

Positive reinforcement can work wonders! With individual students and also with the whole class. You can literally see how the students stand up and "grow".

Who would you rather spend your time with?

And now I would like to ask you an important question: Who would you rather spend your time with? With a person who likes you, who empathizes with you and sometimes even says so? Or do you prefer to spend your time with someone who constantly criticizes and insults you, with whom you have the feeling that this person does not like you at all?

The answer to this question is clear. In fact, it is so clear that I found the questions almost ridiculous when writing them down!

We can win our students over with (initial) acceptance.
This is the key to success with younger students and also the key to reaching the older ones (and it is the same with us adults!). We achieve much more with authentic praise than with negative criticism. Or, as we say, *"You can catch many more flies with honey than with vinegar!"*

When we exercise negative criticism, we reinforce negative behavior. Of course we have to correct our students if they do not behave properly. However, when we emphasize the positive, we can literally see our students "grow". Growth is change. And change and growth are learning.

That's the goal, isn't it?

But I don't have time for this!

Sometimes I hear: *"Yes, but I teach secondary school and I have several hundred students a day. I have to use the time to teach. There's no time for me to be concerned about relationships with the students."*

My answer:
"If you DO NOT build relationships with the students who challenge you the most, you will lose a lot more time dealing with behavioral problems during the school year!"

My proposition to you:
Take the time to establish rapport and a good atmosphere in the classroom during the first weeks of school. Teach the principles of teamwork, respectful interaction with others which results in a feeling of security in the classroom right at the beginning of the school year. Show the students: Teaching is important, but people and being humane are even more important. I guarantee you that you will regain the time you use during this beginning phase many times over during the school year. You will spend much less time disciplining, admonishing and repeating.

Talk less. Teach more.

Some ideas

Five minutes of appreciation

Every Friday at the end of the last lesson we do the "friendly five minutes" in which the students thank each other, e.g. for the fun game during the break, the borrowed pencil etc. I often praise students who are rarely named for something they have done well.

In addition, there is a selected "student of the week", whose photo is clearly visible in the classroom. Student of the week" is chosen because after the break or after the lesson the classmates tell me what they did that was nice, e.g. prevented a fight, handed over some of their food, said something nice, held the door open for others etc. Then he gets a point in the list. I'm allowed to give points too. Whoever has the most points at the end of the week is student of the week.

Works great and puts the emphasis on positive behavior.

Beate F., middle school

Blessing pupils

I am a religion teacher for children and teach all grade levels. At the beginning of each year we have one lesson where a blessing for each student is performed.

Blessing means to give good gifts to someone, to wish him good things. In my case, as a religion teacher I am also giving the student the promise that God will accompany him. To bless someone also means to recognize and name the advantages, the positive qualities of the student.

The children have the possibility to let me put my hand on their shoulder, if they want that, and let me tell them what I like about them, for example "You paint well!", "You took care of your friend when he was sad", etc. Furthermore I wish her/him something for his/her future, for example: "I wish that you always have someone to talk to."

With younger students I do this at regular intervals. When older students leave this school, they receive a blessing from me on their further way, some wish to have my hand on their shoulder, others only want direct encouragement. If these children have already experienced this several times, they can deal with it in a very dignified way.

The most beautiful moment for me was when I tried the class blessing with middle school students. This group had already experienced a lot with each other and had grown together as a group. I thought to myself that maybe the others would like to say something nice to their peers as well. One student stood in the middle of the circle, the others stood behind him as they spoke. Each student encouraged him with words and if he wanted it, they could put their hand on his shoulder while speaking. I was so moved that I had tears in my eyes when I heard the kind words the children said to each other.

It does EVERY person good to hear good things about themselves. We just have to show them how!

Martina S.

A small gesture

A new student who was considered difficult in his old school was changing schools and moving into my third grade class. At our first meeting I could immediately see that he was a very bright and lively child. He came with his mother. We exchanged a few friendly words and they said he would be joining my class in September.

Half a year later, his mother told me how impressed he had been with this first contact because I had brushed my hand lightly over his head. He told his mother after that meeting: "I think the new teacher likes me because she patted my head." This seemingly unconscious hand movement was no longer in my memory. But I can only conclude that, contrary to the reports from his former school, David has fit in very well in his new class!

I was very impressed by what a difference a small gesture can make

Herta R., elementary school

The wooden heart

I use a heart made of wood as a symbol for good behavior in my class. I use it sparingly and usually encourage the children with verbal and non-verbal praise. If they have been particularly well-behaved, I hang the heart wordlessly on the board. This way all the children feel spoken to and praised. Children who have been particularly well-behaved can take the heart home overnight.

The heart has its fixed place on a golden cushion in the classroom and must be placed there again by the respective child the next day.

Christoph M., elementary school

Positive messages to parents

As you said in the training course, we are already doing a lot of things right! That reminded me that while my sister and I were student teachers, we only wrote positive notes on kids' homework.

This really caught on! Every child wanted to have such a note, so they could show it to their parents at home. The children were allowed to stick these notes into their notebooks and have their parents sign it. Reliability, homework, helpfulness, respectful behavior towards the teachers and others were evaluated. So everybody had a chance! And even the laziest one suddenly brought his homework, because he wanted to have a positive note!

Silke G., secondary school

"Praise – Anchor" at the window

I deliberately praise the kids a lot. It does them good and me too because it teaches me to think more positively! I have "installed" a "praise anchor" near the window. I go to this spot whenever I praise my students verbally and/or non-verbally. This really spurs the children on. All I have to do is to move in that direction and you can already see how they sit up straighter and feel proud and happy!

Peter F., secondary school

Positively formulated

I started changing my language four years ago in the first grade. I tried to avoid the word "NOT" and always told the children what I expected of them, e.g. I replaced "Don't run!" with "Go slowly!" or as a reinforcement "No running!", "Stop!" etc. These phrases have become second nature to me now and come automatically.

Result in the class:
The children know the rules much better and follow them much more closely. They use the phrase, "Stop teasing me, pushing me, etc." They also change their own speech patterns and now they say what they want instead of saying what they don't want.

Herta R., elementary school

"Thanks for being so quiet!"

My students were quite well-behaved again last Wednesday, They had two hours of independent work, and each of them was busy with their own topic. While working they would occasionally whisper softly with their neighbor. Totally acceptable. But since I hadn't slept much the night before, even the whispering bothered me. So I wrote on the board: "Thank you for being so quiet and working so well!".

Suddenly it became even quieter. Pearl, you really could have heard a pin drop. When my colleague arrived to teach the third period, she thought that there was no school that day or if something had happened because it was so quiet in the classroom.

Tanja K., Secondary School

Farewell letters

I wrote an individual letter to each of my students at the end of the school year, highlighting their particular strengths. For example, I had a girl who was struggling and trying really hard so she could graduate with good grades. She had remarkable social skills. In her letter I wrote that I was very proud of her and her social skills and I gave a few examples. Her mother told me that she had proudly shown and read it to her mother and that they had both cried with joy.

Another mother told us that her son (14 years old) had hung his letter over his bed so that he could read it often.

Andrea W., High School, Tyrol

Taming difficult classes

This year I was assigned to teach biology to a middle school class that had caused a lot of problems the year before. They were supposedly extremely difficult and unmotivated. I explained my ideas and plan for the year to them. I promised them to include as many experiments as possible if they would actively participate in the lessons. But more importantly, I told them at the beginning of the school year that I was looking forward to working with them for the rest of the year. I gave some "Troublemakers" some justified and honest praise right from the start and immediately had them on my side.

I needed to write a paper for a professional training course. I compiled a student questionnaire and asked this class for their support. The class "ringleader" told me, "Sure, we'd be happy to do it for you." That was quite a compliment!

My positive attitude towards the class was honest (the students would notice it anyway if my behavior was just an act), and I told their homeroom teacher that she had, in my opinion, a particularly lovely class. She was totally astonished and pleased, because obviously everybody else only came to her with negative comments about her students.

I am convinced that every person needs and deserves recognition and respect. This creates a positive atmosphere in the classroom, and in a positive environment, learning and working is fun.

Andrea W., middle school

Ken Blanchard, author of books on management, tells the following true story in his book, "Whale done! - Learning from Whales. How to Motivate Every Team to Perform at its Best"

How do you teach a whale to do tricks?

How do the whale and dolphin trainers at Sea World work? How do they actually get the whale, Shamu, who weighs 7,500 kilos, to jump seven meters out of the water over a rope? This is a real challenge. How can this challenge be compared to the challenges in our everyday school life?

The trainers' first priority is to positively reinforce the behavior they want to achieve - in this case jumping over the rope. They do everything they can to ensure that the whale can experience success. They start by placing the rope on the bottom of the tank so that the fish has no choice but to swim over it. When this happens, he is praised for his positive performance. He is fed fish, stroked and played with. And slowly they raise the rope bit by bit until the whale is jumping 7.5 meters over the rope.

But what happens if instead of swimming or jumping over the rope, the whale jumps or swims under the rope? Nothing. Absolutely nothing. It's ignored. He gets no electrical impulses, neither negative and nor constructive criticism, no warnings and no punishments. Positive reinforcement is the foundation of these spectacular performances. And as the whale swims over the rope more often, the trainers lift the rope higher and higher and higher. Until it is 7.5 meter above the pool.

As with these dolphin trainers, it is also our job to reinforce and celebrate the successes of our learners. The real art here is to be able to estimate the right moment when the rope can be lifted again. Let's do this too. Let us pre-program success. And let us notice when and how high the rope should be lifted!

When I read this story, which is about motivating employees, I thought to myself: *"If this works with managers, and if it works with whales, it should also work with students!* Give it a try. It works!

3 The third commandment

Create an atmosphere of TRUST!

Our Group

We create a fear-free learning environment

In an interview with the "Education Group", the Upper Austrian Minister of Education, Doris Hummer, said that in her opinion, success in achievement and joy in learning are not at all a contradiction, because creating something that was difficult is associated with joy and pride. In order for learning to be successful, according to Councilor Hummer, a fear-free environment is necessary and encourages the desire and curiosity to learn.

I can well remember how my own children were still in kindergarten and joyfully waited for the start of school at the age of six. The closer the first day of school came, the more often they heard statements from acquaintances and also strangers like: *"Now the serious part of life begins!* During the first six years of life, however, a child learns more than in any other period of its life. And the best thing is - the child learns light-heartedly, without any "right" and "wrong". The world is an adventure, and learning is fun. And then, according to many adults, life and learning become "serious" from one day to the next when school starts. The children move from familiar surroundings to a foreign one. Is it any wonder that some children are afraid of "formal" learning.

In order to enjoy learning and school, a fear-free learning environment is essential. If students develop trust in the teacher and in their fellow students, if they know that school is a place where their emotions are respected, where they can take responsibility and exercise self-discipline, we have succeeded in creating a joyful learning environment that inspires learning.

Mistakes are welcome!

When a child learns to walk, it falls down many times. Each time he falls down, the child stands up again and tries again. And again. And again. Until all at once he succeeds, and he takes his first steps. Everyone applauds and rejoices. And most of all, the child himself is happy. A new world opens up. No one would think of saying the first time the child falls down or the second, or even the tenth time, to say, *"You did it wrong,"* or *"I doubt you'll ever learn how to walk."*

But how do we do it at school? When I correct an English test, the number of mistakes a student makes is used to determine how well he can speak English. What he does right is not evaluated. What he does wrong is important for his grade. Students write an essay thinking, *"I won't write more than what is required, otherwise I might make some mistakes and I will get a worse grade!"*

As I write these lines, I once again feel the frustration that our school systems, which are more or less similarly structured all over the world, arouse in me. Do we want all the students who pass through our school system to become average? Do we not want to strive for excellence? Isn't it my and your task as a teacher to help each student to strive for his or her own potential? I consider it my duty and my responsibility. And I hope you feel the same way.

Learning, just like change and growth, means taking risks. If I don't take risks, I feel comfortable in my usual and familiar surroundings, but everything remains exactly as it is and was. Until I am ready to risk making mistakes!

Every Monday at school I presented a poster with our slogan of the week: *"A smile is my style," "The ten most powerful two letter words: If it is to be, it is up to me," "Every day is a new start."Every moment is a new beginning," "T.E.A.M.: Together Everyone Achieves More!"* etc. The first slogan of the year was *"Mistakes are positive!"* When I showed the students this poster they were totally amazed. They couldn't imagine how a mistake could be positive!

We discussed that and then they understood. A few months later, a student made a mistake in answering a question. Like it sometimes happens at school, some of them started laughing about it. Suddenly a little girl in the front row pointed to the sign *"Mistakes are positive"* which we had hung on the wall and said quite objectively: *"We've already discussed this."* And that was that - the others stopped laughing, and we moved on.

We can support our students in many ways to have the courage to make mistakes. But it has to start with us. It depends on how we react when we make a mistake ourselves. How do I react if I misspell a word on the board or if I don't know the answer to a question? Can I admit my own mistakes, my own weaknesses? Can I laugh at myself? Can I say, *"I don't know. I'll look it up tonight and tell you the answer tomorrow."* The days are long past when teachers were expected to know everything! (And the teachers of that time didn't know everything either. They were simply masters at bluffing!)

The pursuit of perfection is a dangerous trap!

Perfection. That's an unattainable goal. There will always be someone who can do things better. The pursuit of perfection is a trap. And it leads to the next -even bigger - trap: comparing ourselves with others. Such comparisons lead to envy. And envy makes us dissatisfied and unhappy. Perfection should not be the goal. It is enough if we simply do our best. More is not necessary.

The highest priority: Getting to know each other

We start every seminar with one or more activities to help the participants get to know each other. Our participants enjoy these activities - partially because they can often use them themselves with their classes. But I have also heard some teachers say that they generally don't like games to get to know each other at the beginning of a seminar. I disagree.

Again and again our participants say how comfortable they feel with us. Sometimes it is so comfortable that at the end of the seminar day they are surprised that the seminar is already over and some of them do not want to stop! They are also very pleased with the group spirit and teamwork. I have often been asked whether other groups have such great dynamics as theirs does. Yes, most of the time it is like that. And the beauty of it is, you can create the same dynamics in your classroom.

That is the content of this book.
The first step is getting the group to work together as a team. To do this, the members of the group MUST get to know each other. When this happens the students move from being a collection of individuals and become a team. If you leave out this step in a teacher training course the result is a dry, left-brained and often boring seminar. And if leave it out in a school setting, it leads to disciplinary problems, bullying, disinterest and boredom.

There are many games to get to know each other, which can be played at the beginning of the school year or in between. Here I have collected some of my favorite activities for you.

Exchange objects

If the students do not know each other's names yet, they write their names on an adhesive label and stick it on the shirt or blouse. Each student then chooses a personal item.

Everyone stands up and walks across the room. They greet each other like this: "Hello! I'm David, and I want to give you my fountain pen." And the person he greets says, "Good morning. I'm Lucy. Thanks for the pen. May I give you my scarf, please?"

It goes on like this until the teacher rings a bell. Then they all sit down with the object they are holding at that moment. Each person introduces himself again and says: "Hello, I'm Magdalena, and this is Martin's ruler." She hands the ruler to Martin.

It is especially funny when the teacher plays along and intentionally assigns the objects to incorrect owners without attracting attention. In other words, in the end, Daniel might say: "I'm Daniel, and this is Manuela's key chain." It turns out the key chain doesn't belong to Manuela but to Halim. And they all have something to laugh at together.

What's that?

On the first day of school, take an unusual accessory with you, e.g. diving goggles, mountain boots or a small bag of sand. Students can ask you questions about the item so that they know what it says about you. Perhaps you have been snorkeling, mountain climbing, or the sand comes from the desert during the summer.

Then have the students write a few paragraphs telling what they have learned about you. The task is to bring their own item the next day that says something about the student. First he shows and explains the object, then the students write short paragraphs about their own object and what it says about them

Why is that your name?

Your name is your business card! Parents spend nine months waiting for their baby to be born and thinking about what they will call the new child. And yet many children do not know why they were called that. At the beginning of a school year I told them that I had been named after my grandmother, that I really like my name because it means "Perle" or Pearl in English, etc. The students were fascinated! Then we asked the students where their names come from. Those who knew told us, and those who didn't, had the homework assignment of asking their parents' why they named them so. They told us in class the next day and then wrote a few sentences about it. A great task, which was also very personal and enriching.

Throw the ball!

The students stand in a circle and throw a ball to each other. Round 1: Each child says his name. Round 2: The favorite sport. Round 3: The favorite food etc.

Snowballs

Students write three facts about themselves on a white sheet of paper, for example
"I have a cat. I like to eat pizza. My mother's name is Helga." Now they make a "snowball" out of the paper. When the teacher rings the bell, the snowball fight begins. When the bell rings again, each student takes a snowball, which is either in their hand or close to it. He reads the three statements and tries to determine the person to whom these statements fit.

Puzzle People

Show your own piece of the puzzle and explain to the class what is written on it.

You're looking at my piece of the puzzle. My name "Pearl" is written on it and also symbols, pictures, numbers and words that describe me. Here the picture is black and white, but in reality it is very colorful. There's a globe on it. It stands for the fact that I love to travel and also that I came from America to Austria many years ago. You can see the screen of a computer on it - I like working on the computer, I like the internet. There is also a piece of paper, a book and a pen on it - I like to read and write books. In my heart are my family and my students. There is also a picture of me standing in the water - I love water and often do water gymnastics. The musical notes are a symbol for the fact that I like singing. And the number 10 stands for the fact that, although I am getting physically older and older, I got stuck in my development at the age of 10!

I explain my puzzle piece and then hand out empty puzzle pieces.
The parts are shown on the next two pages and can be copied. They should ideally be larger than shown here and on thicker paper so that the pieces fit well together. It is nice when both the paper and the pens are colorful. Distribute the puzzle pieces so that there are the same number of piece number 1 as piece number 2. This is important so they can be fit together in a puzzle afterwards.

Students decorate their own puzzle piece with names, symbols, pictures, etc.

When they are finished, everyone can present their piece of the puzzle. The pieces are then glued or stuck together to form a puzzle and hung on the pin board, above which is written: "Our Team".

1 Puzzle People

2
Puzzle People

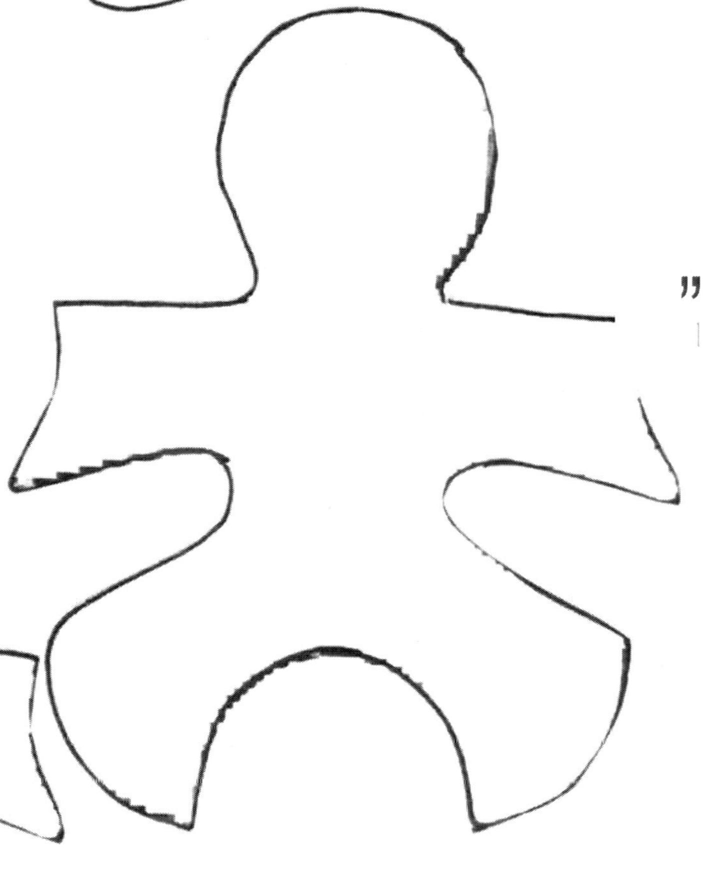

The fourth commandment

Emphasize both their UNIQUENESS as well as

what the students have IN COMMON

Another story:

My glasses - your glasses

A man noticed that his sight was getting worse and so he made an appointment with an old friend who was an optician. His friend gave him various vision tests - reading letters from a screen, looking first with one eye and then with the other, checking if he could read the letters up close or see them better from a distance.

The result: "Well, you are clearly nearsighted. I feared that right away. But don't worry. With glasses, your vision will be perfect again."

"I'll tell you what," said the optician and took off his own glasses, "I don't normally do this, but we're friends and I know you don't have much time... I'll give you my glasses. They're really the very best I have!"

The man was a little upset, but he didn't want to be unkind, so he put on his friend's glasses and looked again at the letters on the screen in front of him.

"But it's hopeless!" he said, "I can't see a thing. Everything is a blur!"

"No, that's impossible," said the optician friend, "I've had those glasses for about five years and have perfect vision with them! Look again! If you try just a little bit harder ...."

"I'm trying," said the friend, "the more I try, the worse it gets! I just can't see anything with your glasses!"

"Well, that's impossible! It must be you. You're doing something wrong!" the optician said angrily, "I never had any problems with these glasses!"

His friend stood up, gave him back his glasses and said, "Look, don't be offended, but I think it's better if I find another optician." With these words he left the office..

"Well," said the optician to his assistant as they watched the friend from the window, "It happens over and over! I do my very best and offer him the solution. He won't accept it. And he's not even grateful for my help!"

We are all different. Just as the man needed different glasses from the ones the optician needed, the needs of each student in the classroom are different. Make a poster with the following words on it:

"Different strokes for different folks!"

Make a poster with those words, **"Different strokes for different folks!"** or make further posters with the words below and hang them up in class. Explain to your students that the words on that sign are the answer to the question: *"Why can he do this and I can't?"*

Our class motto:
One for all. All for one.

Every person in this class is unique.
Everyone has a right to success.

As we discussed in the exercise "Everybody gets a band-aid", fairness does not mean doing the same thing for everyone. Fairness is giving each individual what she needs at that moment and to reach her own potential. If the individual's needs are met, the group itself is socially enriched.

One of my students in middle school was called Armin. Armin was linguistically extremely weak. He had learned two or three languages as a child in his home country, but he was not very good at any of them. When his family immigrated to Austria and he went to school here, he naturally had to learn German. And now it was time for him to learn English too, as all students in Austria learn English for 12 years in school. He was overwhelmed. But what Armin was very good at was drawing. And for this reason I often gave the class English homework that had to do with drawing. They were allowed to do these exercises together as a team and because of Armin's artistic talent, he was, despite his language difficulties, well integrated and was able to improve his English skills through this talent.

Once we went through a chapter from the English book about a ghost named Archibald. The story took place in a castle on a mountainside surrounded by a cemetery. I gave the students a large sheet of flipchart paper and asked them to draw a picture of the story on this sheet. They should then write all the new vocabulary words on the "corresponding" parts of the picture. As an extra task, they were allowed to look up words in their English dictionaries to place more matching words on the picture.

The class was very enthusiastic about this task, which corresponded to their talents and modalities. They came to school the next day with a beautifully labeled picture, most of which had been drawn by Armin. Especially the cemetery, where there was a lovely decorated grave for each of their teachers, was impressive. But I complained, because I was the only teacher without a grave!

"Yes, of course there's a grave for you too, Mrs. Nitsche!" the students replied.

"Where is it? Will you show me, please?"

And then they proudly pointed to a grave with a beautiful floral decoration, which said: *"Mrs. Nice".* That's the most beautiful spelling of my name, Nitsche that I have ever seen!

Each of us is unique...and at the same time we share many things in common

Highlighting commonalities in the classroom creates a feeling of harmony and security. This strengthens the feeling of togetherness and encourages team building, group dynamics and, above all, the trust that supports an atmosphere in the classroom that promotes learning.

Here are a few activities for you to try out:

Learning Style Questionnaires

I distributed the following sheet to the students and gave them a few minutes to answer the questions. Afterwards, I marked one corner of the room as a "yes corner" and one as a "no corner". Then I read out sentence 1. Those who answered "Yes" went to the corresponding corner and those who chose "No" went to the other corner. There they discussed their different ways and habits of learning.

		Yes	No
1.	I need complete quiet when I study.		
2.	I can learn most easily when I hold something in my hand, draw or chew gum.		
3.	I can study better in the afternoon than in the morning.		
4.	I understand things better when they're told to me than when I read them myself.		
5	I move around when I study.		

Of course such questionnaires can also be used for other topics: communication styles, likes and dislikes, opinions. It is important that you emphasize the differences between the various students and that you realize that there is no "one size fits all" here.
No "Right" or "Wrong." We differ - fortunately! - from each other, and the most important thing is that I know what is right for me and have the tolerance to accept others as they are. The additional advantage: students get new ideas about how to learn.

So do I!

The students sit in a circle of chairs.

First round: I am unique!

A student states why he thinks he's unique, like, "I can play the guitar." If he's the only person who can play the guitar, everyone expresses their admiration by saying "Oooh!" or "Aaaah!" But if someone else in the group can play the guitar, that person jumps up, sits on the student's lap and says: "Me too!" And if there are five people who can play the guitar, all five of them sit on his lap!

It goes on until each person has said something where they are unique.

Second round: We have a lot in common!
This is about finding things in common. The pupils sit in a circle. One person stands in the middle, one chair is removed from the circle, i.e. there is one chair fewer than the number of players.

The person in the middle makes a statement about himself, assuming that this statement also applies to at least some other people in the group, e.g. "I like music." All students who share this preference get up and find a new place to sit down. Of course, the person standing in the middle will also try to get a seat. The person left standing without a chair makes the next statement.

The debriefing
Was it easier to find similarities or uniqueness?
When do you want to be unique in life?
When is it better to be like all the others?

I am the only one!

Form groups of three. Each group finds three unique qualities, talents or experiences for each person in the group. Then they find three things that all three have in common. They give their group a name. Then they prepare a poster that doesn't contain words, but only drawings or symbols to introduce their group to the others.

Overlapping circles

Pair up. Each pair gets a sheet of paper with two partly overlapping circles on it. One student writes her name in one circle, the second writes his name in the second circle. In the overlapping part they write what they have in common and in the separate parts each of them writes five characteristics or qualities they do not share.

You're so special.

These suggestions apply to all students in the class. :

- "Now we need someone who has a particularly beautiful handwriting to design the poster. Martin, would you do that for us, please?"
- The students write on slips of paper: "What I'm good at." The teacher collects the notes and reads them aloud. The students guess who is being described.
- Make a class contract and sign it with your hand or footprint.
- Birthdays:
  - Singing a birthday song in different mother tongues or in the language of the birthday child
  - Once a month the birthdays are celebrated. The birthday children each receive a "praise card" from their classmates.

- Design complimentary flowers. Nice things are written on the petals of the flowers.
- Treasure chest: Stick a mirror on the bottom of the treasure chest. Each child in turn is allowed to open the treasure chest and look inside where they see the greatest treasure.
- You're good at this! Circle. A child goes in the middle. The other children say what that child does well, what he likes, etc.
- Children have treasure chests in which they put treasures, e.g. memories of joint excursions etc. https://www.youtube.com/watch?v=bdA1fDDgUkE
- Class tree: Poster with an apple tree. Stick photos of the children on the apples. Every year a new photo is added. On the corners of the poster the class rules are written in keywords: helpfulness, friendship, caution, respect
- Golden letter: everyone writes something nice on a piece of yellow paper and leaves it on that student's seat.

We are a team

The following exercises, which emphasize the strengths and what the students have in common, contribute to the sense of community in the class:

- Theater performances, radio shows, choir, writing books, designing a poster together etc. = We have created something together. When performing musicals, for example, each child can use their own talent as a singer, dancer, actor, CD manager, announcer, costume designer, etc. for the benefit of the group.
- A class becomes partner with a retirement home.
- Hold a Music Camp Week. Preferably in the first months of the school year. The age groups are mixed. Music (choir, band, instrumental groups), dance, hiking, swimming, creative design and pottery, campfire, disco, many outdoor games.
- Specialties from all over the world. The children bring a culinary specialty from their country for a potluck dinner.
- Cultural festival in the school. Include the parents..
- Holiday exhibition: Before the holidays, give the pupils the task of bringing an object from their country of origin. It is presented as an exhibition to the class.
- Forest projects in every season.
- Cooking / eating together.
- Sleep over at the school. Reading night.
- Who am I? Texts from all over the world - for immigrant children. Each child writes a short text about himself. The text is given to another student. Together they translate the text into their mother tongue.

The Fifth Commandment

SET COMMON OBJECTIVES and

ELIMINATE COMPETITION!

Florence May Chadwick was the first woman to swim the English Channel in both directions in the 1950s. In 1952 she wanted to set a new record. She wanted to be the first woman to swim the 42 km from Catalina Island to the California coast.

On the morning of July 4, 1952 the sea was icy. The fog was so thick that Florence could hardly see the supply boats. Sharks approached and were driven away by gunfire. Her body was numbed by the icy cold. She had been swimming for 16 hours. Her mother and her coach were in one of the boats. They encouraged her saying they were almost there. But she could only see the fog. Only 800 meters before she reached her destination she asked to be pulled out.

When she was interviewed later, she said: "It wasn't the cold, nor the icy water that made me give up. It was the fog. I simply lost sight of my goal."

Two months later she tried again.
There was thick fog again, but this time her self-confidence was intact, her faith was unshakeable, and she had a clear picture in her mind. She visualized where she was going and she knew that behind the fog there was land waiting for her. This time she was successful. She set a new record and even beat the men's record by two hours.

Our students also need goals - goals for the lesson, for the semester, for the school year and for life. Goals let you look ahead and they are motivating. They are particularly effective when they are formulated in such a way that the student can see a connection between the subject matter and his or her life.

At school we very often forget to set goals - in class and also at the beginning of the school year. We just start with, *"Let's open the book to page one!"* The students have no guidelines, no overview, no context.

Imagine a company where the director calls 25 of his employees together and says: *"We are now starting a big annual project. This project is very important and will have a great impact on your future life. It also costs a lot of money and we will have to work very hard on it. But I will not tell you what it is about. Let's just start on page one."*

Unthinkable! And that goes for school too!

Goals for the next lesson

"When does the bell ring?", "Is it noon yet?", "Are we finished yet?", "What do we have for the next lesson?", "Can we play outside at recess?", "Are we going to the computer room today?"

Students ask such questions because they want to know what is happening. They don't like surprises. If we give them clear and distinct structures and routines, we support their independence. I always write down the plan for the lesson or for the day. And I also list the materials they need for each section of the lesson. This is always written in the same place on the board.

So they can plan. When they are finished with one activity, they can already have the materials, which are listed on the board, ready for the next one.

Write the date and "daily schedule" on the board. Give the lesson a title preferably in the form of a question. The title should emphasize the relevance of the lesson in relation to its significance in everyday life. And also announce what is coming in the next lesson. These goals should arouse the students' curiosity and encourage them to reflect even before the lesson begins.

At the **end of the lesson,** the goals should be looked at again and those that have been reached should be checked off. This whole process promotes goal-oriented learning, helps the student to plan better, to be independent and to be more conscious of time.

It is generally recommended to keep a few minutes in reserve at the end of the lesson for reviewing the lesson, for self-assessment of participation, etc. But it happens to me again and again that I overlook the time, and while I am in the middle of a sentence, the bell rings. A simple solution to enable the "**end of the hour ritual**" is to set the alarm on your phone to sound three to five minutes before the end of the hour. More on this in chapter 10: "What, the lesson is already over?"

Goals for the coming school year

The beginning of a new school year is exciting for the students. The holidays are over, and new experiences, new subjects, new teachers, a new timetable are awaiting them. Some children are looking forward to the new challenge, others are apprehensive, and some have mixed feelings. A fun "arrival exercise" and an overview of the coming school year can allay these feelings.

The pupils can write goals for the coming year or formulate wishes for themselves and for the class community. In the first few hours of class it is highly recommended to give the students an overview of the material to be covered in the coming year. This serves the same purpose as setting goals at the beginning of the lesson. Together with the teacher the pupils can leaf through the school book and get an idea of what we will be doing in the coming year.

Reviewing objectives

Every new beginning (day, week, semester, school year, etc.) offers the opportunity to take a new path. So it is good to take stock of the current situation, check which of your goals you have achieved and set new ones.

Do our students consider the second semester of the school year to be a mere continuation of the first one? It would be more positive to consider it as a new beginning. That would give the student the chance to take a new path. Take stock of what happened in the first semester to help them develop new goals and a new dynamic for more effective learning in the second semester.

Create questionnaires, have the students write in their school journal, or moderate a discussion about

1. What did I achieve in the first half of the school year?
2. What goals did I not reach?
3. What are my goals for the second half of the year?
4. What can I do to actually achieve these goals?
5. How will I feel after I reach them?

Some ideas

One daily target system

The first ritual is performed right after the beginning of the lesson. After we have greeted the children, they move on to a space in front of the pin boards. This is where we explain the aims and contents of the coming school day.

As visual support for first and second grade, we used symbol cards to indicate what will be happening. There are cards not only for the subject matter but also for activities such as discussion groups, breaks for eating or recess. In the third or fourth grade, we dropped the use of symbol cards and replaced them with words.

Sandra S., Sandra P., Tamara P., Elementary school

The philosopher's stone

My class is exceptionally low-key and they work at a slow pace. At first, I wanted to motivate them to work more quickly, but, then I thought, they are concentrated, careful and diligent. What more could I ask for? What would I do if they finished their work faster? Dish up more work?

Now I have changed the following in my lessons:
I explain the task, which I differentiate according to each child's capabilities and their goals for today. Whoever has reached his daily goal may do whatever he wants for the rest of the lesson.

It was the philosopher's stone!

Elfriede H. elementary school

Eliminate the competition

And another story:

> *An anthropologist explained a game to the children in African tribe. He placed a fruit basket next to a tree and said that the child who got there fastest would win the fruit basket. At a signal, they were allowed to run. When he gave the signal, all the children took each other by the hands and ran together to the fruit basket. While they sat there and ate the fruit, he asked them why they had run there together. One child could have run fast and then had all the fruit for himself. They looked at him and said, "How could one of us be happy when all the others are sad?" Ubuntu!*
>
> *"Ubuntu" is a philosophy of some African tribes, which means, translated:*
> *"I am because we are."*

Eliminate competition in the classroom and work towards common goals. Because of this, there will be no more bullying, no more accusations like *"nerd"* (a word that is strictly forbidden in my classes), and there will be no envy. Instead, a fear free atmosphere will develop in which learning can flourish, an environment in which self-responsibility and self-discipline can grow. Create "Win-win" situations in your classroom.

Yes, I know that there are many out-of-school situations where competition is necessary and encouraged. Some say it's time for the students to get used to it. I don't think that the atmosphere in the school needs to be like that. If students want to or should compete with each other, they can do so in sports. The classroom is a place where every single student should strive for his or her individual potential instead of comparing themselves with others.

Some more activities that emphasize common goals

Counting from 1 to 20

We will count from 1 to 20. I will say the number 1. It doesn't matter which of you says 2 and then 3 and 4, etc., but two people cannot speak at the same time. If that happens, we will start again from 1. You may say a number as often as you like, but one person may not say two numbers in a row. No strategies may be used.

- Variations
  Play the game with open and closed eyes. The group can sit in a circle with their backs to the center of the circle so that the pupils cannot see each other. All stand up and walk criss-cross through the room while the exercise is being done

- The debriefing
  How did you do it? Was it hard? Were you sometimes frustrated? Did anyone take the lead?

Take a step into the circle

This game is similar to the last one. The point here is that the students count from 1 to the number of students playing (e.g. if there are 25 students in the class, the players count from 1 to 25).

The group stands in a circle. One person takes a step into the circle and says, "1". A second person also takes a step into the circle and says: "2". It continues until all 25 students are standing in the circle. No two people may step into the circle at the same time. When this happens, it starts again from "1".

Intuitively forming a series of two

The aim is to form a series of two students in silence and intuitively. The first student stands up and lines up in silence. The next pupil stands up and follows him, and so on. If two students stand up at the same time, the class must start again with the formation of the rows of two.

Blindly form a circle

All close their eyes and slowly wander around the room. Hands are held at chest height, palms outwards to protect against collisions.

After one to two minutes, give a signal that the players should - blindly - connect with others to form a circle where everyone holds hands.

- Variations
  With eyes open, the group builds other geometric shapes. A smiley face, a fish, a swimming fish, you are a loose rubber band, the rubber band stretches, the rubber band tears, etc.

- The debriefing
  - How did you do on the exercise?
  - What thoughts and feelings have arisen?
  - How do you feel now?

Building a team with pair and group work

Let's do it like the wild geese

In autumn, when you see wild geese migrating south in a V-formation, you might wonder why they do this.

It has been found that each bird, when it flaps its wings, creates an updraft for the bird flying directly behind it. By flying in V-formation, the flock achieves at least 70% more range than any single bird could achieve in single flight. Whenever a goose breaks out of the formation, it immediately feels the resistance of trying to make it on its own and returns to the formation as quickly as possible to regain the advantages of the upwind from the bird in front.

As soon as the lead goose gets tired, it rotates back into the flock and another goose takes the lead. The geese in the back rows cheer the front geese on to maintain their speed.

Finally, if a goose falls ill or wounded and falls out, two geese from the formation will accompany it to the ground to help and protect it. They stay with her until she can either fly again or she's dead. Then they take off and fly with another formation to catch up with their own group again.

Next time you see a flock of birds, remember... It is a gift, a task and a privilege to be a member of a team.

In today's society, more and more teamwork is required. The ability to co-operate and work together contributes to a harmonious classroom and is also important as an important skill for our students' future. Partner and group work also bring many other advantages, both for the individual and for a class's group dynamics. Among others:

- The students get to know each other better - even those with whom they otherwise would not come into contact with.
- Students who like to be in the center of attention are less likely to disrupt lessons because they get more attention within the group itself
- The pupils identify more closely with the class and one another.
- The motivation and self-confidence of weaker pupils is strengthened.
- Students who are stronger help those who are not so strong.
- Group work is learner- and not teacher-centered
- The teacher has more freedom to help where help is needed
- Social skills are strengthened
- Students learn to express themselves, make decisions, take responsibility, share, listen, solve conflicts
- The self-esteem of all the participants is strengthened

What is cooperative learning?

Cooperative learning is an extension and refinement of pair and group work. Students form teams. The team members support each other in their work and the team achieves results. They must work together to achieve the group's goals. All participants are equal and share responsibility for the results. If one team member does not do his or her part, the whole group feels the effects. The successes are not only in the cognitive area, but also in social competence. The team members learn empathy and learn to put themselves in the position of other group members. They learn to respect the other, his opinions and themselves. They take responsibility, learn skills such as the ability to solve problems, make decisions, trust themselves and others, give feedback and exchange and reflect. Everyone wins if the group is successful. This kind of learning can be used in every type of school and for every age group. Vocational schools, for example, form the teams as "companies", and then put what they have learned into practice in their own company.

What do I do if they get too loud?

Many teachers tell me, *"Yes, but when I use group work, the students get so loud."* Yes, that's true. When you teach interactively and communicatively, the noise level automatically increases. But if you use the principles of noise control, which are here and in Chapter 6: "We've got rhythm!" you will easily be able to control the noise level.

As already mentioned, I can increase the volume of the class to become louder or softer with my own voice. For example, if I use my voice to stay just a bit below the volume of the group - and then my voice gets louder and louder, so does the class. The effect is the same as the wind blowing under the wings of an airplane. If the wind then increases, it will lift the aircraft. The same thing happens often in the classroom. We want the class to become quieter, but we make it louder. The class automatically reflects our volume. We achieve the opposite of what we want. But if we are aware of this phenomenon, we can turn it around, to our own and to the class's benefit.

Several years ago Michael Grinder held a seminar for me, my colleagues from the Pearls of Learning Institute and some other interested teachers. There were about thirty of us. One morning he divided us into two groups. He gave one group, which was sitting in the right half of the room, some questions to discuss with each other. He also told them that during their discussion he would work with the other fifteen teachers sitting on the left side of the room. Then the groups would swap roles.

So they started to discuss the answers to the questions with one another. Michael turned to us sitting on the left side of the room. He turned his back to the other group and started to talk to us about the effect of the teacher's voice volume. The group behind him was busy with their discussions and did not listen to his words. As Michael talked, he gradually became louder and louder. And so did the unsuspecting group behind him! He increased the volume until he and the group behind him were almost shouting! And then he lowered the volume - again gradually - until he and the group behind him were whispering. We, the group on the left, were left aghast with our mouths open in amazement! By the way, the teachers in the group on the right said in the feedback session that they had not noticed at all that at times they were almost shouting and at other times whispering during the conversation.

You can do this with your voice – believe me, it's amazing. But music can also be used as a volume control. This is especially useful for group work. The volume of the group automatically adjusts to the volume of the music. This means that we can regulate the volume of the group using music in the background - without it even being noticeable. When I slowly turn up the background music, the group gets louder. And if I turn the music down, the group becomes quieter. There are only a few exceptions to this rule, e.g. if the members of a group are performing a very interactive and loud activity. Then they no longer notice the music in the background.

Some ideas

Regulate the noise level with music

During the drawing lesson I now always play a CD with quiet music. The pupils are still allowed to talk when they work, but they are not allowed to be louder than the music. When it is time to end the lesson, I turn the music up for a short time. This is the signal for "time to clean up". And when they are finished I slowly turn it down again.

Claudia M., secondary School

Music and signal card "Whisper"

In individual, group and pair work, I have introduced the idea that there is often soft music playing in the background. Today I used it to lower the noise level in the class. And it worked!!! When individual students talk loudly during group work, I don't admonish them anymore. I simply walk past them holding up the signal card "Whisper". And they immediately lower their voices - isn't that amazing?

Peter F., secondary school

Today I can only whisper!

Last November I had almost no voice due to a cold. I remembered what I had learned in your seminars, but had not dared to try it before - I actually did not really believe that it would work.

I entered the room and stood in silence, with a friendly smile in front of the class and waited until they became quiet. For reinforcement I put my finger on my lips. And it worked. Everyone was so surprised that the class actually disciplined themselves (bump in the ribs, "Shh, be quiet, we want to know what's going on!") and soon there was total silence.

Then I thanked them in a very low whisper (without exerting myself) for the silence and shortly explained that I had no voice but would like to work with them silently today. If everyone kept as quiet as right now, it would surely work. When it got louder again in some classes, my silence and the finger on my mouth were enough to get them back on track. In my senior class (25 students aged between 18 and 19) they even said at the end: "The class today was really cool. We're surprised how well we can work when it is so quiet!

Ingrid S., vocational schools

Some ideas:

- Designate one person in each group as a "noise regulator". It is their task to keep the noise level below a certain, previously agreed upon volume.

- You can indicate the current noise level yourself with a "traffic light". If you attach a green card with a magnet to the board, the noise level is OK. Orange warns that it is getting louder. Red is clearly too loud, and if it does not immediately become quieter, the group work is stopped.

- There are free "noise level apps" for smartphones. For example: https://play.google.com/store/apps/details?id=kr.sira.sound&gl=AT Discuss this with students before group work. How many decibels are acceptable for this task? Show the students how the app works and then put your device on the teacher's desk. If the students aren't sure if they're too loud, let them control the volume on the app. It works like magic!

- If the noise level of a group is too loud, you can silently place a "Whisper Card" on the table where this group is working.

"How should I deal with groups who chat instead of working?"

Here are a few ideas from my book, "A Nonverbal Recipe Book for Talked-Out Teachers"

- Go to the group and offer them help
- Point to or knock next to the topic written on the board
- Sit or kneel next to their desks and listen to the conversation with interest
- Write the topic on a piece of paper and silently put it on their table
- Put a "red thread" on the table
- Point at your watch
- Give them special tasks such as designing posters etc.
- Smile and ask, *"Should I bring coffee/cocoa and cake?"*

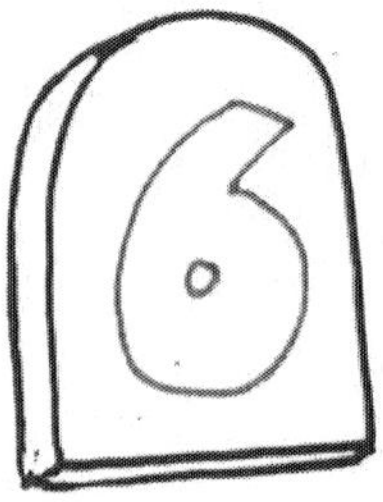

The Sixth Commandment

Let the students do something SIMULTANEOUSLY!

Simultaneous action contributes to group rapport. At the beginning of a course, I can provide a starting point for developing group rapport by asking all or most of the participants to do something at the same time. For example, I write the seminar times on the board and mention that they might want to write down the times because they are not listed in the script. The moment several participants reach for their pens at the same time, the first steps towards establishing group report have been completed.

Some ideas

Here are activities that can be done simultaneously to increase group rapport:

- speaking in chorus, clapping, singing, breathing exercises, repeating movements or clapping sequences, praying, reciting poetry, circle dances, karaoke, reading aloud in chorus
- everyone, including the teacher, paints silently to music
- gymnastics exercises, autogenic training
- breathing, meditative or stillness exercises, power breathing, guided fantasy
- Whenever you tell a story, the members of the class automatically and unconsciously breathe simultaneously
- Pass on handshakes while standing in a circle

Breathe consciously

The students sit down comfortably. The teacher leads the breathing technique:

"We are relaxed and inhale calmly through the nose. We take our breath deep down into the stomach and feel it increasing in volume. We hold our breath a little. Now we breathe out again very calmly through the mouth."

Repeat several times, OR inhale for five seconds, exhale for eight seconds.

Group freeze

The students move wordlessly through the room. One person freezes. As soon as the others notice that a person is standing still, they freeze too. They remain like this until one person starts moving again.

Conductor breathing

The teacher takes the position of a conductor. The group breathes together and the teacher conducts. Inhale. Hold. Exhale.

Hands up!

Everybody stand in a circle. Hold hands. Close your eyes. Hands up - breathe in slowly. Hands down - exhale even more slowly (exhalation should always be longer than inhalation).

Action journeys

Do a "journey" with the entire class with movement - we climb a mountain, climb over the rocks etc. (either as a guided fantasy journey or imitating the movements of the teacher).

Horse Racing Game

Everyone sits in a circle and pats their thighs with both hands. This sounds like horses' hooves. The game master performs the following movements, and the group imitates it:

- The horses go to the starting line (clap their hands on their knees)
- Starting signal (teacher whistles)
- The horses run off (clap their thighs violently)
- Right turn! (continue clapping and lean to the right)
- Left turn! (continue clapping and lean to the left)
- Jumping over a small obstacle (clapping and make a small jump)
- Jumping over a big obstacle (clapping and jump up out of your seats)
- The tourists are taking pictures of us! (hold up cameras and shout "Snap! Snap!")
- Jump over the moat"
- Fall into the moat ("Blubb! Blubb! Blubb!")
- Run on (clap your thighs violently)
- We ride past the grandstand: Applause and cheers
- We overtake the last opponent: panting and with the tongue hanging out looking backwards at the opponent
- The last stretch (clap your thighs even harder)
- We won! (cheering)
- Victory photo (pose and smile)

Ghost Dodgeball

My students love to play ghost dodgeball. They are not allowed to speak or (if they succeed at it) laugh etc. If someone speaks, I put a stopwatch in his hand and he steps out of the game for one minute.

Susi H., elementary school

Musicals

An experience that was important for the class cohesion and which helped them to get to know each other better was our musical performance at Christmas. The joint planning, preparation of the stage design, creation of various posters and the rehearsals were great fun for everyone. The children kept singing the Christmas carols until Easter!

Angelika K., elementary school

The Seventh Commandment

Tell METAPHORICAL STORIES!

Everyone, young and old, likes to hear stories. No matter if I ask schoolchildren or adults, *"Would you like to hear a story?"* I always hear an enthusiastic *"Yes!"*, and see an eager expression of joy on their faces. Telling a story changes the atmosphere in a room to one of harmony and enjoyment.

Seminar participants have often told me, *"A few months after the class was over, I looked at my notes. And do you know what I remembered best? The stories you told us."*

And so it is. If you want something to go into long-term memory, put it into a story. If you want to make people curious about today's material, tell them an introductory story that leads up to the topic. Or use the suggestopedic texts on my website (www.pearls-of-learning.com) to teach subject matter.

If you would like to change the behavior of the class or of individuals, but do not want to be overbearing, tell a story about when you were younger or an exciting story about your own life: *"When I was your age...* With these words you will cast a spell over every child. By telling a story instead of admonishing a child or the class, you avoid resistance and your students go along with your wishes.

Two Danish primary school teachers who attended my courses at the European School in Brussels told me that they have a dog puppet named "Hund". Hund is always doing naughty things and getting into trouble. The pupils love him! They always cheer when he appears and ask: *"What has he done now?"* Amazingly, his pranks bear a very strong resemblance to various negative incidents that have occurred in the classroom. For example, if there had been a birthday party and a child had made fun of the birthday cake, it turned out a few days later that Hund had also gone to a birthday party and done exactly the same thing. Very impolite! There is a second hand puppet, the snail, who always takes his time. He thinks things through and does everything slowly and deliberately. And afterwards Snail always has a dialogue with Hund. *"Why did you say that? Don't you understand that his mother might feel hurt by your words? If you have good manners..."* The pupils love this naughty little dog and join in with Snail giving well-intentioned suggestions. And, lo and behold, not only the dog behaves better, but the children do too! Surprisingly, the person who shows the most enthusiasm is usually the child who behaved poorly! And it is all done with absolutely no resistance on the part of the student.

Another example is this contribution from a teacher for children with difficulties:

The way out of the swamp

A teacher reports: ...I work a lot with metaphors because the children can accept and understand the comparisons quite well. For example: If a student doesn't change her behavior despite our encouragement, I tell her a story. She listens. And you can also have her act it out.

"Imagine a deep, deep swamp. It's wide, you step into it and slowly begin to sink. You don't have the strength to swim out. There are people on one side. They are your teachers, parents, etc. They hand you a board to hold on to. They call to you and motivate you to grab the board. If you accept it and help with "leg movements", you will be able to get out of the swamp. Then you can move into the future you desire: a positive life with a secure job, a boyfriend, a car, etc.) That will be nice. You'll be able to fulfill your dreams."

I also sketch this on the board and have the students re-enact it. The student usually shows where he is and in which direction he is going. Often the student changes his behavior or goals during the story or a little later. Through the use of a story, they can accept help and are ready to cooperate.

Ulrike E., secondary school for children with behavioral difficulties

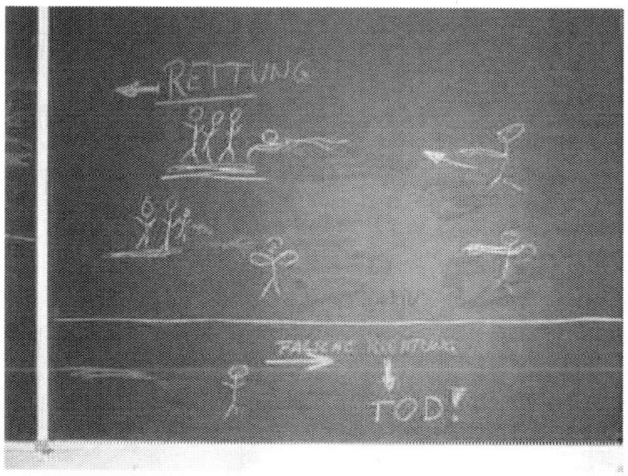

Stories cast a spell over the listeners

Storytelling has another huge advantage: If you can tell stories in a good and mesmerizing way, the students will be captivated. They sit on the edge of their chairs and - most importantly: everyone in the room unconsciously breathes in the same rhythm. In the last commandment we discussed the effect of simultaneous activities in the classroom. Of all the things a group can do simultaneously, breathing is the most effective. When you are telling stories, you and your students are automatically breathing in rapport. This is very, very powerful.

Some ideas

Reading Rug

During the first year of school each child receives a reading rug for his or her birthday, on which I have embroidered his or her name. When their assignments are finished for the day, the child is allowed to take his rug, lay it down where it is comfortable for him read until the bell rings.

Andrea G., elementary school

Practicing reading

The children sit in a circle with the reading text. Each child has a glass stone. In the middle is a basket. The children organize themselves and decide who will read first, etc.

The first child puts his glass stone in the basket and begins reading. Another child puts her stone down, the first child finishes reading the sentence and the second child continues. After all the children have read aloud, all the stones are in the basket.

Having lost all sense of time

...encouraged by my success with nonverbal techniques, I decided to read the students a legend. I placed my chair in front of the window, turned off the big lights and turned on a classical music CD as background music.

Then I asked the children to find a comfortable place to sit, not to run around, not to have things that make noise in their hands. When a child played with pens, I got up quite dramatically, fetched a "stress ball" and pressed it into the child's hand: "You can press it very hard, it's quiet and doesn't disturb anyone when it falls down! And I started to read.

This was a total success.
My place to read aloud is in front of the window. When I carry my chair here, the class immediately goes into "reading mode". Two children jump up and close the door, which is otherwise always open, and turn off the light to make it cozy in winter.

On the first day, I covered twenty minutes reading aloud. We only noticed how late it was when a colleague and mother of one of the children in the class opened the door and asked: "Don't you want to stop for today?

Petra F., elementary school, Vienna

Hand puppets tell stories

I often use a hand puppet, "Willie", a little koala bear when teaching social skills. Recently we had a lesson about how to cross the street.

"Willi and I went shopping yesterday. We had to cross a busy street at an intersection with a crosswalk and a traffic light. Willi was looking every which way and wanted to cross the street without looking to see if a car was coming. He didn't look at the traffic light. He didn't check ....."

Before I could talk any further, some children called out to Willi: *"This is very dangerous Willi! You must look!"* So I asked the kids to give Willie some advice. They did. And they explained exactly what needs to be done when crossing the street.

Monika S., elementary school

Fractions with Miss Riedi and Pirate Kral!

The day before yesterday I had the topic of fractions in one of my math groups. My colleague, played the role of the noble Miss Riedi, I was the dark Pirate Krall. In my story, I kidnapped Miss Riedi. I had hidden twenty chocolate pieces in an old box that served as a treasure chest. Miss Riedi promised the pirate 1/5 of her treasure if he would let her go. So one student was assigned to put the treasure on the desk. He gave the pirate his share of the treasure and the pirate then released Miss Riedi. A happy end!

Johanna K., middle school

The Eighth Commandment

Pick them up where they are: PHYSICALLY and MENTALLY!

Move closer to the students

Fortunately, the times of exclusive frontal teaching are over. Nevertheless, we still often stand in front of the class when we talk with our students. Try it once in a different way. For example, while you are telling a story, move from one point in the room to the next. Observe the students' reactions. They will listen closely and follow every move you make. Where will you go next? And what will you say when you get there? Or move from table to table. Stop at each table and ask the class a question. Anchor certain facts in their minds at various spots around the room.

An important tip, especially for secondary school teachers:
A primary school teacher is usually in her class for several hours a day. She has contact with each child at least once a day. Subject teachers, on the other hand, only have 50 minutes time and there will be many lessons where there is no one-on-one contact between you and each of your students. In this case, it is very important that you stand close to each student at least once every lesson. Try it. You don't have to address the student verbally, but your closeness, the eye contact and, if it fits, a friendly smile is noticeable and involves the student in the lesson.

Enter their mental space as well

Try to empathize with their world. Put yourself in their shoes. What do they think? What do they perceive? If they ask strange questions, try to understand where the question is coming from. Often there are misunderstandings that our adult thinking does not pick up on.

A teacher told me about her own son who was six and in first grade. One day he came home and was visibly upset. When she asked him what was wrong, he said, *"The teacher doesn't like me!"* She kept asking for details, and he told her, *"We did a math test. I did all the calculations correctly and she gave me the worst grade, a five. That's how I know she doesn't like me!"*

Then the mother said, *"Let's look at the test together."* So they did, and she discovered it was a test practicing subtraction. For each minus sign, her son had drawn a vertical line through the minus to make it into a plus. Then he added the two numbers together.

His mother asked why he had turned all the minuses signs into plus signs.
His answer was: *"Addition is easier than subtraction. And even though I added everything correctly, she give me a five. So therefore I know she doesn't like me."*

Fortunately, the mother was able to clear up the misunderstanding - because she immersed herself briefly in his world and his way of thinking. If you can feel yourself into the needs, hopes, fears, anxieties, experiences, questions and/or doubts of your group and students, it will be much easier to reach them. Do not ignore their fears. If they express them and encounter understanding, they will disappear.

Here is a very interesting e-mail about a secondary school class's ideas about a perfect timetable:

Dear Pearl,

Today I had an experience in class that might interest you. I worked on a worksheet with the students. ...and I asked them to draw up a fantasy school timetable. The pupils should first think about when their school day should begin (nobody started at 8.00 am – they all wanted to start later). Then they should consider which subjects they would like to include in their ideal timetable. They could use the traditional subjects and they could also invent new ones.

It was very noticeable that there was only ONE student who had completely banned traditional subjects like math, German, English, biology, physics etc. from his timetable. All the others included these subjects, but with a smaller number of lessons than in reality.

BUT: All the students wanted to have much more physical education with sports such as dancing, swimming, ice skating, music, hockey, horseback riding, gardening etc. Although I was not surprised by these statements, it became clear once again that our school system is not satisfying our students' basic needs.

The evaluation demonstrated very clearly how students judge their ability to concentrate. The question came up several times during the activity if they could schedule an hour break some time during the six hours of lessons per day.

They were also asked to list afternoon activities. I found the results surprising. Only two students listed computer games or television on one afternoon per week. The other activities listed were going to the cinema, outings -mostly sports related – with family and friends.

Beate F., middle school

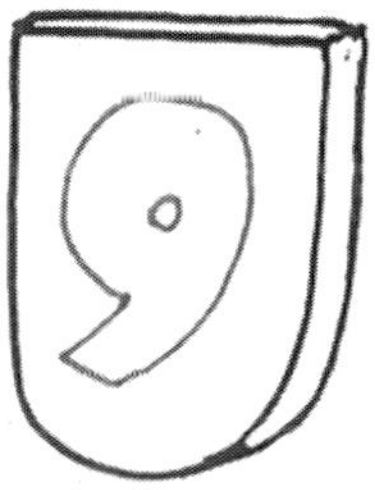

The Ninth Commandment

Get them INVOLVED!

Studying in America costs a lot of money and for this reason while I was a high school and also as a college student I worked during the holidays and the school year. I held a wide variety of jobs! And I believe I actually learned as much on these part-time jobs as I did during my studies!

My first job was in a drive-in ice cream shop that was next door to our high school. There were times - before or after a football game, for example - when we had to make hundreds of ice cream cones, banana splits and sundaes with all kinds of different toppings as quickly as possible and we had to calculate the cost in our heads. Sometimes, especially at the beginning, I made mistakes with the ice cream confections: instead of chocolate sauce I put nuts on a sundae or instead of a small ice cream cone with strawberry topping I might have produced a big one with colored sprinkles. The boss trained me in a quite unusual way. If I got an order wrong, he opened the door to the freezer without comment and put my "mistake" inside. I was "allowed" to eat all the mistakes later. That sounded very tempting at first, but as the series of ice cream creations got longer and longer, my craving for ice cream died away - and surprisingly, I started making fewer mistakes!

But there were also times when there was less to do. We would clean the equipment and get everything in order. When this was all finished, we waited for customers. There was nowhere we could sit down and do anything else. We just stood there and waited for the next customers. After several weeks I came to the conclusion that I actually liked the time when we were fully occupied much better than the empty times when time was just dragging on. During these slack periods, it was not the boss who was my working partner, but usually another student who worked part-time. Without any constructive work, we came up with the funniest (and also most stupid) ideas, such as producing crowns for each other made of whipped cream.

It's no different at school. As long as the students are busy, everything runs like clockwork. But as soon as nothing is happening, they come up with entertaining ideas and often get into mischief! We can avoid that by making sure we keep them busy and involved.

I can't hear anything!

How often did I write something on the board at school, and immediately the kids were calling out: *"I can't see the board, Mrs. Nitsche!"* (a teacher recently told me that her standard answer to this statement is: *"I'm not transparent yet, but I'm working hard on it").* Very rarely, however, have I heard: *"I don't hear anything",* although I believe that this is actually very often the case. Sometimes when I was standing right next to a student while she was answering a question, I couldn't hear her. I also often sat in the back of the classroom while colleagues were teaching. I could hear the teacher. Not the student. It doesn't matter how interactive we make our lessons - if students can't hear and understand what their peers are saying, their attention will drift away. Would it be different for us? If you came to one of my lectures, no matter how much the topic might interest you, and I gave the lecture in Chinese, you wouldn't pay much attention.

What can we do so that the students listen to each other and also to us and are interested in what is happening?

We can do elocution exercises

I often did speech exercises with the students. I told them, our voices need to be like arrows. When a student spoke to me, I would point with my index finger behind me. That was the signal: *"Shoot your voice like an arrow at a point behind me."* Or we'd play with our voices while reading aloud: I would read loudly, dramatically and clearly, and they would then repeat the words at exactly the same volume and in exactly the same tone of voice.

We can pay attention to the seating arrangement

The seating arrangement you prefer so that everyone is involved is individual and depends on many factors. If the students sit in rows, you should be aware that the student in the last row is unlikely to hear students in the first row speaking. This problem disappears immediately when the students sit in a circle. They see the person they are talking to and direct their voice towards them. In middle school, we preferred to place the desks in a U-shape, with individual rows in the middle of this formation. It looked something like this:

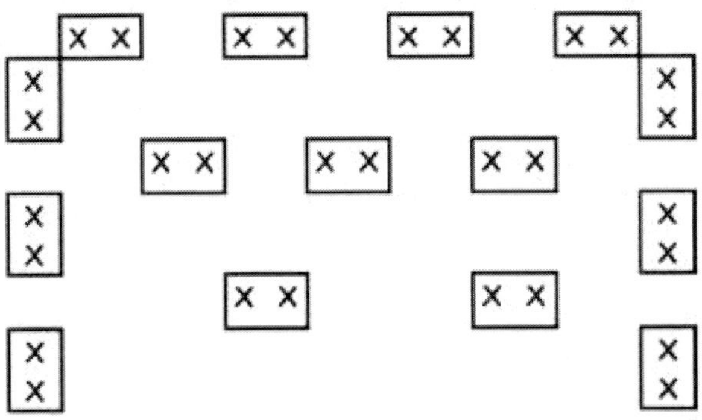

This was an ideal solution for us. It was more communicative, everyone was involved in the lessons, and if we wanted to form a circle quickly, we asked all of the students to stand up and sit on the desks that formed the outer circle. . It's incredible how much more communicative this seating arrangement is. The students see and hear each other much better. It immediately creates a different and much more intimate atmosphere.

Change the seating arrangement regularly.

- We change the seating arrangements often especially at the beginning of the school year. In this way the students get to know each other better and new friendships develop. Outsiders are integrated. I make it clear at the beginning of the school year: *"In our class, everyone works with everyone else!"* If the students don't like that, or it doesn't work out well, then the seating plan is only for a week or so and will change quickly.
- Everyone can choose their own seat for the week. The only stipulation: *"You must sit next to someone you haven't sat next to yet."*
- Draw lots for seats. Draw the names of the children. Features such as the zodiac sign or the color of socks determine the seat neighbor. Cards with numbers are assigned.

Partly fate. Partly choice.

After many different and sometimes very elaborate "attempts" I have developed the following way to arrive at a new seating arrangement.

It is a combination of fate as well as choice. It is also occasionally dependent on the conditions I set, for example, every boy must sit next to a girl or Andi should be in the first row or everyone chooses a new neighbor or children who were in the first row, should now sit in the 3rd or 4th row, etc.

This is my favorite variation:
Everyone takes all of their belongings and stands around the front, the back or the sides of the classroom so that all the seats are empty. I draw a name card and that child chooses a seat. This is repeated until all the children have seats.

IMPORTANT: This all happens in total silence. If a child speaks who already has a seat, he must give his chosen seat up. If a child speaks who is still waiting for his turn, her name card will be put at the bottom of the pile.

Afterwards any changes that are necessary, for example, if a very tall child is sitting in front of a shorter one, etc. can be made.

Christa O., High School

Other seating variations ...

Here are some seating arrangements for selected activities:

Onion formation

The onion

The pupils form - either standing or sitting - two layers of an "onion". There is an inner circle of students, facing outwards. The remaining pupils form an outer circle facing the inner circle of students. In this manner each student in the outer circle has a partner in the inner circle.

The teacher gives the students a question to discuss or a task to perform. The partners work on this task together until the teacher rings a bell. Then the outer circle stands up, says goodbye to their partner moves one person to the right and greets his new partner. The partners now get a new task to solve.

The Onion is a very communicative way to do controlled pair work. The students can work with a great number of classmates – without the activity becoming chaotic.

Two rows

Another form of controlled pair work is when the students line up – either standing or sitting - in two rows facing one another. The person they are facing is their partner for the next task. When they are finished, the teacher rings a bell. The first person in the left (or right) row moves to the back of his line and the other move forward to the next partner.

The goldfish bowl

Several students are chosen to perform a given task, for example, a short role play. The rest of the students sit in a large circle. The "performers" sit in the middle of the circle. The outer circle is the "goldfish bowl" and the performers are the "fish".

And of course there are the more common forms, such as sitting around a table, in rows, in a circle, in the shape of a horseshoe, etc. Try different variations for different activities and see what effect they have on the group dynamics in the classroom.

I'm finished!

There is always at least one student in each class (and also in adult classes) who finishes faster than the others. Generally this is not the goal. If we are practicing conversation in a language arts class or there is a discussion in small groups, it doesn't make sense to do the exercise as quickly as possible. The students need practice in the (foreign) language. In a discussion, it is useful if several points of view are taken into account. I tell the learners that it is not about speed, but about practicing speaking or generating new ideas, and then I direct their conversation in that direction.

If a student finishes a worksheet in math faster than the others, and if the worksheet is done correctly, the student obviously needs more of a challenge. There are a lot of possibilities and ideas of how to keep the students constructively occupied in the meantime. The following ideas come from teachers in our courses:

Weekly worksheets for different subjects

Here the teacher puts together all the exercises, worksheets, puzzles, reading tasks etc. for the whole week, makes a cover sheet with instructions, copies it and gives this weekly plan to the students on Monday. Some exercises are compulsory, others are voluntary. Some are done together during the lesson, others as homework and the students can work on them when they have time between activities at school. At the end of the week the weekly plans are collected.

These weekly plans have many advantages. Students can schedule their own work and learn to plan ahead. They also provide something to do for the students who always finish exercises faster than the others.

Book in your desk

We went to the school library at regular intervals to borrow reading material for use at home and in class. Every student has a book in his or her desk. If he finishes an assignment earlier than the others, he may take the book out and read. We encourage the students to take out their books at the beginning of the lesson as well. They can continue to read until the lesson is about to start.

I also always have a book with me. We introduced the idea that if everyone was reading quietly before the lesson started, we all – including me – were allowed, as a reward, to continue reading for another five or ten minutes.

Bonus worksheets

Once, my colleague in middle school English class told two girls that they needed some extra practice with personal pronouns and she would give them an extra worksheet. I offered to go to the teachers' room to copy the sheets. As I left the class, I asked, *"Does anyone else want an extra worksheet?"* My colleague and I were left with our mouths hanging open when seventeen kids put up their hands! Not only did they want the sheet, but most of them brought this finished task with them the next day!

This experience made me realize that we very often underestimate our students. We often assume that the students do not want to work - and our own assumptions are actually limiting them and preventing them from realizing their true potential. Therefore we started providing additional worksheets in the classroom. If a student finished earlier than the others, he was allowed to take a worksheet and fill it out. For the completed sheets there was often a stamp or sticker (stickers are extremely motivating. As we all know, most students - even the older ones – would sell their soul to get a sticker for a homework exercise :-).

And what else can they do? There are unlimited possibilities! For example, they can make an educational game or a puzzle, or start their homework earlier, relaxing in the cozy corner, correct arithmetic sheets for the teacher, embellish exercise books, help a weaker child with the task at hand, complete helper activities in the classroom such as cleaning the boards, sorting, arranging etc.

My students can't sit still!

When we have to present a topic in class, there will often be students who can't sit still and listen for any length of time, there are various things you can do:

Some students are easily distracted. The slightest disturbance is enough - *"Look! A bird is outside in the tree,"* and these students are immediately elsewhere with their attention!

To be able to concentrate well, many students feel the need to do two things at once. These students can't just sit and listen. They need a second activity or movement that they do on the side. You can put a crumpled ball in their hands. Under no circumstances should the ball fall to the floor or fly across the room. To keep the ball, it must stay with the student - otherwise you take it away. Or you can give him a small piece of plasticine. Or you hand out mandalas which can be colored while listening.

- An American colleague and the guru of interactive training in management, Thiagi (a.k.a. Dr. Sivasailam Thiagarajan, Ph. D.), writes a monthly free newsletter and has written books on interactive lectures. See http://www.thiagi.com/index.html Many of Thiagi's suggestions for management training can easily be applied to school settings, especially in higher grades. Among many other ideas he suggests asking a great number of interactive questions (see below) scattered throughout your presentation and to have short, active stages such as : *"Turn to your neighbor and discuss..."*.

Use non-verbal techniques to engage your students during the presentation:

- Maintain constant eye contact with the class. If a teacher's eye contact with the class is interrupted for more than six seconds, she will lose the class's attention.
- If a disturbance occurs, just stop talking and wait. Silently.
- Encourage active participation: *"Who has ever experienced this?"* - Show of hands.
- Use inviting, open posture, facial expressions and gestures.
- Stroll through the classroom as you speak. Stop dramatically in different places at various important lecture points.
- Take into account the students' learning styles and also include various presentation styles.
- Allow, acknowledge and welcome questions.
- Address the students by name.
- Have keywords and phrases repeated aloud by the whole class.
- Wink, smile, nod.
- And do anything else you can think of to make the students think and listen actively!

Ask a lot of questions

The type of questions you ask has an impact on younger and also older students and their willingness to answer or participate in class.

Ask rhetorical questions

These are the questions to which you do not expect an answer at all. The students answer these questions inwardly, and their attention is thus with you.

However, caution is advised with younger students.
They usually see EVERY question as an incentive and prompt to answer.

If I have a group of adults and ask in the morning if they had a nice evening, they nod, or if something really unusual happened, they will tell me.

When I ask the same question in a 1st grade class, I get 25 detailed answers: *"Yes, teacher, I have to tell you! The dog peed on the carpet ...*"Children at this age take everything literally.

Ask easy questions too

If we always ask difficult questions, the same students always answer. They are fully involved in the class. But the students who cannot answer the questions do not feel involved at all. Either they stop paying attention or they come up with creative ideas about how to disrupt the lesson.

Ask questions that arouse their curiosity:

What do you think I brought for you today? Would you like to know what happened to me on the tram today?

Ask questions that show a connection between daily life and the material to be learned.

Apply the principle of WIIFM - What's in it for me? When students know why they are learning something and what it will bring them, they see the meaning behind it and are more involved.

Ask suggestive questions:

The questions should also make the students curious and encourage them to think. "Have you ever wondered why the air above the ground is much warmer, for example, when you climb up the ladder?"

It is also important that the lead-in questions to a new topic can be answered in the affirmative with "YES". If you ask questions that interest the majority of the students, they will join in more easily than if the students are either loudly or inwardly say "No!" which subconsciously leads to resistance. Use the art of positive suggestion when asking questions.

The Tenth Commandment

INTEGRATE THE OUTSIDERS!

A teacher asked the kids in her class to take out a piece of paper. She asked them to crumple it up, throw it on the floor, to stamp on it, to be angry with it and do anything to it except to rip it. Then she asked the pupils to pick the piece of paper up again and to very carefully smooth it out. Try to make it look like it did when we started. They should look at it now, how dirty and scarred it was. Even if they told the paper how sorry they were, it would never be the same as it had been before.

It's the same when people are bullied. Even if we are sorry later, the scars are there forever.

Have you ever been an outsider?

I was - and still am - not an athletic person. When I was in school we played a lot of team games. Every lesson began with selecting teams. There were always two captains who took turns choosing the members of their team. Usually I was the last person to be chosen. This was torture for me. I suffered before, during and after every gym class. Fortunately there were other things I could do well. But the gym lessons have remained as a lasting unhappy memory.

We also have students in our classes who are total outsiders. They suffer. They have developed defense mechanisms to protect themselves, and sometimes these mechanisms make it even more difficult to reach them. They often take the role of *"I want to be alone and I don't want to have anything to do with the others anyway."* They reject contact because it hurts less than being rejected. Very often they do this so convincingly that even the teacher believes them.

A classic experiment: Blue eyes or brown eyes

An American elementary school teacher, Jane Elliott, conducted an experiment with her third grade class in a small town called Riceville, Iowa in the 1950's. In this experiment, which has since become world-renowned, students with blue or brown eyes are called inferior or superior for a period of one day. Taking their eye color as the criterion, they are able to experience life as a member of a minority group for one entire school day.
The reactions were shocking.

There are several articles on the Internet about her experiments. Here are two of them:

In the article Jane Elliott says that her class had completely changed from a group of twenty lovely children to a group which cruelly ostracized about half of their classmates within ten minutes after the experiment had begun. These films and Jane Elliott's work show how quickly our behavior can change and how the outsiders, the classmates and also the teacher contribute to the situation.

What are the outsiders' strategies?

I have listed a few games on this topic below. You can play these with your students. But beware: The experience goes very deep. After playing these games in teacher training seminars, the participants made the following comments about their own feelings and reactions during the game:

- Some initially fought against the outsider role. They wanted to integrate, but they soon resigned and accepted their role within the group. They simply observed what was happening.

- Some formed their own clique. This made them feel stronger. They rejected integration, even if the group wanted to accept them later. This is how gangs develop. They then take revenge on society and on those who excluded them.

- Techniques they used spontaneously to try to become a member of the group.

  - They paid compliments and tried to ingratiate themselves. .
  - They resorted to physical means to try to become a member of the group.
  - They got loud, they sang, they played the role of the clown.
  - Some became aggressive.
  - The girls tended to pull back or to show off while trying to join into the conversation.

What can the other students do?

What can other students, compassionate observers, do to help those who are being excluded? They do not need to tolerate this behavior in silence. Students should feel free to turn to a teacher and ask her to intervene. There are in all probability other students who also sympathize with the outsider. It is easier to do something about it together, with the teacher's help, than alone.

What can the outsider do himself?

The outsider should stop and think why this is happening. Why are others excluding him. When does that happen? Is it always the case, or does it only happen in certain situations? What do his classmates get out of torturing him? Is it malice, or is he doing something in particular that bothers them so much?

If changes are justified, the outsider should try to make them. Otherwise, let him be true to himself. It is not necessary for him to change his personality simply to placate his attackers. Where are there other youths or children like him? At the football club? A chess club? He should actively seek another circle of friends that is good for him. He should talk to his parents, his teacher and guidance counselors about it.

What can you do as a teacher?

A lot! Teachers are the most influential factor in the integration process. Remember above all:

- **You are the role model!**
  Treat everyone - especially the outsiders - with appreciation and respect. Students learn their social behavior by imitation. Unfortunately, the models they usually have are quite often not positive ones. There are many homes where the parents do not give the student a sense of warmth and security. Consciously set a counter model. The students are constantly watching you. Both your verbal and non-verbal messages are accurately perceived - partly consciously, partly unconsciously - by the class. You set the tone for dealing with other people and also with outsiders.

- **Emphasize their strengths**
  This strengthens everyone's self-confidence – that of the outsider and of the observers. Provide opportunities where he can show his strengths. Admit and stand by your own weaknesses as a teacher/human being in the classroom, e.g. *"I'll never be a pro footballer", "You can do it much better than I can!* Here, as everywhere, the emphasis should be on positive behavior and strengths. On a one-on-one basis talk to the student what his strengths are and what has worked well so far. Consider his strengths can be transferred to other situations.

Social learning

Set priorities: Discuss the characteristics and values which are essential for a good classroom atmosphere. Attention, respect, tolerance, consideration and helpfulness among others. Make it very concrete. Many students recognize the names of the values but they do not really know what they mean. Include metaphorical stories, role plays and activities that convey these values. Use social learning as much and as often as possible. The material can be packaged into group-dynamic, social learning games that encourage cooperation rather than competition for almost any subject - e.g. English, German, history, math, religion.

How to form groups or teams.

Random group and team formation ideas:

- Count off.
- Distribute cards with different colors or shapes.
- Distribute different colored jelly beans or pencils. All those who have a red gummi bear...
- Decorate worksheets with colored dots. All the blue ones go together, all the...
- Deal out a deck or part of a deck of cards. All kings go together, etc.
- Draw lots. Exchanging is not allowed.
- Before the students come, stick different colored candies under the seat (or if you don't come before the lesson, have them pull the candies out of a bag).
- Cut postcards into puzzle pieces and distribute them. Students have to find out to which postcard their puzzle piece belongs.
- Find things they have in common. (toothbrush color, number of buttons, eye color, etc.)
- Hand out riddles and their answers on cut up slips. "Find your partner."
- Hand out memory cards.
- Distribute cards with calculations and results (e.g. "1 km" and "1000 m").
- Hand out cards with "wave", "cough", "walk on tiptoe". They mime what is on their card and form pantomime groups.
- Cards with "You're happy/hungry/thirsty..." Mime and find the others in your group.
- Hand out cards with songs on them. Walk through the room singing or humming. Everyone who sings "Happy Birthday", "O Sole Mio", "The National Anthem" etc. belongs to that team.
- Students line up in a row: by height, hair length, etc. The first three work together, the next three, etc.
- The last person to be selected is the captain the next time.

How does it feel to be an outsider?

This is followed by some games to promote communicative and social skills and to integrate outsiders. The principle behind these games, which can be played several times and with variations, is that everyone in the class should feel at least once what it is like to be an outsider.

I have played a number of these games with teachers in training courses. Some of the games took a completely different turn from what I had imagined. We didn't have an outsider problem in the seminars, and I only wanted to play the games so they could use them themselves later in their classes.

That's not what happened. The reactions while playing were varied and sometimes extreme. In a large group, where there were four teachers who volunteered as outsiders, they banded together. They first banished the rest of the group from the seminar room with vehemence, and then they ran after them through the garden to the edge of the forest!

During the debriefing, the participants were amazed at their own behavior and the strong feelings the game had evoked in them. These games are very powerful. You have to keep an eye on the way the game is developing. When you are playing the game in class, you should neither choose those who are really outsiders nor the pack leaders to play the role of the excluded students. It is also very important to choose "outsiders" you can rely on to speak openly and honestly about what they experienced or are experiencing. And you can, of course, stop the game at any time.

The debriefing is the most important part of any group dynamic game and may, under certain circumstances, take much longer than the game itself. Usually the discussion is more productive if the debriefing questions are answered first in small groups and then later in the large group.

Role-playing about prejudices in the group

Ask the students if they can imagine situations where some people are excluded from others in a group. Can you imagine what it feels like to be excluded?

Divide students into small groups them a situation where a student is excluded. All groups work on the same example. They should think of a solution for the situation. They play through the situation and the solution a few times within the group so that they can empathize well with the roles and improve the solution if necessary.

Then the small groups perform their scenes for the large group. As a debriefing session, the different solutions are looked at more closely and compared.

The Points Game

Let the students stand in a circle, facing outwards. Explain the process to the pupils: "You will stand in a circle, looking outwards, and close your eyes. I will put a sticky dot on each of your foreheads. Only when I have finished, may you open your eyes again. No talking during the game."

For example, if you have a group of 25 students, you will need six red, six green, six blue, six yellow dots and one black or other colored dot.

Carefully select the person who will be "the odd man out". This should be neither an outsider nor a pack leader. Give it to a person who can express himself well, who will speak the truth and who is emotional but will not overreact.

After you have finished sticking the dots on their foreheads, say, "Open your eyes and turn around. Please do not speak. Now you may begin." Keep your instructions vague. It's important that you don't say, "Please sort yourself out," or anything like that. The students will first look at you a little helplessly, and then they'll start dividing into groups by color. The person with the single colored dot will be left over.

Do not end the game too quickly. Wait and see what the group will do with the person who is left over.

The debriefing takes place first in small groups. The outsider chooses a group and joins in with them. Then the discussion takes place in the large group.

Discussion questions:

- What did you feel at the moment when you discovered someone with a dot in the same color?
- Why did you sort yourselves into groups?
- You sorted yourselves into groups, each of which had the same color. Could you perhaps have grouped yourselves differently?
- How did you feel?
- Did you help each other to find the appropriate groups?
- What about "the odd man out"? How did you feel / react toward him?

We're all in the same boat!

The students look at the illustration on the next page. They consider which figure it represents and why.

(The following illustration may be copied)

"The self-disciplining classroom." Pearl Nitsche

Illustrator: Andrew Wright

Red dots - Green dots

Give each student either a red or a green dot. They can stick it on their clothes in a clearly visible place. There should be about the same number of red and green dots.

Tell the students that we are planning a big party. The students with the green dots will sit together with pencils and paper and discuss the planning for the party. They should make a list of all the tasks that need to be done for the party. The students with the red dots sit down with their backs to the board, close their eyes, pause for a moment and think of - without speaking - all the ideas they can come up with for the party.

Once everyone is in position, write secret instructions for those with the green dots on the board:

> "Shhhhhhhh!
> In a few minutes, those with the red dots will open their eyes again. We will discuss the festival. Please IGNORE the people with red dots. Don't talk to them. Pretend they're transparent. And now continue with the festival planning."

After a few more minutes, ask the students with the red dots to open their eyes. The two groups should sit together in a circle and talk about the festival.

After about three minutes, end the discussion.

Debriefing questions:

- How did you feel? Ask the red dots and the green dots.
- What happened? What did you do as a green dot and why? What did you do as a red dot and why?
- When the green dots declare that they have followed the instructions, show the red dots the secret instructions.
- We only played for a few minutes. What if your whole life was like those minutes?
- What would have happened if there had been more red dots than green ones?
- What does this exercise tell us for the future? For our behavior here in the group?

Black sheep

The students walk through the room and play "welcome scenes". They shake hands, smile at each other, say a few words to each other, say goodbye, walk on, greet the next student they meet, have short conversations with each other.

- **First round:**
  One or two pupils who have volunteered to play the role of the "excluded" - is/are not considered. The game is either over after five minutes, or if the student has succeeded in shaking hands with another or getting into conversation.

- **Round two:**
  Again, one or two volunteers are appointed. This time the other students hate these two. They can express this verbally, but they are not allowed to touch the outsiders.

- **Followed by a class discussion:**
  - How did the outsider feel? What did he think during the exercise?
  - How did he try to make contact?
  - Has the way of communication changed in the course of the game?
  - How did the other group members react to this?
  - How did it make you feel?
  - Have you ever experienced a similar situation?

Table Leg Number 3:
STRUCTURE! STRUCTURE! STRUCTURE!

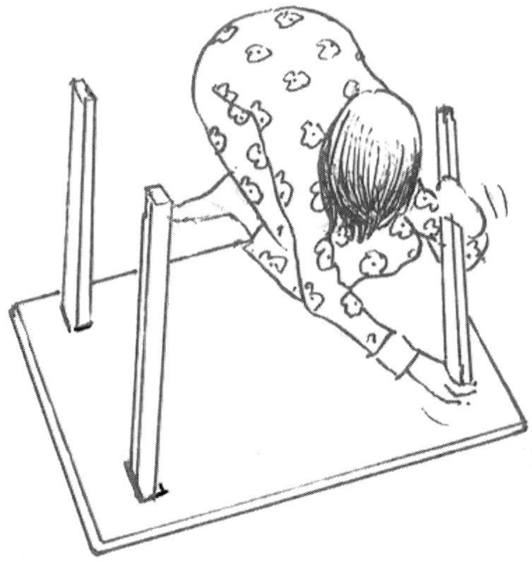

If rules, procedures, daily routines and desired behavior are clearly formulated, understood and practiced by a class to perfection, problems that are common in other classrooms or situations have no chance of arising. And, therefore, the need to discipline students will be eliminated. A structured classroom is a pro-active classroom. By setting up detailed structures - be they anchors, routines or defined limits - the students know exactly what is expected of them and how they should do it.

In this chapter, we will take a closer look at anchors and structured sequences in the classroom. You may know some of these processes from my book "Nonverbal Classroom Management". Here we will take a look at how teachers actually use these practices in the classroom. However, each situation and each class is different. Experiment with this information and create your own routines - step by step. There is a great number of suggestions here. Have fun trying them out!

"First determine the destination and the way to get there so that others know what to expect"
Sir Francis Bacon

8

What is a structured classroom?

The two keys: Structures and Relationships

These two elements, structure and relationships, are the keys to a self-disciplining classroom. In the last chapters we discussed the relationship level, which is the first key. Students' main motivation for going to school is for relationships and friendships - with each other and with their teachers. When they feel that we like them, they are motivated and help to create a classroom where disciplining is not necessary.

The second key consists of structure and recurring routines. Successful classroom management requires schedules, routine procedures, rules and rituals. This means that students always know what to expect in certain situations. The result is a smoothly flowing and harmonious classroom experience.

The advantages are obvious:

- Daily repetitive rituals and structured processes give learners a sense of orientation, support and security in everyday school life. This results in a fear-free learning environment.
- An "automated" classroom saves time, confusion and disciplinary measures.
- Structures offers boundaries. As a result, disciplinary measures are rarely necessary.
- Rituals promote identification with the class and the school.
- Social skills are strengthened and the quality of life in and outside the classroom improves.

- There is always the possibility of a new beginning: every hour, every day, every semester, every school year is seen as a new beginning through ritualization. This means that students can leave burdensome memories and failures behind and to start again with new energy.

Established routines and structures in the classroom are like railway tracks. They show pupils clearly and unambiguously the pathway to successful action. There is no deviation. The students have a clear goal, a map and precise instructions on how to carry out the desired action. Thus, success is guaranteed. Since the process is repeated over and over again, it is also automated. This is positive for the students and also for us: the students feel comfortable. Classroom management becomes more efficient and takes less time.

The more difficult a class, the more structure is needed.

Rituals promote self-confidence and trust

Our primary special education school is for students with acute psychological crises and behavioral difficulties. There are about eight children per class. Each group has two teachers who work together closely with a multidisciplinary team in the psychiatric or social/therapeutic fields.

One of the most important pedagogical factors for working with these students is a strongly ritualized daily or weekly routine. Structure and a manageable framework provide an overview and orientation. Rituals bring relief and stability. They promote students' self-confidence and self-assurance. They provide reliability and a sense of security, which is absolutely essential when working with these children. In addition to a daily routine the qualities of openness, understanding and a positive attitude are essential.

Sabine H., Special Education

Rituals give the students support

Rituals in the classroom provide structure, give support and enable trust. They signal constancy. What is valid today will also be valid tomorrow and was valid yesterday too.

Sandra P., Tamara P., Sandra S., elementary school

Be pro-active not reactive

Again and again I hear questions like:

"How do I keep the students quiet?", "What should I do with a kid who is out of control?", "What should I do if the students ignore me?" or *"How do I get students to pay attention in class?"*

We all know these situations. Actually we are asking ourselves these questions too late. Yes, we can solve the problem and turn the situation around. But this is much easier to do **before** it becomes a problem. This is called pro-active behavior.

Being pro-active means nipping problems in the bud before they even begin. If we wait until there is a disturbance in the class, the situation is already too far advanced. Then my only choice is to react to the student's behavior, i.e. I am on the defensive. If I take action before the negative behavior starts, then I am still in the sphere of influence. Nothing has happened yet, and if I act cleverly enough, the student does not even notice that he has barely missed a disciplinary action!

If I do not succeed in nipping the disturbance in the bud, I have no choice but to move from the sphere of influence to the sphere of power and discipline. When I discipline a student, I respond to his actions. In other words, he has misbehaved and I have no choice but to switch to the sphere of power and react to it. When I react I am on the defensive and he is in the stronger position.

There are two types of pro-active measures:

1. "spontaneous" interventions (more on this in the next Table Leg Number 4: Setting limits. giving support!)

2. and systematic interventions by means of the use of predetermined routines in the classroom.

Pro-active measures prevent negative behavior arising in the first place. This means that if we are pro-active enough, we would (at least theoretically - apart from occasional slips) never have to discipline in the classroom again.

This second kind of proactive measures, the systematic use of rituals, routines and anchors in the classroom, helps the class to bond as a group. They let you transition from one step to the next more quickly and smoother. Disturbances do not usually happen while teaching the lesson itself, but rather during the transitions from one activity to the next or at the beginning or end of the lesson.

Anchors: Magic in the classroom

I would like to give a brief overview of the use of anchors in the classroom, a very important and central topic here. You can read more about it, including numerous examples, in my books "Nonverbal Classroom Management" and "Nonverbal Recipe Book: First aid for teachers" and on a film clip with Derrick and me on YouTube: (https://www.youtube.com/watch?v=vKjzknWxLUo&t=15s).

When a teacher repeatedly and systematically uses a non-verbal signal in connection with an event, a concept or an idea in the classroom, the signal and the concept become anchored. Words become superfluous. The non-verbal signal is sufficient and the pupils react accordingly. These non-verbal signals can occur in many different forms: e.g. as movements, sounds, rules, symbols, images, customs, ceremonies, contracts between teacher and pupils or as recurring rituals in the school day and school year. These anchors create an inner state in the pupil, which promotes learning as well as building up a certain expectation (e.g. *"Now the math lesson begins!")*. This happens automatically - without words.

Think of typical phrases that you use often, perhaps several times a day, in classroom management. Here are a few examples:

- "Be quiet!" – *Simply place a finger across your lips*
- "Monday's homework assignment is..." – *always write it on the same place on the board.*
- "Now it's time to clean up!" – *Cleaning up music*
- "Worksheets in the binder!" – *Binder in one hand, worksheet in the other*

With non-verbal anchors - be they visual, auditory, kinesthetic or place anchors - you can permanently delete these sentences from your vocabulary. (What is important is that you simply DO it – without words accompanying the anchor)

Keep your anchors clean!

It is important that anchors are kept "clean". This is done by executing them systematically and with precision. When you set a place anchor for assigning homework, you must ALWAYS assign the homework on that spot. If you put on a nice magic hat to signal that you are going to tell a story, you must not put the hat on for any other event. If you give a hand signal to create silence in the classroom, you need, first of all, to take the time to give the signal and secondly to wait until the class is totally silent. In this way - if anchors are used cleanly and systematically - they will remain in your teacher's toolbox as a wonderful and almost magical tool!

Some ideas:

Attention and calmness

Anchors have greatly improved our class environment! Right after our seminar I taught my team colleagues how to do the anchor for getting the class's attention. I showed them how to do it and we also used the You Tube Video. The kids quickly calm down at the beginning of the lesson. They need 3 to 6 seconds at most. They are much more attentive and more concentrated when the lesson begins. They reacted to the anchor immediately, just like you said they would. Thanks!

Martin G., high school

But we don't want to stop!

The other day, we were busy with artwork, and because everyone was enjoying it so much, I thought I would put on some nice music. I walked towards the CD player, and suddenly a student said, "Oh, are you turning on the music? Does that means we are finished? Please don't play it yet. We want to work some more."

Ulli H., middle school

A classroom full of anchors

We save so much time now using anchors in situations where in the past a lot of time was wasted talking, cajoling, and disciplining. Now it only takes seconds to get the students to react appropriately. It is also sometimes very funny to observe how the children react when certain anchors in the daily rhythm have been "forgotten" by mistake. They immediately reproach the teacher, "Wait, Mr. Smith! You forgot to put the poster on the board! I'll do it for you!" or: "You need to play our music and then we can shout Yes!!" etc.

For the last seven years I have been working mainly with children whose mother tongue is not German or English. These classes are multi-lingual so I use a lot of non-verbal elements to communicate. It works like magic:

Here are some of the acoustic signals I use:

- I play MUSIC to indicate that they should sit down and be quiet
- I play "The Pink Panther" as a signal to clean up after art class.
- Creative writing is done with classical music in the background.
- I use a rattle, e.g. a filled wooden egg, to signal to the students they should move their chairs into a circle.

I use the following visual anchors:

- When my index finger and middle finger point to my eyes, it means "Look at me!"
- I hold one hand behind one ear and the other "zips" my mouth shut. That means..: "My mouth is shut, and my ears are open!"
- When a child wants to go to the toilet, he or she shows a "W" with the thumbs and index fingers of both hands placed next to each other. This "W" means: "I have to go to the WC!"
- We have a poster with a chair and an arrow pointing upwards on it. When I put this on the board, it means "Put the chairs up on the tables".
- We are the "bear class". We have pictures of bears that are either writing, painting or working. The picture I'm holding up shows what we're going to do next.
- I lay a golden treasure chest on our round red study carpet. Sometimes there is a note, a picture or a symbol inside. This is a signal that says, "We're going to learn something new now!"

And I use the following place anchors:

- My "pay close attention" anchor is at the front in the middle of the room
- My discipline anchor is next to the sink. Here I stand with a frozen posture and a very serious expression on my face
- Two bright yellow adhesive dots next to the door signal that this is the place I use to talk to another teacher or adult. As long as I am standing here, the students should not interrupt us.

Gabriele S., Preschool

It's so much easier without words

My "pay close attention anchor" is my teacher's desk. This is where I like to stand or lean when I give important information or assign work.

When I place my teacher's chair in front of the board, my students know: Now she is going to tell us a story. This is also the place where I read and act out my suggestopedia texts.

When standing in the hall, I hold up my hand and slowly count with my fingers (without words) from 1 to 3. At the number 3 they are standing in an orderly and quiet line. I also give them the signal to move into a circle by blinking. It's amazing how well this all works. And how proud the students are that they can do it so well.

Iris G., elementary school

Symbols on DIn A4

I printed out large symbols on colored DIN A4 paper and laminated them. I use them in class as symbols for silence, working volume, listening and writing. If I lose or misplace them, it's not a problem. I simply reprint them. I don't say anything while using these symbols. I lean the symbol on the board and simply knock or point at it.

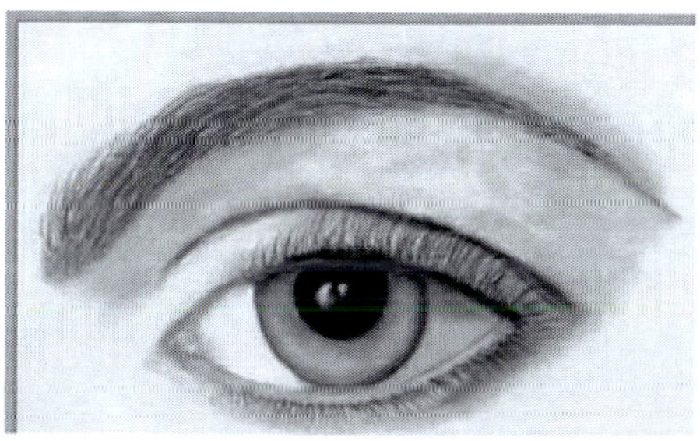

Ilse S., high school

There's no need to talk!

When one or more kids get a bit loud, I use various symbols:

- Yellow and red cards,
- Smilies with laughing or sad mouths,
- Smilies with angry faces,
- Smiley face with the finger pointing to the mouth. We take this one with us when we go on excursions and used it in the dining hall when it got too loud. It worked like a charm.

I like to work with exaggerated gestures - they are striking and funny too. For example silent shouting, fake sighing or crying. Sometimes I feel like I'm on a cabaret stage. But it works!

Margit W., middle school

And what do the students say?

Peter F., a middle school teacher, asked his students to evaluate him at the end of the school year.

Here are the comments of a 14 year old pupil:

Dear Mr. F.!

What I noticed and liked this year

- you wrote all the material we would need for the three hours of lessons on the board.
- you used music to signal what we would do next. You always turned it on at exactly the right moment
- you showed us notes or pictures about what we should or should not do: "Chewing gum.", "Keep it down."
- you praised us so much.

This was the very best of the four years we were here. The ideas you had were really great. I especially liked the music you played at the beginning and end of the lessons. It was also great that you didn't say anything when we were too loud and just shot a softball at us with a friendly smile. Then we knew we had to be quiet, but it was in such a friendly way. No one felt offended.

The most important sign was by far the one that said: "Log off PC at the end of the lesson!" or "Shut down PC at the end of the lesson!" Because last year we were never sure what we should do. We always had to ask. Then maybe a couple of kids weren't sure and in the next lesson, you had to shut down all of the PCs yourself. This year, because of the sign, we knew exactly what we were supposed to do. That was much better.

Now I would like to say a bit about your teaching style:
Talking to you is like talking to a bright student. If I don't know what you're talking about, you explain it right away. You're very humane - and you're also very funny. For me you are the best teacher, and I think it is a great pity that I only had you as a teacher in computer science.

Nevertheless, the year was great and I wish we could continue. Thank you!

Best regards, Andreas M.

Some further comments from Peter's students:

- I found the summary on the board about the day's lessons very good.
- Actually, you are my favorite teacher because you are nice to children and you never raise your voice. It's also a good idea that you always write down on the board what we are going to do during the lesson.
- I thought it was a good year. What I liked are the songs and the way you try to solve problems without being angry at the students.

Structures are ritualized procedures

A structure, as we will call it from now on, is a sequence of actions or a ritualized process. It is a detailed behavioral model for procedures that are regularly performed in the classroom.
- be it once or several times a day, a week or a month.

The first thing the teacher does is to find out in what situations more structure is needed. What does not run as smoothly as you would like it to? What leads to unrest or chaos in the classroom? Where do disruptions occur? Let's take, for example, getting the students lined up in a double line to go to the library. The teacher asks herself how this can be done in an orderly way. She analyzes this procedure, divides it up step by step into sequences and then teaches it to the students. They practice together until it becomes automatic. This procedure is explained in more detail below.

NLP, Neurolinguistic Programming, as already discussed, is sometimes called "A Model of Excellence". The structures we are discussing here are models. They are recipes. They are precisely prescribed procedures that bring structure and order to the classroom. They are rituals. Students appreciate them because they know what is happening and what is expected of them. They offer us the opportunity to manage the classroom peacefully, effectively and, above all, proactively with models rather than disciplinary measures. In this way we are able to use influence instead of power - and resistance disappears. You can use the models described on the following pages - if appropriate and desired - or you can easily adapt them to your personal needs in the classroom.

What are these routines good for?

When aircraft pilots are trained, they learn routines that are used in emergencies. A light on the control panel lights up and the pilot and his crew react with the appropriate routine to avoid a disaster. There is a series of steps for every crisis situation, which are carefully practiced and, if necessary, implemented.

It's no different in a hospital. Every operation has a precisely prescribed procedure, which the surgeon carries out to the letter. A fire alarm drill in school also consists of a series of procedures that are carried out automatically and accurately. If you stay overnight in a hotel, the escape plan in case of a fire catastrophe is displayed in every room.

This is exactly how we should conduct classroom management procedures. The teaching profession is, in my opinion, the most beautiful profession in the world. But the prerequisite for this is that you have your class under control. Anchors, structures and other pro-active measures make this possible. If you automate the management process, you can then give free rein to your creativity when working on content.

How does it work?

Structures determine the behavior we want to see and experience in our students. They are like a map or a path that demonstrates for them what we want from them. Because the path is used again and again like railway tracks, they always stay the same, a regularity, a constancy and a feeling of security is created. Routines are effective and they save time. They are one of the most powerful and helpful tools a teacher can have in his toolbox. Success is guaranteed because the students know exactly what to do and perform it automatically, without discussion.

The first step

Think about it. What's the problem? Which time-consuming processes happen day in, day out and could be made into a routine procedure? Some examples, which will be discussed in the following chapters:

- How do you start the lesson?
- How is the homework assignment specified?
- How should the workplace, the games cupboard, exercise books be organized?
- What do you do if you need to go to the bathroom?
- If someone was absent, how does he find out what he needs to do as make-up work?
- What do you do if you come to class late?
- How do you get your students' attention?
- How are excuses, homework, milk money, etc. collected?

What administrative tasks get on your nerves? What procedures involve too much talking on your part? What situations confuse your students? Explain these routines to your students as described below and practice them with the class until they can do the procedure perfectly.

I have heard some teachers say: *"But I don't have time for that! We have to start with the material right away!"* But in the long run that doesn't make sense. If you practice these structures with the students at the beginning of the school year, you will save yourselves a lot of time. And - much, much more important - you will enhance the positive atmosphere in the classroom and spare your voice and your nerves!

Teach the students the routines that are needed. Practice them until they become second nature. Write them on a poster and hang it up. If it doesn't work perfectly, point to the sign and ask, *"What should you be doing right now?"* And it will happen. Your classroom is now on autopilot!

The exact instructions now follow in detail:

1. Note the goals. Be concise.

It is important that students know **exactly** what is expected of them.
It's not enough for me to say, *"I want you to form a double line quietly."*

Define the challenge precisely for yourself:
What do you mean by "quietly"? Does it mean they can talk quietly while in line? Or does it mean they should be totally silent? Where does the line start? Do they all line up at the same time? How are partners chosen? When standing in line, how far apart should they stand? And so on.

Sometimes we assume that students know more than they actually do. It is therefore important that I have a clear picture for myself of what I want them to do. How can I explain this in a way that the students can reproduce the process exactly? It often happens that our students know WHAT to do, but they don't understand HOW to do it.

First you define the problem. Then you plan the procedure step by step.

2. Explain to the class why they should learn this routine

For example:

> *"When we go to the gym, we pass many classrooms. We don't know what the students are doing in those classrooms right now. Maybe they're writing a paper. Or maybe their teacher is doing a guided fantasy with them or telling them something important. If we walk by and make a lot of noise, we'll disturb them. We wouldn't like that and we don't want to bother them with noise."*

3. Demonstrate what the students should do

It is important that you tell them what to do – rather than what NOT to do. Otherwise you will bring confusion into the instructions - and, as we know, the brain does not understand the word "NOT". For example, if it is raining and I tell the students NOT to forget their umbrellas, the chances are great that many of them will not process the word NOT and they will come without umbrellas. It is much better to say, "Remember to bring your umbrellas."

If possible, show your students exactly what you want them to do. Or, even better, let some of the students demonstrate it. Model exactly what you want. While you're doing this, talk about the procedure so that students understand the steps.

> *"Here, right by the door, the row begins. As you can see, I'm standing here on the third tile away from the wall. Remember, I'm standing right..."*

And then have the students do the same. As they demonstrate, emphasize what they do right or wrong.

> *"Let's take a good look at how the front row is doing. Great! Susi and Martin stood up very quietly, pushed their chairs back under the table and came forward without talking. And now Florian and Anna are doing the same ... now the whole first row is standing and waiting for the second row to line up behind them ..."*

Encourage the students to think about what they are doing by peppering your explanations with meaningful questions in between so that the students think:

> *"How did the second row do? Did they walk forward calmly? What is the distance between the pairs? Oh...something's wrong in the middle of the row. What should we do differently? Yes, some students need to stand up straight. How does it look now? Great! You did a great job!"*

4. And now practice, practice and practice!

Time their routine with a stopwatch. Write down the best scores. Ask the students if they think they can do it faster and better. Close your eyes and say you will count to 10. Have the class zip their lips and line up without saying a single word. They tell you when they're done. How many seconds did they need? Practice until they are perfect and the structure is automatic.

5. Repeat the routine whenever and as often as necessary

After a while, it may happen that the structure gets sloppy. Then it needs to be reviewed until it once again runs precisely like clockwork. Some students will get it immediately. Others need longer. Here you can introduce a "buddy" or a "helper system".

What do we do if...?

You can repeat the structures at regular intervals in a variety of ways. For example, make a card or board game and name it:

"What do we do ..."

- ... when we have visitors in class?
- ... when we get in line?
- ... when we clean up the classroom?
- ... if you have to go to the bathroom?
- ... if you were absent yesterday and you need the worksheets that were handed out?
- ... if you need something but the teacher is talking to someone else?
- ... if you come to class late?

or:

- How many sharpened pencils should I have in my pencil case?
- Who is first in line?
- Where does my backpack belong?
- How do I talk to an adult who asks me to do something?
- Who is responsible for cleaning the board?
- How do we hand in homework?
- When do we hand in homework?

Or assign role plays to small groups. They should demonstrate to the others how something is done the right way as well as how it is done incorrectly.

Or you do it the wrong way and let the students list all the "mistakes" you made.

When should rituals, anchors and routines be introduced?

The sooner the better!

Some elementary and middle schools have "taster" days to introduce kids to their new school / class in the spring before they start in the fall. This is a great opportunity to introduce several anchors which they can practice during the summer. For example, when the teacher raises her left hand and the index finger of her right hand, it means that the students should be quiet.

In the first weeks of school we set the tone for the whole school year. Teachers with the best functioning classrooms spend most of the first two weeks establishing routines and boundaries, a positive learning atmosphere, goal setting and group dynamics. Feel free to neglect the curriculum a bit during these first weeks. The time you gain by establishing a structured classroom will pay off many times over. Like the hare and the turtle - slowly but surely you will create a classroom in which students exercise self-discipline and you will no longer need to play the role of "policewoman" in your classroom.

Can I introduce new structures during the schoolyear?

Yes, definitely. You don't have to wait. It's NEVER too late to change something that doesn't work. You can and should change your processes, expectations and strategies whenever you feel they are no longer effective. First you think about what you want to change. Tell the students the problem and also the solution you have considered. Students may have additional ideas that you can incorporate into the solution. Then proceed as above, until the new process is well "installed".

Are there situations where I should omit the routines?

This is a very important question.
The answer to this is yes. Leave out the anchors and routines on right-hemispheric school days.

And now you're surely asking yourself, *"What is a right hemispheric school day?"*
These are the days when everything is different from usual, when things get a bit chaotic, for example the week before the Christmas holidays, the day when the school doctor gives vaccinations, or when the photographer takes school photos.

On these days it is good to leave out the routines and anchors. You have invested a lot of valuable time in introducing these structures, and the great danger on such days is that they might be violated. If the anchors and structures are not followed precisely, they will be "contaminated". So on right hemispheric days, do everything differently than usual. Change the seats around so that the students are facing the windows instead of the board. Concentrate on group processes and dynamics, on interactions. Do not present new material, but practice what you have already learned in playful and creative ways. In this way your anchors and routines will remain intact and you can then use them effectively again on the next "normal" school day.

9

Let's get started!

Arriving

How the day or the lesson begins determines what the rest of the day will be like.

At the beginning of the lesson our students are physically present, but often their thoughts are far away from our lesson. It pays off to use this time to help them **arrive** and get into the **right mood.** Pick them up where they are. If the class is too lively, calm them down with concentration and relaxation exercises, and if they are still half asleep, wake them up with warm-up exercises.

Once again, we can compare this to the hare and the turtle. It takes a bit longer to get started on reaching your goals for the day, but it pays to have the students with you mentally. If they are fully present, you can get a lot more done than otherwise.

Start the lesson nonverbally

Let us first take a look at the non-verbal aspects of beginning a lesson.

The Credible Posture & Voice

https://www.youtube.com/watch?v=_VbNOhd3xhE&t=303s

You walk into your class and ...

What's going on here?
No student is sitting in his seat! The pupils are laughing, talking, playing, romping, listening to music, eating their snacks and lunches, and discussing excitedly about the math test in the last period. Everyone is busy. No one even notices that you are there.

- You go to your attention anchor at the front of the room.
- You stand straight and freeze your posture.
- Your feet are parallel to one another and pointing forward.
- Your weight is evenly distributed on both feet.
- You stretch out one hand (or both hands if it is particularly loud) holding them parallel to the floor. The hands and your body are also very still.

Some students have already noticed you and are starting to pay attention. Others are still talking.

- You say, *"Good morning, ladies..."*
- Your voice is a bit louder than the noise level of the group.
- Pause before continuing to speak
- *"...and gentlemen.* You speak these words in a whisper.
- "*We will now begin.*"
- This sentence begins in a whisper and gradually increases in volume till it reaches your usual voice volume.
- The class is quiet and the lesson can begin.

The steps

Now let's take another look at this sequence and go through the technique again step by step.

1. The teacher has adopted a visual and silent BODY POSITION.
2. She also used very FEW WORDS.
3. She has shown the students the behavior she wants them to imitate.

One of the most important principles in classroom management - not only at the beginning of the school day or lesson, but in EVERY classroom situation - is the following:

The class mirrors the behavior of the teacher

If I stand silently in front of the class, the class will unconsciously imitate me and calm down - even if it takes a little longer the first few times I use this technique.

Using your voice

4. Use your VOICE in an optimal way to attract the attention of the class.

If the students see you when you enter the room, it is usually advisable not to say anything. You adopt the frozen posture and make eye contact with the students. Remain frozen and do not say anything! We lead the students to be still by being still ourselves.

In the scene described, however, the pupils did not even notice that the teacher had entered the room. Therefore she had to use her voice - or any other loud noise. Here it is important that you are very shortly louder than the students.

We can guide the volume of the class to make it louder or softer using our own voice. Here too, the class reflects us. The louder we get, the louder the class gets. Therefore it is important that we direct the noise level with our own voice to where we want it to be.

1. For students to notice you, your first words must be louder than the noise level in the room. This will surprise the class and they will become quieter,
2. The second step is to pause. By becoming silent, you show the class what you expect from them,
3. Now you can lower your volume to a whisper.
4. As you greet the class or begin speaking, let your volume glide up until your voice has reached its normal volume.

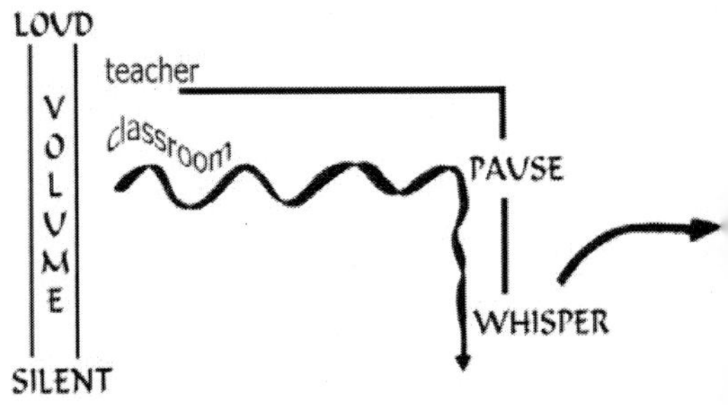

Let your first words reflect the group's modality/modalities

The preferred modality of a group –visual, auditory or kinesthetic- is very often dependent on their age.

Primary school children are more likely to be kinesthetic, middle school students auditory (or a mixture of auditory and kinesthetic), and with the onset of puberty the visual phase begins.

If you address the main modality of the group (or, even better, all the modalities) with your introductory sentences, you will gain their attention much faster.

That is, if the group is mainly visual, words like *"Please look at me"* will be effective. If the group has auditory tendencies, you may prefer to say, *"All ears to me, please."* or if you want to address all three modalities, use, *"Please everyone turn to the front, look at me, and listen very carefully.*

And now back to our opening scene - the sequence was ...

Emotionally neutral and very concise

If you stay within the sphere of influence, the students will not resist you or your wishes. They know exactly what you want from them - their attention. You are calm. You are not excited, angry or nervous. Your aura of positive, natural authority is enhanced. You are not judging their behavior and therefore there are no power struggles. It is very important that we remember to remain in the area of influence and not of power.

Very often teachers (mostly on an unconscious level) consider getting the class's attention as a kind of disciplining measure - Especially if the students are loud and boisterous. If our students communicate with each other at the beginning of the lesson – even if it is at times loud and boisterous- this is not negative behavior. Therefore if you believe getting the class to be quiet and to listen is a disciplinary measure, you are no longer in the sphere of influence. Disciplining is using power. And it often results in either active or passive resistance. Getting attention should belong to the sphere of influence and not power. And should always, if possible, be the preferred way of dealing with any kind of challenge in the classroom.

Avoid power struggles! As long as you stay in the sphere of influence you are on safe ground. But in the sphere of power, you are on the defensive and therefore in a weaker position. The students misbehave, for example, and you must react. You have no other choice. Your aura of positive, natural authority has been challenged and is endangered.

After the scene described above has played out several times, it becomes routine. It is an anchor. An anchor is a reflex. The more often it is used, the faster it works. This means that if it is used properly, gaining your class's attention will have become a challenge of the past.

Introducing a structure to mark the beginning of the lesson

The more often the beginning of the lesson is performed in a ritual manner, the faster and more smoothly the students will become centered and concentrated.

Anchors are the first proactive step.
The second step is the introduction of structures, i.e. action sequences, routines and strategies with which the class, for example, begins each lesson in a "ritualized form". This completely eliminates situations in which you used to have to admonish and rebuke the pupils.

Here are just a few of many anchor examples to give the signal that the lesson is about to begin.

visual anchors
- write the date on the board
- quietly close the classroom door
- give a signal like a conductor with your hands, while smiling to "Stand up!"
- Stick a symbol card on the board with a magnet

auditory anchors
- a triangle, a singing bowl
- a musical instrument
- a bell, a rainmaker
- a jingle or a theme song
- Ready - Steady - Go!
- Rhythmic clapping or tapping

place anchors
- At the beginning of the lesson, always stand on the same spot
- place the class-register on the teacher's desk
- Form a morning circle (also for secondary school)

There's a lot to do after the bell rings!

When I started teaching at the commercial academy in Vienna, many things in the Austrian school system were new to me. Now I appreciate most aspects of that system, but one thing I don't like is that in Austria middle and high schools the teachers move from one room to another. In the U.S., teachers generally have their own room for their classes or subjects, and students move from one teacher to another. This makes it much easier for the teachers. The teacher does not enter the students' territory but the students come into the teacher's.

That makes it more difficult here in Austria. In the breaks I have to return to the teachers' room to get whatever materials I need for the next lesson. Because we cannot be in class at the beginning of the lesson, the bell has lost its anchoring effect (although it still works VERY well as an anchor at the end of the lesson!). The students have (perhaps) heard the ringing of the bell, but when we enter the classroom at the beginning of the lesson, they are mentally still in the break. This is natural. We, as adults, would react in the same way.

While teaching my 14 to 19 year old boys at the commercial academy, I discovered (almost by accident) a brilliant structure to use for the beginning of the lesson. This procedure completely eliminated the need to get the class's attention at the beginning of the lesson! I introduced the structure by telling the students one day: *"I think you have far too much homework."* This statement immediately got the entire class's attention. *"And yesterday, in the middle of the night,* "I continued, *"I came up with a great idea! I even got up out of bed so I could write it down - otherwise I might have forgotten it!"* Less homework! They were sitting on the edge of their seats with so much enthusiasm!

"Every time we start a new chapter, your assignment is to write the new English words and their German equivalents into your vocabulary notebook. This is a very important task and must be done. But maybe we can do it at school instead of at home. And now to my idea! As you know, I can't always be here the moment the bell rings. Sometimes there are important discussions with the teachers, or often some of your parents are here to talk to me. This is basically lost time for our lessons, so I thought maybe we could make good use of it.

What do you think about this idea: As soon as the bell rings, you can take out your vocabulary notebooks and start writing? You write very quietly and silently until I come. I will still need a minute or so to take roll and put my things together before we start. When I am finished, I will give you a signal –I will knock three times on the board – to let you know that we can begin. You write as far as you get. The next time you pick up again where you left off. And you will have saved yourself one homework assignment per chapter!"

It worked like magic! It was once again a win-win situation: the students had fewer tasks to do at home. They were calm and concentrated at the beginning of the lesson. And I was able to start the lesson without stress and excitement. The most beautiful thing was the feeling of harmony that spread throughout the classroom. They were working diligently together towards a common goal. We were a team.

Some time ago I did an afternoon session on non-verbal classroom management in the same school, the commercial academy, where I had begun my career as a teacher. In the meantime, more than thirty years had passed. A former teacher colleague is now principal at this school. When she introduced me to her teaching staff, she told them that once ten minutes after the start of a lesson, she passed an open classroom door in the corridor. The students sat in the classroom as quiet as mice and were working hard. Surprised she asked, *"What teacher should be with you now?"* The students answered, without being distracted from their work: *"Mrs. Nitsche. But we can't chat now - we have to write vocabulary words."* Amazing, isn't it?

I told this story to a group of teachers in Styria, a southern part of Austria a short time later. They explained to me that they were also using this technique in their classrooms - with some refinements:

The Styrian "time-keeper" variant

The students are silently writing in their journals as the teacher enters the room. One student is "The Time-Keeper.", whose job it is to write down the number of minutes (and, if you like, seconds) that the teacher needs before starting to teach. At the end of the school year or semester, they add up the minutes and are allowed to make a wish for this time, e.g. play games in English or go for an ice cream cone together.

The condition for this is that the class must complete a task given by the teacher by the time the teacher arrives, e.g. writing in the journal, writing arithmetic exercises in the notebook, etc. The teacher enters the room, places her things on the teacher's desk, take out what she needs for the lesson and writes the lessons' goals on the board. She then stands in front of the class and gives a signal to stand up. Everyone stands up and the lesson begins.

Helmut B., vocational schools

A few variations:

At the start of the lesson, or even better beforehand, write **visual instructions** for an activity they should begin immediately after the bell rings. This could be some math problems, a riddle or a puzzle. Or the students have five minutes at the beginning of the lesson to write in their journals These journals can also be used at other times. They are the private property of the students and they do not have to share the content with anyone. Or it could be instructions for the first activity in the lesson: *"Please get out a pencil, a ruler and your atlas.* Or write the homework on the board and the students can start to do it in those minutes before class starts. Or each student has a book in their desk and may begin reading when the bell rings. They may continue reading until the teacher is ready to begin.

Some more ideas:

How our day begins

- Classes start at 7:45. I am sitting at my desk at 7:30 and welcome the kids as they come into the room.
- The homework, tasks, etc. to be handed in are written on the board. There is a designated place to leave these things.
- The schedule for this day or for this lesson is written - always in the same place and in the same color - on the board. Next to each item the materials required are also listed. As soon as a student finishes a task, she silently prepares the materials needed for the next task.
- The students put their homework on a designated place. Each child has a number. The notebooks or the assignments are numbered accordingly. The task of "notebook counter" is changed at regular intervals.
- The pupils prepare their desk: Pencil case, books, notebooks, reading material in the desk, hang up the backpack, etc. parents' booklet underneath, put reading material in the desk compartment.
- Afterwards, the children can talk, playa game or complete a worksheet. Unfinished worksheets are placed under the work surface or mat. They can be completed later.
- When the bell rings, the students go to their seats and stand behind their chairs. I am standing quietly in the front. We wish each other a good morning!
- The goals for today, which are written on the board, are discussed.

Brigitte S., elementary school

Some variations:

- When the bell rings, the students take out their reading material and read quietly for five minutes. The teacher then draws a student's name from a stack of cards. That person tells the class what he has just read.
- After the greeting, a song or rhythmic exercise is performed together.

How we start the day

In my elementary school class, the children themselves write the daily order points from our weekly schedule on the board before class.

- I stand still behind my teacher's chair and wait until the children are ready to start. It's amazing how fast it happens now.
- Then I step in front of the teacher's desk, paying close attention to my very still posture and body tension.
- Only when it is completely quiet do I start to speak. I make sure that I am concise and don't repeat myself.
- Leaning on the edge of my desk means: "Organizational matters are being discussed."

Petra F., middle school

Rituals in preschool

Rituals in the morning are a very important part of the beginning of my lessons!

- The children arrive at 7.45 a.m. I greet each child personally.
- They enter the cloak room and take off their jackets and shoes before putting on their school house shoes
- Drink water and use the WC
- After the bell rings, they prepare their desks and have a few minutes of play time before we begin
- Then we sing a song with movements or we dance to wake up.
- I have an egg-shaped rattle which I give a signal with. This means we all meet in the daily morning circle. We sit around a small round learning rug.
- We shake hands and greet each other.
- Then we inquire about how each child is feeling. Sometimes the children simply report. Or we can put out a "feelings thermometer" and the children mark where they are on the thermometer with a colored stone.
- We start the school day at 8 a.m. with a series of short gymnastic exercises.
- With older children the exercises - including yoga, chi gong, brain gym and also classical exercises such as jumping jacks are selected led by the student of the day.
- Discussion of the daily program. For example, I often hide an item in a small treasure chest or under a colorful cloth indicating the topic of the day. Of course, Bear Bobo, our class mascot, is always present and takes part in the conversations.

Gabriele S., preschool class

Brain Gym Plus!

Several classes at our middle school use Brain Gym ® as a way of beginning class or whenever the kids are in need of a movement break. Brain Gym, developed by an educationalist, Dr. Paul Dennison PhD, highlights the importance of movement for learning. It uses simple cross-over movements to integrate the whole brain, the senses and the body. It can be used to improve a wide range of learning, attention and behavior skills.

Paul Dennison, Gail E. Dennison
Brain Gym ® cross-over movements in learning

Carla Hannaford
has developed another movement approach based on the body's role in learning

We start with a few of these simple exercises as a preface to the lesson. In the first position we use crossed legs and intertwine our hands. We hold this position for a few seconds and then switch to a second position with legs shoulder-width apart, the fingertips of the hands touching each other and making a "dome". Hold this again for a few seconds. Then we loosen our hands and stand in a normal position.

I start by saying "Good morning!" and the students respond. A big smile. And then we sit down and start the lesson.

When I introduced these activities to the pupils, I told them a bit about brain science. There are two halves or hemispheres to the brain. Each is responsible for something else and both of them together are important for learning. These two halves want a connection that they can't make on their own. We create it easily and automatically through these cross-over movements. That was enough explanation for them for the beginning and they truly enjoy the exercises. Afterwards they are calm and concentrated.

Romana S., middle school

Beginning with praise

I start every lesson with specially chosen music. The pupils can hear the music while they are in the corridor and they come running into the classroom. Within seconds they are all standing quietly in their places and I can go to my "praise anchor" next to the windows and praise them properly for the first time in this lesson. It's a very positive way of beginning the lesson.

Peter F., middle school

I want to hear the clock tick.

At the beginning of the lesson I write the lesson's topic on the board. Meanwhile the students take their places and become calm.

I'll stand next to the teacher's desk and wait until everyone is quiet. The students know it is our goal that it should be quiet enough for us to hear the clock ticking. Sometimes I hold up a pin. When it's totally quiet, I drop the pin. And they are quite pleased that they can actually hear a pin drop!

Manuela F., middle school

The calm before the storm

I start every lesson with "the calm before the storm". We stand and wait until it's totally quiet. I stand to the left of the desk. The signal to sit down is when I slowly blink.

Christian B., middle school

A small mishap

At the beginning of the lesson I always play "Poisson Rouge" by Saint Privat Riviera. My song to end the hour is "Lemon Tree" by Fool's Garden. They don't listen for the bell anymore but these melodies have replaced the bell as their signals.

The following happened yesterday:
It was recess. The weather was bad and the kids had recess in the classroom. At the moment I have two student teachers accompanying me. I came into the classroom at the end of recess to help them prepare so that the student teachers could immediately start teaching at the beginning of the lesson.

I turned on the music and discussed a few more tips with the student teachers. Suddenly I noticed that the pupils were not reacting to the music. They continued to play, gossip and eat without a care in the world. I was so surprised. Why weren't they reacting to the signal song?

I was about to say something when I noticed that I had accidentally turned on "Lemon Tree", the signal for the end of the lesson. I quickly switched to the opening song. Immediately the kids became quiet, got their things out for the lesson, sat down in their seats and were waiting for me to start the lesson. And the bell hadn't even rung yet! Magic!

Doris A., middle school

I'm floating on a cloud!

Fully motivated after the wonderful stress-free and informative days in our seminar, I started Monday morning with a totally positive smile. With palms down, chin lowered and calm eyes I entered the very difficult class, 4a. I didn't move a muscle until everyone was quiet. It worked and was utterly amazing.

Maria A., high school

10

What? The lesson is over?

It happens to me again and again that I am in the middle of a sentence and the bell rings. The students have the tendency to jump up and race out the door. One of the first rules that I introduce in my classes is

The teacher - and NOT the bell –
determines the end of the lesson!!!

Nevertheless, I don't want to end the lesson just like that – in the middle of a thought or sentence. It is much nicer and also more effective if both the beginning and the end of the lesson are ritualized. So I came up with a solution.

I set the alarm on my smartphone to ring three to five minutes before the end of the period. Such an alarm is also an anchor! Or I can instruct a student to call my attention to the fact that the lesson will be ending exactly two minutes before the bell rings.

Review the goals

You can use these final minutes to review the goals that were written on the board at the beginning of the lesson. This gives structure to the lesson and contributes greatly to motivation and work efficiency. It allows a review of the lesson and a self-evaluation of the work. Together with the students, check off the goals you have achieved. You can let the students assess their own cooperation (thumbs up or down, smiley cards, etc.). At the same time you can give advanced notice or a preview of the next lesson. Make them curious so that they are already looking forward to the next lesson! This process at the end of the lesson promotes goal-oriented learning

Some ideas:

The timekeeper switches on the music

I end the lessons with a song that I have on a CD. This is their signal that they are now allowed to collect their belongings and prepare everything for the next lesson. Since I have the tendency to overlook the time, I am very thankful for my timekeeper to remind me that the lesson will end soon. The student I consciously chose for this task has ADHD syndrome and this task has strengthened his sense of self-worth.

Sometimes it happens that the students get carried away and get a bit wild when clearing up. Then I press the pause button on the CD player and freeze my posture. The pupils know that if this happens, they must freeze their movements too. Only when the music is heard again may they continue.

Gerhild V., secondary school

Selecting the correct music

Initially, the music anchor did not work very well at the end of the lesson. I had allowed the students to choose the music and it was much too aggressive. So we switched to a calm and soft music. Lo and behold, the result was amazing! Chairs were placed quietly on the desks, the school bags were closed quietly and there was not a hint of aggression.

Franziska S., secondary school,

The Pink Panther

At the end of the day we play the theme song from the Pink Panther. That is the signal that it is time to clean up. The students sneak around the classroom putting things away. Before we did it the first time, I explained exactly what they had to do: Put everything that you will need tonight into your backpack or on the weekend, put everything else where it belongs, put your chair up on the table, etc.

Monika S., elementary school & special ed

Looking at the clock

At the end of the lesson I pointedly look at the class clock or my wristwatch - this is the sign for the pupils to gather up their school things. Some students are still working very hard and not looking at me. I go to them and point to my wristwatch.

Daniela G. middle school

Final music anchor

I have chosen lively Greek music as our final melody. The children clean up and put the chairs on the table. However, this music is so lively and makes you want to move! The children dance while cleaning up!! That's fine for me because everyone is happy and leaves school with a smile on their faces!

Petra F., elementary school

Farewell circle

This ritual was introduced at the request of the children!
We read a story together. Sometimes it is a complete story and sometimes we continue with the story over several lessons. It is a beautiful, calming, shared experience. We end with the words in chorus: "We wish you a wonderful afternoon!

Gabi S., preschool class

Reflection

The end of the lesson is a good time to reflect on the lesson we are finishing up and anticipate the coming one. This can be done quite simply by...

Line up, eyes closed and reflect

...the students, either sitting in their seats or standing by the door, close their eyes for a minute and reflect on what they are taking with them from today's lesson. At the end of the minute, the teacher gives a signal: rings a soft bell, strikes a triangle or gong or plays soft music. The students leave the room without a word and are only allowed to speak at an agreed place (the cloakroom, in front of the school building, etc.)

Andreas M., secondary school

What am I taking with me?

A nice ritual at the end of the lesson I call "What am I taking with me today?" We form a standing circle. Each of us thinks of two words or short phrases we are taking with us from the lesson. I start with the first word, and while speaking I put my right hand on the left shoulder of the person standing to my right. This person does the same with the person standing next to him on the right, etc., until the person standing next to me on the left puts his right hand on my left shoulder. Then the same process begins with the second word to the left. Finally, we stand in a tight circle with our hands on the shoulders of our neighbors. I will now end the ritual by saying: "Have a nice day". The students answer: "We wish you a nice day too!" It is a nice summary as well as a lovely conclusion.

Edith S., vocational schools

End of the week

The end of the school week can also be ritualized:

- Write in journals,
- Celebrate success,
- Fill in questionnaires, concerning the class's cooperation during the past week

The Friday Ritual

Every Friday I write a list of today's tasks plus what we still need to do or finish up for the week.

After our morning rituals, we agree on what bonus activity we will do once we have ticked off all the points on the board. For example, the students might want to exchange stickers, go to the garden, sing certain songs, etc. The democratic majority rules!

CAUTION: My kids wanted to leave out recess so that they could reach their goal faster. I was not enthusiastic about this idea, so every Friday there is one fixed point on the board: "Spend recess together".

The pupils have learned that they need to help the slower ones to reach the common goal. There is also hardly any chatting on Fridays. They know that they will have enough time to chat after their work is finished!

Ines G., elementary school

Circle Talk

Circle Talk, where the students sit in a closed circle of chairs, gives us time for reflection and provides a calm, positive anchor at the end of the day. What did you like about today? What did we do well today? What can we do better tomorrow? What are you looking forward to tomorrow?

We do Circle Talk on Fridays too. At first, everyone says what they're proud of at the end of the week. Then we sit quietly for a few moments, and everyone thinks about a wish for the coming week. We keep these wishes to ourselves. The students whisper their wishes into their hands, and at a signal from me we open our hands, blow the wishes up in the air and thus release them.

Susan J., bilingual middle school

End of the semester

Do your students see the second semester of the school year as a mere continuation of the first semester? By means of rituals we can give them a different perspective. Discuss with them that the second semester is a new beginning. It gives the students the chance to take a new path. Take stock with your students to help them develop new goals and a new dynamic for more effective learning in the second semester.

Create questionnaires, have the students write in their school journals, or moderate a discussion about

- What have I achieved in the first half of the school year?
- What did I want to achieve but didn't?
- What can I do to actually reach these goals?
- How will I feel after I have reached them?

By means of this ritual the students are summing up and completing the past semester and enabling a fresh start in the coming one.

End of the school year

Various rituals are already in place at the end of the school year: the closing conference, more relaxing activities with the class, which also combine learning with fun, the distribution of certificates - and then off to the holidays! In addition, however, we can use this time even better to take stock and reflect.

Guided fantasy: Our school year

You can either prepare a list of events during the past school year or you can brainstorm a list with the students. Have them sit in a comfortable position. Close their eyes and lead them into a relaxed state. Play relaxing, meditative music in the background. Speak slowly and leave a lot of pauses giving the students time to internalize your instructions or to form pictures of the keywords in their minds:

We will now take a short trip through the time we spent together this year. Sit down comfortably, and if you like, you can close your eyes...

I will now read you various keywords. These words may bring back memories and images of our time together during this school year. Let the images come and look at our school year like a film that is running before your eyes...

Choose appropriate words about positive experiences during the past school year and read them slowly. Allow several seconds between the keywords so that the students can get an idea of what they experienced and relive it.

And then lead the students back again.

Now our fantasy journey is slowly coming to an end. You have experienced a lot in the past school year. These wonderful memories will stay with you. And as you slowly return to the here and now, you store these memories safely in your mind.

Slowly begin to return to the here and now.

You take a deep breath. And release it. You feel the chair ...

I will now count from one to five.
With every number I say, you feel more and more awake and alert.
1...2...3...4...5

Start to come back into this room by moving your toes. Your fingers. Legs. Hands. Arms. And stretch...

11

Giving instructions

Who hasn't experienced this?

You would like the class to write an essay on the topic "My vacation". You give them the instructions, but are interrupted several times by questions:

> *"How long should the essay be?"*
> *"How much time do we have?"*
> *"May I please go to the bathroom?"*

Finally, you've explained everything. Now ask the students if they have understood everything and if there are any further questions.

Lucy asks:	*"Lined or plain paper?"*
Thomas asks:	*"Should we write with a fountain pen or a pencil?"*
Murat asks:	*"How long should the essay be?"*
Ali asks:	*"Where do we write it?"*
Martina asks:	*"Lined or plain paper?"*

Frustrating, isn't it?
Our students have a tendency to think with their mouths. They often do not listen and find it much easier to ask questions than to think. It's up to us to teach them to *think first, ask later.* Various anchors and structures help us to do this.

Two anchors

The first step in giving instructions is to establish two place anchors:

The first anchor is for giving instructions.
Even if you (hopefully!) no longer teach exclusively in front of the class, it is a good idea to define a place at the front of the room where you present particularly important information. If you use this anchor systematically, the students will immediately react. Some will even pick up a pen to note what you say just because you are standing on that spot.

The second anchor is the place where you answer questions. This is the place where suggestions, questions, proposals, discussion and exchange are welcome.

The credible or the inviting voice?

These two voices and postures can be seen in the You Tube Video:
https://www.youtube.com/watch?v= VbNOhd3xhE&t=346s
Both of these variations are good – depending on the situation.

The first voice is called the "**credible voice**".
I use this voice when I discipline in the classroom, have a serious conversation, want to gain attention or, as in our example above, give instructions. This voice carries the message: *"I am talking now. Please listen carefully."*

The second voice is called the "**inviting voice**".
This is my voice when I want to discuss something with the students, when a discussion, questions, suggestions and proposals are welcome. This voice encourages conversation and exchange.

My posture and movement determine which voice is generated.

With the "**credible voice**" I have a straight and very still posture. My feet are parallel to each other. My chin is tilted slightly down. My head is also still because of my still posture. This silent head posture has a direct influence on my voice, which is monotonous and often goes down at the end of a statement.

People who have a credible voice can assert themselves easily. When they talk, others listen and then take action. The disadvantage of this voice is the quality and also the quantity of communication. The conversation falters and there is little echo or feedback.

With the "**inviting voice**", on the other hand, there is a slight up and down body movement, a bobbing, which is rhythmic and symmetrical. The arms and hands move rhythmically and are held close to the trunk. Often you can see the palms of the hands. The head and also the voice move slightly up and down in rhythm with the body. The voice generally goes up at the end of a statement – making it sound like a question.

People who have an inviting voice are sociable masters of communication. Their conversational partners become communicative and no matter what topic is being discussed it usually results in a congenial conversation. The disadvantage of this voice, however, is that people who use it frequently sometimes find it difficult to assert themselves. Statements made in an inviting voice are discussed and questioned. And in the end, often nothing happens because of all the discussion!

IMPORTANT: Different situations require different voices.

In our example above, you want the students to be calm and listen carefully while you are telling them what they need to do. Therefore, stand quietly on the "instructions-anchor". Wait wordlessly until you have the attention of all the students, and then speak in the credible voice. As you speak, write down all of the essential information on the board.

Visual instructions are influence - Auditory instructions are power

If the instructions are very complicated, or I get lost in too many, often unnecessary words, the only person who is in the picture when I stop speaking is me. And if I am the only one who knows what needs to be done, I am (unintentionally) in the sphere of power. On the other hand, if the instructions are written on the board, everyone is informed as to what is expected of them. That is influence in contrast to power.

It is therefore important that ALL essential information, both when giving instructions and for homework, projects and school exercises, is presented in WRITING on the board. Explain the process verbally only once, while simultaneously writing down the essential information on the board.

It is even better if at least part of the information, e.g. the required material, is already listed on the board beforehand. This way, students who have finished another activity early have the possibility to prepare everything in advance. The transition from one activity to the next becomes more fluid.

While explaining, pay close attention to clarity and accuracy. Avoid generalizations and use as few words as possible. Explain what is to be done step by step and write the most important information on the board.

To make the written instructions even easier to understand:

- Always write instructions on the board in the same place.
- Use simple words for instructions and also different colors and symbols - this appeals to both sides of the brain!
- If the students need a book or notebook, hold it up or lean it against the board for the students to see. Write the page numbers on the board.
- It has also proven to be a good idea to make and laminate color copies of the book cover. These can be attached to the board with magnets.
- For the 1st grade, where the children cannot yet read, you can use magnetic stuffed animals or symbol cards.

Once you have completed the instructions, go to your second anchor, the "answering questions" anchor. Change your posture so that you and your voice are inviting.

If the students ask you an important question that you forgot to mention, write this additional information on the board.

If a question that you have already answered and written down the instructions to is asked again, **DO NOT REPLY TO THE QUESTION a second time**, but point **wordlessly** - with a (friendly!) smile – to the answer on the board. Students often think with their mouths. They do not think about it - it is much easier to ask again. With such techniques we are teaching our students to think for themselves and reason.

When all the questions have been answered, go back to the "giving instructions anchor" and resume the credible posture and voice. From this place you give the instructions for the transition to begin work. This process, called MITS (Most Important Ten/ Twenty Seconds) is covered in the next chapter.

Some ideas

Giving instructions
...to get the full attention of the students while working

- Strike the triangle once,
- Students stop working and sit down, look at me and listen,
- When I'm done with the explanation, they can go back to work and chat with each other.

I was fascinated - I teach in eleven different classes, and this worked in every single class. We refreshed this process once in the first lesson of the new semester and once again it worked perfectly for the rest of the school year.

Angelika K., elementary school

Pausing while speaking is the most powerful non-verbal signal
When I explain the rules of a game in gym class, the pupils sit around the circle markings drawn in the center on the gymnasium floor. I sit in the circle too. If anyone makes a whispering remark - even if it is only in a whisper, I immediately stop talking in the middle of a sentence or word and wait, without looking at the child in question, until everyone is quiet again. I do this repeatedly, no matter how often I am interrupted and no matter how much time we lose. It takes three weeks at the most, until really everybody gets used to it. That is not lost time if you consider that for the next four years I will have peace and order while explaining something in gym class.

Elfie K., middle school

You can do it without talking!
Last Tuesday, I took a chance. When explaining a task I deliberately forgot to mention one important step. I didn't want to say anything while the students were working, so I, without saying a word, wrote the "forgotten" step on the board. I wondered if anyone would notice.

Every single student completed this step - without me saying it verbally!

Peter F., secondary school

Writing instructions on the board
In the past I often used so much energy explaining and using much too many words saying what the students should do. It was exhausting for me and answering all their questions cost me a lot of strength.

Now I write the topic and the necessary steps before the bell rings on the board and try to be very precise. Occasionally I also hand out scripts or I show pictures as explanations. They still ask a lot of questions but seeing as the answers have been written on the board, I simply knock on the board next to the answer with a friendly smile.

Christian G., middle school

Non-believers

Pearl held a workshop at my school last spring. That was the first time I had heard about "Nonverbal Classroom Management". I was fascinated and took some more of her seminars that summer.

During the summer I also met with some of my school colleagues at a restaurant. They asked me about the seminar and how I liked it. Of course there were also some colleagues there who were not convinced by these teaching methods. When I asked them why, they said: "I have tried that "Getting their attention anchor". I could have stood there all day and nothing would have happened." I realized that they had no interest in this topic, so I let it drop.

A bit later I needed to leave and wanted to say goodbye. I noticed that my colleagues were engrossed in a conversation, and I didn't want to shout "Goodbye! So I thought to myself: "Try what you learned in the seminar. Let's see if it works for adults too."

So I placed myself in front of my colleagues, took a rigid posture, my palms were facing the floor and I looked at everyone once without saying a word. Within seconds everyone was calm and looking at me.

Then I smiled and said, "Have a nice vacation!" I turned around and left.

So, it does work!

Monika S., Special Education

The Magic Word

We agreed on a word which is called our "magic word", for example the word "zucchini". When I explain something to the students, I say, "When I say the magic word... what was the word?" The students yell, "Zucchini!" "That's right." When I say that word, it is the signal to begin working. It works like a charm!

Everyone listens with eager anticipation to my words, because they are waiting for the magic word. If they start before I have finished with the explanations I ask if I had said the magic word. And when I say it, they begin working. We change the magic word once a week and the students can choose the word if they want to.

12

Elegant Transitions

moving from the teaching phase to seatwork

Wrong

Correct

Just imagine ...

You are just finishing the informative part of the lesson. The students are attentive and quiet. And now you say: "Please take out your English books, a ruler and a pencil." Suddenly it becomes restless and loud. Schoolbags are emptied, the contents of desks are searched through and everyone needs to ask their neighbor a question: "What page?", "What book?"

And once again, you must get the class's attention.
Transitions from teaching to seatwork or transitions in general very often lead to restlessness in the classroom.

... or imagine ...

The lesson is going well and the students are listening attentively. One child raises his hand enthusiastically. You call on him and he says, *"Can I please go to the bathroom?"*

The flow of your lesson has been disrupted and you need to restore that concentrated state the class was in before the interruption.

This chapter deals with the elegant and seamless design of transitions, the avoidance of disturbances, as well as the teacher's behavior during seatwork - so that the class can work in a concentrated way!

Rule number 1 for all these activities is:

**Conduct yourself, both verbally and non-verbally,
the way you want the students to behave.**

When my students at the commercial academy really got down to work, they were so concentrated that you could have heard a pin drop. I enjoyed this silence so much that I instinctively barely moved. I knew that if I started moving around the classroom, the silence would be broken. As with all processes in the classroom, the class is a reflection of the teacher. So if I want that silence to be maintained, I have to act accordingly!

Transitions - MITS

Michael Grinder, educator, trainer and one of my greatest mentors, has developed a concept for the transition from teaching to seatwork. He calls it "MITS" or "Most Important Ten/ Twenty Seconds". What he means by this is that the transition from teaching to seatwork determines how productive the seat work phase will be - this transition lasts twenty seconds for older students and only ten seconds for younger students due to their shorter concentration span.

You can start now

In the last chapter we discussed giving instructions. You established two anchors - one for giving instructions, where you should not be interrupted, and one where you stand when you encourage the students to ask questions. You wrote all the essential information on the board and answered any questions the students had. Now you want the students to start working. They should not ask any more questions. Stand on the instruction anchor, and say one or two short sentences with the credible voice as a signal that the students should begin: *"No more questions, please. You may begin now."*

After you have uttered this sentence, freeze in the credible posture and remain standing very still for ten to twenty seconds. In this way, you non-verbally demonstrate to the students the behavior you expect them to exhibit.

During these ten to twenty seconds, do NOT answer any questions. While you are still frozen, give a hand signal to students who put their hands up to show them you will soon be addressing them (in the meantime, the student will probably come up with the answer on his own anyway).

Seatwork

When the ten to twenty seconds are up, loosen your posture and walk - slowly - to the students who have their hands up. If they ask a question, the answer to which you have already written on the board, point wordlessly to the answer. To get them to look at the board, you will have to shortly break eye contact with the student, who asked, and look at the board.

If you talk to students while they are doing seatwork, always speak in a quiet, private voice. And move slowly. You are like a motorboat moving across a lake. When the motorboat moves quickly through the water, it makes many waves that stir up the water. The students are moved back and forth by the waves like little corks. But if the boat moves slowly, the water remains calm. And so do the students. The same is true in the classroom. If you are too fast or too loud, you will pull the pupils, who are working well, out of their concentrated state!

The teacher should be almost invisible during seatwork. Personally, I think that we offer too much help to the students while they are working quietly from their seats. The students start fulfilling the task we have given them and we immediately shoot out to them like marathon runners offering help. How can they become independent and solve problems on their own if we always step in?

I introduced them to the concept that if they need help during this phase of the lesson, they should let me know. During the first few minutes while I'm standing in front of the class, they have to work alone. This teaches them to reflect. Very often they can answer their questions themselves if they take a minute or so to think about it. After five minutes I sit down at the teacher's desk. If a student has a question, he or she may come to me. Only one student at a time is allowed at the teacher's desk.

Mini-MITS

About halfway through the seatwork period I get up and walk slowly through the class and glance at what the students have done so far. As far as possible I do this non-verbally. If I see mistakes, I simply point to the mistake wordlessly. If a student has misunderstood something, I point to the corresponding item on the board. To keep the rest of the class in "working mode", after helping one or several students, I do what Michael Grinder calls a "mini-MIT": I take one step away from the student, freeze my posture for a few seconds and let my eyes wander through the class.

Some ideas

Correction during seatwork

For viewing, reading or correcting dialogues or texts I have a table in the back of the classroom. When it is not in use, it is placed on the back wall of the room. If I plan to look through, read or correct texts in the course of a lesson, I move the table about two meters away from the wall and add two chairs, one for the student and one for me. The pupil whose text I'm going through sits there. The others are busy reading or writing at their desks.

This gave me the opportunity to talk to students in person, or to really come to grips with their individual language problems. This reduces the stress on the student in that his "mistakes" are not being discussed in front of the others. The relationship between teacher and student is open, honest and improves.

Elfie K., middle school

Singing bowl during seatwork

Striking the Asian singing bowl serves as an acoustic signal for the beginning of seatwork and it is a signal to work quietly. If something important needs to be said while the students are working, we also use the singing bowl. At the end of the seatwork, I strike the singing bowl twice. This means we are finished with seatwork, please get your things together.

Christoph M., elementary school

The clothespins

My students each have two clothespins with their names on them. At the front of the board are two signs: "Help" and "Done". If a student needs help or is finished, he hangs his clothespin on the corresponding sign. This way I can help where it is necessary, and I also have an overview of the progress of the exercise.

Susanne M., middle and high school

I'm done!

"What should I do next? I'm finished!" As discussed in the 9th commandment "Involve them!" there is at least one student in each class who finishes first, long before anyone else. A number of ideas were described in the 9th Commandment. In addition, you can make a list of activities that they can do on their own. It's good to do this as a brainstorming activity together with the students. Do this at the beginning of the school year. Laminate this list and hang it up in the classroom. If a student "forgets" and asks you, point to the list without saying a word.

Some ideas

- Always have a library book in your desk
- Help with some classroom duties (e.g. keeping the class library in order, watering the plants)
- Write a story. (List some title suggestions)
- Draw illustrations for a book
- Think up some math problems
- Help someone who is not finished yet and wants help
- Write a song about what we are learning
- Provide them with a folder or box with additional worksheets.
- Doing some prescribed work on the computer
- Learning games on the computer. See for example Compass Learning Odyssey: http://www.compasslearning.com/ . There are a lot of apps with learning games for every age group. This is individualized teaching at its best!
- Relaxing in the cozy corner
- Correct simple arithmetic worksheets
- Classroom helper activities: delete, sort, cut things out, laminate, etc.
- Long-term projects such as class newspaper, slide shows, production of books, etc. This works especially well with highly gifted students, who usually finish earlier and need challenges in the classroom.

There's always something to do!

That depends, of course, on the subject I am teaching. Most of the time, I ask the student to do some extra work for the task the class is currently doing. For example, the student can make a list of adjectives from the story they are reading or come up with additional arithmetic problems. But I always have some other activity ready. For example, the student can make a felt flower or a macramé bracelet. This is quickly done and gives the student something to do until the others are finished. A third possibility is that I let them help to make a bulletin board or cut something out.

Sara E., elementary school

And other things you can do...
I often have short educational games. Books or magazines are available for reading. Riddles are usually also included. Often there are also things from the previous lessons, which can be finished or corrected.

J. Bock, elementary school

Integrate the hall into your classroom

Every child has a book or one from the class or school library to read. The child who finishes early can take the book somewhere in the reading corner of the room or to a special spot for reading in the hall. This is a welcome break from the group, and in the hallway you can also read aloud together without disturbing others. Other ideas: Two children play a board game without words, chess, jigsaw puzzles or flashcards, look through notebooks, make improvements...

Stefan R., middle school

A lot of ideas!

- Games, plasticine, puzzle books, sudokus are laid out and can also be solved in silent partner work.
- Students are allowed to work on their portfolios, continue working on design projects.
- Design a cover for a special book.

Teachers at the elementary and secondary School

Surprise eggs

Collect the plastic surprise egg containers (or have the students collect them). Write additional tasks on pieces of paper for students who finish faster and put one piece of paper in each of the surprise egg containers. Place all the eggs in a clear bottle or container. A student who finishes earlier may take a task from the bottle. This is fun and is an incentive for the students to work faster!

Ursula S., secondary school

13

Getting their attention – and keeping it!

You are teaching and suddenly the students become restless. What can you do to get their attention again?

Since this topic is dealt with in detail in my other books, I will only touch on it here.

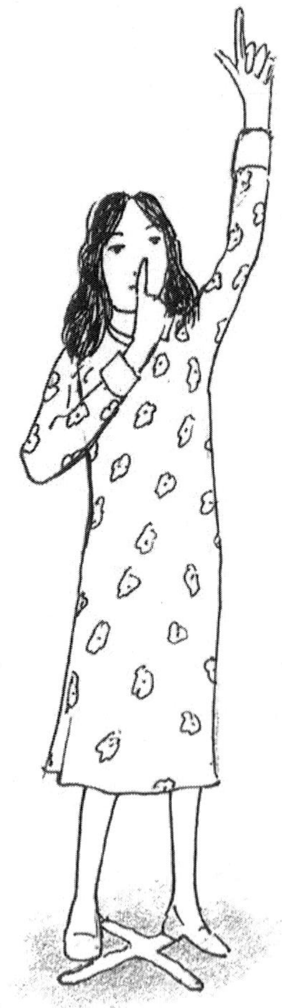

When I'm standing on this "X"...

When I was still teaching in middle school, I set an anchor by marking – without speaking - an "X" on the floor with masking tape.

The students were very curious!
"What does that cross on the floor mean, Mrs Nitsche?" they asked.

I replied dramatically, *"This is my 'Silence Spot'.*
Whenever I'm standing here, I want you to be quiet as a mouse! ALWAYS!!"

It worked like magic!

I often show this technique to the teachers in my training courses. Recently I received the following e-mail:

Was Armin in your class?

Dear Pearl,

Two days after our course, I was standing in front of the class and wanted to make an important announcement using what I had learned from you. I had forgotten to bring the masking tape to make an X on the floor but decided the anchor would work even without the tape. I stood up, had a very still posture and pointed to a spot in front of me on the floor. After a few seconds of total silence in the room, I explained to the pupils: "Please, listen closely. This is a very special spot. Whenever I stand here, I want you to be as quiet as mice because I have something very important to tell you."

A few minutes later, Armin, one of my liveliest students, jumped up and burst out with a good tip for me, "Miss W., I have an idea! You could stick an X on the floor with masking tape. Then when you stand there, we know we need to listen carefully!"

For a moment I was speechless! So I'm writing now to ask you if Armin has ever been to your seminar? I immediately took a tape and put this cross on the floor. It works perfectly! And Armin is very proud!!

Marlene W., Elementary school

1 - 2 - 3 - zap!!

When the class got too lively, my colleague, Franz, always counted out loud *"1 - 2 - 3 - Zap!"* When the students heard these words, they would freeze into statues. The colleague would wait two or three seconds, and then continue the lesson as if nothing had happened. The children "defrosted" and listened attentively.

Everyone who can hear me, clap their hands!

I was at a congress and took part in a workshop with about 300 other teachers. We were doing group work and were, as could be expected, very loud. When the speaker wanted to end the group work and continue his lecture, he stood in front and said at a normal volume: *"Everyone who can hear me now, please clap your hands.* He paused while several participants who had heard him clapped their hands along with him. And then, *"All those who can hear me now, please clap your hands twice."* And everyone in the room clapped twice and was totally quiet.

These techniques can also be used in crisis situations

Some years ago I gave a lecture at a teachers' conference in Germany. There a teacher who had been in my class a number of years earlier, raised her hand and told the group the following experience:

She teaches at a vocational school where a former student came to the school during a break, shot the headmaster of the school and then shot himself. Since this happened during recess, the other students were aware of what had happened. Many fled in panic through a window and over a flat roof into another school building. A group of about 250 students were assembled in the auditorium of this building. The police had arrived, psychiatric help was there and the situation was under control. The only thing left to do was to fetch the students who were in the auditorium. The police asked the teacher, who was telling us this story, to go into the auditorium and send the students to the appropriate classrooms.

She told me that she went into the auditorium with her heart pounding. How was she to get the attention of these students, who were quite naturally overexcited and completely beside themselves? She went into the auditorium, climbed up a few steps to the stage at the front of the room. Suddenly she remembered my words and the story I had told in our workshop a few years earlier.

She stood in front, her posture frozen, and said slowly and clearly: *"All those who hear me now clap their hands once." Pause. "All those who can hear me now, please clap your hands twice."* Everyone was silent and looked at her expectantly. Then she continued with her convincing posture and voice and said: *"The police are already here. Everything is under control. The students from the 1C please go to room 47, 1D go to room 47, etc."*

The students turned and silently followed her instructions. And we, who were listening to her story, had goose bumps.

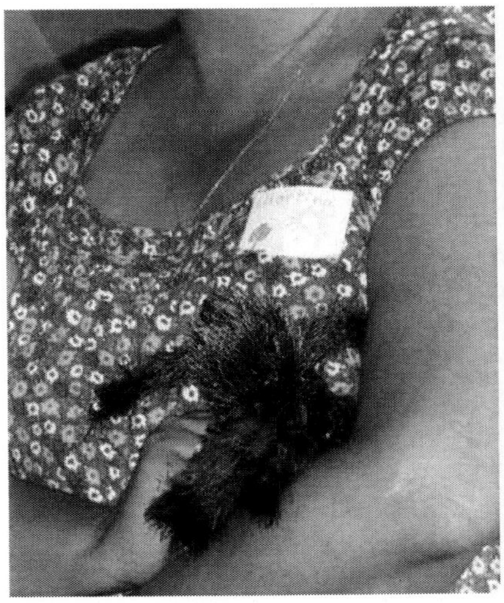

Fridolin the spider

This is a contribution by Martina, religion teacher for children with behavioral problems in grades 1 to 9:

"Hello, I'm Fridolin!

I am a little tarantula hand puppet and I accompany my teacher, Martina, to her classes.

Unfortunately, many people are afraid of me. They think I'm ugly and shout funny words like "Ewww!!!" when they see me. You can imagine how sad that makes me feel. But thank goodness, many kids at our school like me a lot.

Actually, I'm afraid of noise myself. When it gets loud, I hide in my cave under Martina's arm. I only come out again when everyone in the class is completely quiet. Martina always says that I am her best anchor, whatever an anchor is?

In the meantime I know that there are many little people who feel the same way I do. They feel small, ugly, often unwanted. Therefore they are happy that there are other living beings who feel the same way. At some point, when I have already spent some time in the classroom and dare to go outside, provided of course that it is quiet, then some children even want me to sit on their shoulder or stroke me a little! Imagine that! Me. I'm so happy that sometimes I stroke the back of their hands with my soft legs. In class it is always so nice and quiet...

I think the kids like me..."

Unusual, beautiful hand puppets available at: http://www.folkmanis-handpup- pen.eu

S.L.A.N.T.

When my own children were teenagers, they attended a wonderful summer program, Super Camp (www.supercamp.com). Here they learned learning and communication techniques for teenagers. They were thrilled - and they still benefit today as adults from what they learned there. One technique they used there to increase students' concentration and attention is called **S.L.A.N. T**.

The trainers introduced this technique by asking the students if their teachers at school ever complained that they were not interested. All of them answered with a loud *"yes"*, but it was not clear to them why their teachers would think such a thing. Any teacher though, who teaches teenagers knows how students of that age sometime behave in the classroom. They look bored, they loll about in their seats. Raising a hand takes much too much energy. Suddenly the students, whom we sometimes had to tame like little lions in former years, become totally lethargic in their teenage years.

The trainers told the kids, *"If you'd like, we can teach you a technique - S.L.A.N.T. You can use S.L.A.N.T. to trick your teachers!"* Trick teachers! Of course everyone was interested. The coaches explained:

*The **"S"*** *stands for "**Sit up straight**."*
*The **"L"*** *stands for **"Lean forward."***
*The **"A."*** *stands for **"Ask questions".***
*The **"N"*** *stands for **"Nod your head"** and*
*the **"T"*** *stands for **"Talk to the teacher"***

If you do all this, your teachers will firmly believe you're interested!"

And so it was. As already mentioned, your posture determines your inner state and your mood. The key to why this works so well is that by adopting an interested posture the students actually became more interested and motivated.

I told this story in one of my teacher training courses. A few months later, a teacher told me

> *"You know, Pearl, my son was endangered of failing in math. Whenever I went to talk to the teacher, he would tell me, "Your son is simply not interested in math. He isn't motivated." After our training course, I went home and taught my son S.L.A.N.T. The last words I said to him before he went to school every day were "Remember S.L.A.N.T.!"*
>
> *In his report card he got a 'B Plus'! And the next time I went to the math teacher, he said: "It's incredible how he has changed. Suddenly he's interested in learning math!"*

The Wah-Wah Whistle

I have a so-called 'Wah-Wah-Pipe'. When I knock on it, it resonates for a while with a pleasant tone - just long enough for the students to stop what they are doing and go to their seats to sit down. I keep this whistle in a box next to the sink. Whenever I walk in that direction the sink, the children run to their seats, even if I only want to wash my hands!

Martina S., elementary school

Raise your arm

In gym class, whenever the children were running around excitedly and were very loud, my colleague used to blow a shrill whistle so that everyone's ears (including mine) hurt. That was his way of signaling that the students should come and line up.

He was absent from school for a time, and I introduced a new, much more gentle, anchor. I simply stood next to the door and raised one arm. The children quickly noticed the signal and came running. This even works outside on the playground, where they are playing, scattered throughout the very large garden! Then I raise my arm. If I want them to sit down, I make a semicircle with my hands in front of me without saying a word. Within seconds everyone sits down. This is much quicker, and above all there is no noise or stress.

One day I was talking to a colleague in the garden recess and I must have raised my arm while talking, without realizing it. Suddenly the whole class was sitting in a semicircle in front of us - without words and full of expectation!

Daniela G., secondary school

Give me a signal!

I teach boys gym and sports. Boys are generally loud and very energetic and it was taking us forever to get them to change their clothes quickly before gym class.

One day I had this idea. I told them, "I'll pick you up for gym by knocking three times and standing outside the door of the locker room. When I hear no sound from all of you, I'll pick you up. It worked right away.

I have now used the same technique in the classroom when the students were too loud and noisy after the break. I just put my head through the door to peek into the classroom. I look very surprised and then close the door again. I wait outside the classroom until it has become absolutely silent. It works wonderfully!

Elfie K., middle school

Raising my hand

After we have sung a song in music class, the students start talking cheerfully as if it were a break. In this case, I raise my hand. There are always students who notice this and then raise their hand as well. It doesn't take long until everyone has raised their hand and stopped talking. With a smile and a "Thank you!" for the quick reaction I continue with the lesson.

I also use this hand raising in other lessons. It has also happened that the students did it on their own initiative, when they felt it was too loud.

Gerhild V., secondary school

Multiple anchors

Some ideas on how to get the class's attention:

- Stand on your "silence anchor"
- If the class becomes restless, simply stop talking, or drastically lower the volume of your voice to a whisper!
- When working with the LCD projector: simply switch off it off and wait.
- A touch on my singing bowl is a sign for instantaneous and absolute silence. Especially for group work, time to clean up, in between ...
- In some classes we have keywords for basic rules (e. g: "one person speaks at a time", "wait your turn", "let him finish"...). These are presented on posters in the classroom. Simply point to the respective poster.

Regina H., religion teacher

"L" is for "lists"

When teaching interactively, there is often a certain amount of working noise during the lesson. When I want everyone to return to their seats, I write on the board a capital "L" (representing the word "listen"). As soon as the students see this sign, they calmly return to their seats and wait for further instructions. This is a tremendous help for saving my voice, and interestingly enough, this sign is noticed very quickly.

Andrea W., middle school

The quiet ball

I have a nice spiky little plastic "calmness ball"! The kids love it because it's so pleasant to hold. The kid who is holding the ball is permitted to talk. If someone speaks out of turn, I simply wave the ball at her. This ball has another plus: the pleasant feeling of holding it makes the children want to talk more. Since using it, they express themselves much more precisely. And if you have kids who want to talk too much, just use a timer that indicates when a student's talking time is over.

Ulli H., elementary school

The doorbell

The bell, either a hand bell or an electric doorbell, is on the teacher's desk. During free work, students use it when they feel disturbed by loud work noise. They press the bell and directly call on the troublemakers, e. g: "Alexander, can you please be quiet, I can't concentrate!" This is always accepted, and they can work in peace and quiet!

Katrin M., secondary school

14

The homework is...

Kurty, the homework rooster

Turn assigning and collecting homework into a routine. For example, always write the homework in the same place on the board. You can also mark it with a symbol – for example, a simple drawing of a house, a book or simply the letters HW for homework. Some teachers write the task on a large calendar. In this way the students know on which day the homework was assigned and will be turned in. It has also proven very useful to set a fixed rhythm with fixed days for homework.

In the bilingual middle school we have two boards in each classroom. One is the usual board in front of the room. The other is a smaller board that is fixed to the wall at the front of the room to the right of the large board. All homework assignments, important messages and notices, etc. are written on this board. The students are not allowed to write on this board or delete anything on it. Only teachers are allowed to write or delete anything here. So if someone was absent, they simply check on the board and know what work needs to be made up.

Have a box where you keep leftover worksheets and handouts. If a student was absent, she can take the worksheets she needs out of the box. This box and the homework board save the teacher a lot of talking time. She does not need to carry the worksheets around with her. And the student becomes more self-sufficient.

Other suggestions made by teachers in our courses are

- A homework book located on the teacher's desk in which all of the teachers enter what homework assignments they gave.
- All the students as well as the teacher have a small homework notebook in which they have written down every homework assignment. When it is time for the students to enter a homework assignment, the teacher holds up her own notebook - without saying a word.
- The homework assignments can be entered into the calendar on the teacher's desk.

Wording of the homework assignment

The homework instructions should always be worded in the same way. Introduce the class to the abbreviations, symbols and color codes you will be using. For example, the exercise might always be written in blue. In elementary school, you can determine a color coding for the different subjects, e.g. English is blue, math is green, and other subject lessons are yellow.

Repeat in your own words

One teacher told us that the students in her class were allowed to take turns being the "homework students". At the end of the school day, this pupil sits on the teacher's chair and waits until it is completely quiet in the room. Then he repeats the homework for the class.

It is to be recommended - especially if the task involves several steps or is complicated - to have the assignment repeated orally by one or more of the students. In the age groups we are dealing with many of our students are auditory. They are like parrots. They can repeat sentences accurately and reproduce the sound and volume of others' voices. This does not mean, however, that they understand what they are saying. It works much better when they rephrase the instructions. Therefore, it is always good to have them repeat important information in their own words.

Handing in your homework

This should also be ritualized. In our classroom we had a certain space - a shelf or a table - in the classroom where the homework books were placed BEFORE the lesson started. We would not accept them after the bell rang. However, our students had a one-day extension deadline. If they did not submit their homework on the day it was due, they were allowed to hand it in before the following lesson. The only condition: they had to take responsibility for handing it in themselves. We did not remind them or ask them for it. If the homework was there, it was fine. If not, the student got a minus. It worked well, and it was encouraging to see how our students took responsibility for their own work.

Some ideas

Homework supervisor and his assistant

At the beginning of the school year, the place where homework was turned in as well as a homework assistant were determined. This student had the following duties:

- He counted the number of homework assignments turned in,
- He determined who had not turned in the assignment,
- And then noted whose homework was missing

After a certain period of time, the homework assistant takes over my job of being the homework supervisor and appoints another child as his assistant. The assistant takes over the tasks listed above. This responsibility is always passed on until the whole class has had a chance to do the job.

Doris G., high school

Homework checkers

The homework notebooks are numbered. When checking, it is then immediately visible which notebooks are missing. One or two students are responsible for checking which homework notebooks have been handed in.

Susanne R., secondary school

Homework poster

The "homework poster" also works well: It only says "Homework please!" and a list of the students is attached. I put it on the table, and the students bring their homework notebooks, opened to the correct page, and stack them in order from bottom to top.

While the pupils are doing seatwork, I quietly call one child after another to me and look at his homework together with him. I can explain, praise or be pleased about a particularly "good mistake". A "good mistake" can then be utilized to explain something to the whole class. If, for example, Andi's mistake shows me that he needs to learn how to use clauses beginning with the word "because", I can explain this to the whole class. I thank Andi for his "good" mistake which has helped the whole class learn something new.

Kathrin R., secondary school

Kurty, the Homework Rooster

In my elementary school class, we have an auditory homework anchor. It is a stuffed animal called "Kurty, the Homework Rooster". As soon as Kurty crows, the students know, "It's time for the homework assignment!" They put everything down at lightning speed and focus their attention completely on Kurty. He explains the homework assignment to them. After he has finished and all questions are answered, as a "reward", the rooster then begins to dance!

Starting in 3rd grade of primary school, instructions for the homework are given visually. Nevertheless the kids insist on the rooster and his dance in third and fourth grades too.

Elfriede H., elementary school

15

Circle Time. The rules of good conversation

Winnetou was always in the picture!

The seating circle has its origin with the American Indians. Whenever there was something important to discuss, the Indians would sit in a circle and either hand an object from one person to the next around the circle or put it in the middle of the circle. The one who holding the object in his hand was allowed to speak his personal "truth". Only the person holding the object was allowed to speak.

The seating circle was part of the Indians' democratic process. They considered the circle, without a beginning and without an end, to be sacred. The individual's hierarchy within the group ceased to exist within a circle. Each person was equal. They believed that no single person possesses the whole truth, but that each individual carries a part of the truth within himself. This truth was collected in the seating circle from the community. The statements were not evaluated. The members of the tribe did not try to convince the others or speak for or against anything. The process strengthened the sense of community and with the collected "truths" the tribe, led by the chief, was able to make decisions for the entire group.

Circle Time at school

In elementary school Circle Time is a common and very powerful ritual, and it is very advisable to include it in secondary school as well. It is generally used once a week. Monday, another new beginning, is particularly suitable for this. The pupils can be picked up at the beginning of the week and everyone is "back in school". Afterwards, the teacher can give the students information about the week's activities and responsibilities. And, if possible, the class could have a second Circle Time to summarize the week's events on Friday during the last lesson.

When I introduced Circle Time to our middle school class, I told the students the story above about the Indians. Our anchor for forming a Circle Time was the hum of a small singing bowl. When the students heard this sound, they stood up without speaking and sat down on the desktops of the outer tables, which were set up in an U-shape. Of course it would have been possible to move the tables away and form a "tidy" circle of chairs with the other tables in the room. We sometimes did this, especially during more serious meetings, but it was quicker to sit on the tables. This simple form of sitting in a circle had an amazing effect. There was an immediate sense of connection that greatly enhanced the community or group spirit.

Before beginning I announced the three rules of conversation practiced by the Indians. We all silently made the corresponding movements.

1. Speak directly (pointing to the lips with the index finger) and honestly from the heart (pointing to the heart)!

2. Hold your tongue for a moment while you speak. Speak clearly, distinctly and only the most necessary words! (Hold the index fingers of both hands in front of you at a *short* distance from each other)

3. Listen carefully! (Make a circle round your own ear with your index finger and your thumb)

And then we started with the sitting circle's agenda of the day.

Other rituals

Other signals can also be used for the Circle Time. The teacher can, for example:

1. the ringing of a gong or a bell,
2. a symbol card showing that a circle of chairs should be formed,
3. painting a circle in the air with your hands or fingers,
4. draw a circle on the board,
5. the teacher puts her chair where the circle should be formed.

What is done in the circle?

Communication is of the utmost importance. The circle represents a group process that enables direct, honest and effective communication. Group dynamics are promoted. The content can consist of activities such as singing a song, telling a story, prayers, concentration exercises, explaining the rules of the game, organizing, telling personal experiences from the weekend or working through problems that have come up within the class community. Decisions can be made, projects planned and conflict solutions can be worked out.

The advantages

The benefits of a seating circle are the same for our students as they were for the Indians.

- **The seating circle is a haven of peace:** the students "gather" here, they feel protected and come to rest.
- **The contact to each individual is guaranteed** because every voice is heard and eye contact is made with everyone.
- **The hierarchy within the group is eliminated:** Everyone - including the teacher – is within the circle and has equal rights.
- **Rituals bond the group:** The following can function as anchors: seat cushions on the floor, the gong, a speaking stone, microphone or an object that is passed around. If you have some students who are very talkative and want to monopolize the "stage" for themselves, use an hourglass to limit the speaking time.
- **Group dynamics are enriched:** The group works together and a sense of belonging is created. Problems can be discovered and discussed.
- **Social learning is enhanced:** students learn how to conduct a conversation, how to speak in front of a group, how to summarize ideas and try out feedback techniques. Circle Time is a living example of the democratic process. It allows the students to get to know each other better and to develop interest and compassion for each other.

Some ideas:

Circle in the air

On Monday morning my class and I perform a very nice ritual. We all stand up. I say "Good morning!", and draw a circle in the air with my hand. That is the signal that we will now quietly sit in a circle. One time one of the student's three year old brother was visiting us. I asked him to stand next to me in front of the class and whispered in his ear that he should draw a circle in the air with his hands. He did that, and it worked just as well when he did it as when I did.

Christoph P., elementary school

My key ring

Instead of the usual speaking stick or speaking stone I use my keys. That's very convenient because they are always at hand and they are also a powerful symbol (class key, conference room key etc.). Only the person holding the keys is allowed to speak. When someone is finished speaking, she places the keys in the middle of the circle, where the next person who wants to contribute picks them up.

Elfie K., middle school

16

Raise your hands. Don't call out!

How much students participate is often dependent on the age group you are working with.

When students start school they are eager to answer questions. They all want to participate. Now! When I ask a question - and sometimes even when I don't ask a question at all! - they want to answer. They are like unruly little tigers, and one of the first challenges is to keep them from calling out and begging, *"Me! Me! Please take me, teacher!"*

And then comes the day, when their behavior completely changes. The students, who a few months ago were almost untamable, have become lifeless zombies, who only hang listlessly in their chairs. It takes way too much strength for them to raise their hands.

In addition, although they look very "cool" on the outside, they are very insecure inside. The days when they enthusiastically volunteered without having a clue whether the answer to the question was correct or not are over. They don't want to embarrass themselves. They have also become critical of EVERYONE and EVERYTHING. They are bored. "Enthusiasm" is a foreign word they've never heard before.

Raise your hands? Or don't? Indicate it non-verbally

Sometimes raising hands is absolutely necessary, but there are also other situations where it is not necessary at all. If the students are used to communicating within the group, discussions can take place quite naturally without putting up hands. But how do you let them know if they should raise their hands or not?

Of course, we can tell the students that. But it's so much easier and more effective to indicate this wordlessly with hand signals. We do this once again either with the "inviting posture" or with the "assertive posture" and showing the students what you expect. I raise my own hand as a signal to show them what they should do.

In any case, the following must be observed: Open palms indicate that they should *"TALK!"*

If you are having a discussion and want the students to contribute, keep your hands open and show the palms of your hands often when talking. This open hand position also allows you to bend your fingers slightly and move them towards yourself so that more contributions are called forth.

However, if you are lecturing, gaining attention, disciplining or speaking a serious word to the class and do not want to be interrupted, do not show the palms of your hands. If you want the students to raise their hands, imitate this behavior by raising your own hand wordlessly.

Sometimes it is good to create distance

When we teach and a student asks a question, we have the tendency to automatically get closer to the student. But actually we should do exactly the opposite!

When I get closer to the student, I automatically exclude the others. If I turn my back on some students, they immediately start chatting and I have to get their attention again. Going closer to the student also gives the impression that I am having a personal conversation with him and thus, non-verbally, give the other students permission to start their own conversations with their neighbors.

When I am standing in front and a student near me raises his hand, I first act as if I had not seen the hand at all. As I continue talking, I slowly walk away from the student. Then I turn to him and the whole class and say: *"Steven, what did you want to ask?"* That way I am looking at the whole class and they all feel addressed and included.

Give recognition for all contributions

When a student raises her hand to answer a question, I ALWAYS acknowledge her whether the question was answered correctly or not. This recognition - whether for individual students or for the whole group - is extremely motivating. If students' cooperation and efforts are appreciated, they work harder. You appreciate your class and they appreciate you. You are in rapport with one another. When students feel appreciated, they dare to take risks. When they take risks, they are willing to make mistakes. Making mistakes means learning!

The recognition for correct answers can be verbal: *"Super!", "Great!", "You can do it!"* etc. or non-verbal: thumbs up, a smile, a wink, etc. If the answers are wrong, it can also be: *"That's not quite true, but I see you're thinking along with me", "Thank you for making this mistake! "I think there are many others in the class who make exactly that same mistake." "Thank you for showing me what we need to work on!" "Almost right, but not 100%"* etc.

Raise hands rather than calling out the answers.

When I started out teaching middle school, I had a class that was constantly calling out the answers rather than raising their hands. As a result, it became more and more chaotic, and I could feel myself losing control of the class. A structure or ritual was needed!

Step number 1 for establishing a structure:
Ask yourself: "Where do you have a problem? Where are things not running as smoothly as you would like them to?" This shows you where you need to develop a structure or procedure.

So that is what I did. The solution didn't occur to me immediately. Very often I developed it in a series of steps over a period of a few weeks.

Almost every lesson in this class started with a vocabulary review. If a student answered the questions correctly, she got a plus, and if the answer was wrong, she got a minus.

Step number 2: I changed what I had been doing and developed a new structure.
I stopped giving minuses for incorrect answers. I corrected the mistakes but there were no more minuses. This emphasized the point that we only learn by making mistakes.

There was only one exception to this policy. If a student called out the answer without raising his hand and being called on, he got a minus.

That was a good solution:
I explained why to the students and they understood why we were establishing this new policy. This procedure reduced the number of called out answers to a minimum. And students who were shy or afraid of making a mistake became more involved because if the answer was incorrect, they were simply corrected. Minus points were unnecessary anyway. When it was time at the end of the grading period to determine grades, it was quite obvious if a student had twenty pluses and another only four, which students had mastered the material.

This was much better, but it did not completely solve the problem:
I constantly had to look at my student lists to enter the pluses. And, as every teacher knows: if you break eye contact with the class, you will quickly lose their attention. It is said that if a teacher breaks eye contact with the class for more than six seconds the class's attention is elsewhere and needs to be regained.

Step number 3: Refine the structure if necessary.
Therefore, I made a new class list and passed the work and responsibility on to the students. They should make the entries. That worked - but only to a limited extent. The idea was so well received that EVERYONE wanted to keep the list and at the beginning of each lesson we ended up discussing who would have the responsibility of entering pluses and minuses. But we also quickly solved this problem: We did it alphabetically.

At the beginning of the lesson I gave the list to the appropriate student. She carried out the task conscientiously (the students were meticulous. They never cheated, and the only questions that came up were occasionally *"Was that a plus?"*). At the end of the lesson I took the list back.

And a structure was born! A structure that led to a much calmer classroom!

Some ideas

I raise my own hand

I used to have to constantly reprimand students who called out answers. Now when I want the students to raise their hands, I simply raise my own hand. They understand immediately. They raise their hands and everyone stays focused.

Herbert S., secondary school

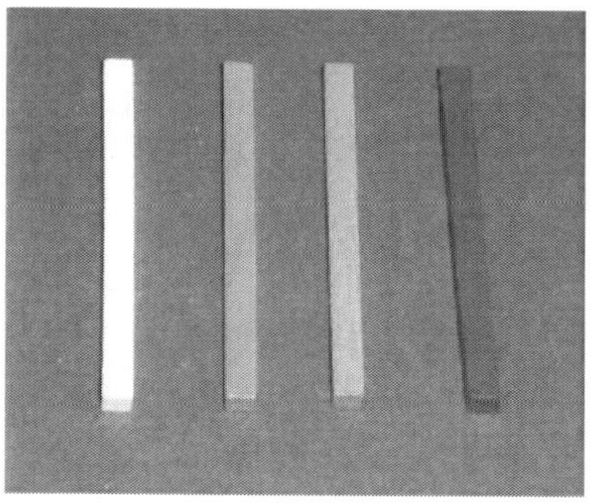

Raise your hand markers

I have, like many other teachers, a magic school bag, where there are many "accessories" for emergencies. One of these items is a collection of colorful wooden sticks. There are about fifty of them in a small bag.

I teach religion in many different special education classes and school levels. It can also happen that due to the children's restlessness or simply having a bad day, they simply forget behavior patterns such as raising hands.

Then I pull out my "hand raising sticks" and ask the children how many they think they can manage today. Good. Let's try. The class (and not the individual student) collects sticks for raising hands. For every time that the teacher calls on a student and he answers, the class has won another stick. And if someone calls out the answer without being called on, the class loses a stick.

The class is very eager to get as many sticks as possible. And they have never asked what reward they might get for this. Just doing it well, is incentive enough!

Martina S., teacher of religion and special education

Raising hands:

In order to stop them spontaneously calling out, the students raise one hand and place the index finger of the other hand over their lips. This sounds incredibly childish, but they always grin so that any resentment or anger immediately gives way to a smile. In the meantime it works automatically. And the pupils have noticed how much more pleasant it is to work in peace. They even ask the teachers in other classes if they can do this!!

Christian H., middle school and high school

More tips for good communication

- List “good conversation” points on a poster. Then point wordlessly to the appropriate rule, to be followed
- If a student calls out without raising her hand, the teacher looks at her with a smile and raises her own hand.
- The teacher raises her hand and snaps her fingers, stomps, clicks her tongue, etc.
- Look at the student dramatically and raise your own hand
- Use an object – a ball, a stone, etc. Whoever is speaking holds this object in his hand. He then passes it on to the next speaker.
- Place your finger or your hand on your mouth.
- The person who is speaking stands up.
- If several students raise their hands at the same time, number them to determine the order in which they can speak. “OK. *You're first, Helmut is second, Anna third, and Martina fourth."*
- Pass a golden microphone around
- Hold your hand to signal *“Stop!”* to the interrupter. Encourage the speaker to continue talking with an inviting hand movement.
- Extend flat hand towards the child, fingers on lips or a flat hand facing downwards signals to the child: *"Do not speak now!"*
- Ignore the ones who do not raise their hands. Call on those who raise their hands.
- Arrange with the students: If you knew the answer and didn’t get called on to answer. Praise yourself by patting yourself on the back.
- Draw an imaginary student on the board. *"This is Hugo"* Hugo gets a minus for each answer called out and a plus for each time someone raises their hand and answers.
- Show a signal card or object (e.g. a picture of a student raising his hand, an empty glove that you wiggle up and down
- Every time someone calls out, ring the bell.
- Show happy and sad smileys
- I call on the first pupil. Then that pupil calls on the next and so on.
- Call on someone by blinking at her, massaging your ear lobe or with another non-verbal signal
- Place the "speaker’s chair" in the front of the room when discussing, explaining problems etc. The person who wants to say something, goes to this chair and sits down on it, he may then talk
- Everybody write down the answer to the question and then say the answer in chorus
- Determine which student will answer before the question is asked
- Students work in small groups and answer questions

17

In the hallway, during recess and on class excursions

Nonverbal anchors and structures are particularly suitable for recess supervision and excursions. In such situations the students are busy with each other and the acoustic perception is very limited. In addition, there are many distracting impressions from the outside that affect the students. Therefore, nonverbal techniques are much more effective here than verbal ones.

Running and other rowdy behavior in the hall

- When students run towards me in the corridor, I stand in front of them and raise my hand as a stop signal. Or I point at their feet.
- In most cases, a warning glance, a clap or waving your index finger to the right and left and shaking your head *"No" is* sufficient to stop undesirable behavior.
- We had a sign in the corridor saying "Parking" and underneath it was a chair. Students who got too rowdy had to sit in the "parking lot" for five minutes.

End of recess or the break:

We usually sent the students to class one or two minutes before the end of the break. This gave them time to get everything ready, and we could start classes more punctually.

- Wordlessly and invitingly pointing down the corridor towards the room (once while doing this I said a single word - *"Go!"* The student looked at me in surprise and then said: *"Went - Gone!")*
- My fingers "walk" and show the way to the classroom.

Some ideas

Timekeeper

Two students are designated as timekeepers. They are responsible for ensuring that all the students are in their seats at the beginning of the lesson and that the teaching materials for that lesson are ready. For each successful day there are two minutes of good time, which are noted in the calendar, i.e. in the best case ten minutes can be collected per week.

Our trial has been running for more than half a year now, there has only been one single day (!) on which it didn't work.

Karin B., grammar school and secondary school

How and where does the break take place?

It is often during the breaks that arguments, brawls and other undesirable behavior occur among the pupils. This carries over then to the classroom atmosphere and events in the subsequent lessons.

Personally, I believe that we often have incorrect assumptions about what students want to do in their "free time". We leave the organization of recess up to the students. My own experience and the experiences of my colleagues and seminar participants show that the students actually appreciate a structured arrangement – with choices - for recess.

One teacher at our school offered the pupils relaxation and meditation exercises during recess. She set up a room called the "Room of Silence" with some cushions and a CD player. Soft music was playing in the room. Upon entering the room talking was forbidden. The teacher did a guided fantasy with them, and afterwards the students went to their classes quietly and relaxed.

Participation in these meditative breaks was of course voluntary. Several teachers who have tried this idea have had the same experience. They assumed that the number of children who voluntarily gave up a break from play would be negligible. They were amazed. There were so many pupils, both in primary and secondary school, that each child could only have a turn once every three or four weeks!

There is always something happening at school. Our students yearn for peace and quiet. But they are not able to create this peace in the school by themselves. To do this, they need our help. During the breaks, we need to offer the students choices. Let them choose between quieter and more lively activities. Many of the teacher training events I hold take place in schools. In these schools I have seen a great number of approaches to make recess and breaks for their students enjoyable. Here are a few examples:

- Active breaks are held in the gym or the assembly hall
- Cozy reading and/or chatting corners are set up along the corridor
- "Game Zones" are in the hall or in empty classrooms. There are puzzle and board game tables, in a room where the partially played game can be continued during the next break, table football games, creative zones, rest areas and fitness equipment sponsored by various companies are available to the students in the assembly hall, etc.

The students appreciate these - once again structured - entertainment opportunities. The breaks are spent meaningfully and the disagreements that otherwise occur in the unstructured break are eliminated.

18

Form a line

How do we form a double line within seconds?
In Chapter 8 we discussed how a structure can be used to have pairs form lines. Here are a few more ideas on this topic, which teachers have shared with me:

The bunch of keys

I use my bunch of keys with several keys as a signal that the students should get in line with a partner so that we can move from point A to point B, be it to the computer room, the music room, the gym or the cinema etc. in an orderly fashion. I do not need to use my voice at all. I signal with my keys and the students become quiet, stop talking and get into line all by themselves. On the very first evening during our last ski course, it got quite loud in the dining room. One of the students said to me, "Mrs. K. Don't you have your keys with you?"

Elfie K., secondary school

The Victory Sign

I often organize field trips and it is necessary that pupils line up quickly in a row of two so that I can count them. That is why I introduced the Victory sign. I also explained the meaning to the students: "Victory" means to me: "We did it!" This sign is really magic to me because it works so well. In a short time everyone is counted and we can continue with our program.

Here is a short example:
On a field trip last school year - two colleagues and I were on the outing with my own class and two other classes. We wanted to gather our students together for the bus departure. It was almost embarrassing: the other two class leaders were shouting in front of a snack station, and it took an eternity until their two classes were standing in line. I stood there quietly, showed my "victory sign" and without saying a word my group was lined up in a row of two!

I said nothing, but I could see from the looks on my colleagues' faces that they were impressed. At the next best opportunity I explained my trick to them, because I think it is important not only to keep positive techniques for oneself but to pass them on to those who want to use them too. Some of my colleagues have also used the key signal and are also pleased that it works so well.

Andrea M., secondary school

Some more ideas:

- Silently and dramatically put your finger on your mouth. Point at the door. Hold up thumb and index finger as a symbol for two rows.
- *"I'm curious if you can get in line very quietly - WITHOUT Saying A SINGLE WORD - in ten seconds."*
- Have them line up according to various criteria, such as date of birth, catalog number, everyone wearing something red, window group, door group, etc.
- Clap your hands twice and keep both hands upright and parallel to each other.
- Show a symbol card with e.g. two children standing next to each other.
- One finger in the air is called "goose march".
- Thumb and index finger in the air is called "row of two".
- This signal "thumb and index finger" in the air can also be used to control the volume. Slowly bring the thumb and finger together. The closer together they get the quieter it should become.
- The teacher closes her eyes and counts slowly up to 5. The pupils line up - without talking - and should say when they are finished (usually they are finished by 3!).
- The teacher blinks at a child. The blinked at child lines up. The teacher or the child who is already lined up blinks at the next person, etc. There must be absolute silence while this is done!
- Play a music anchor or a certain melody on the xylophone.
- If I stand next to the door, that means we will leave the class now and everyone has to stand in line quietly.

... and walk quietly down the hall!

Now they are lined up but how do we get the students to move quietly and in an orderly way from one room to another? Here again is a selection of anchors and also structured procedures to choose from:

Count the seconds

First, we quietly line up in twos in the hall or inside the room. Then we estimate the number of seconds we will need to get to the music room, physics room, cloakroom, the gym, etc. They close their eyes and silently count along as I count from 1 to 10 seconds. Then we start. Everyone counts silently as we walk toward our goal. The students continue counting until I say "stop". They enter the room quietly and sit down on their seats without speaking. They write down the number of seconds. We can then have a short discussion on how long it took.

It is always astonishing how well-mannered and civilized this process is in comparison to the former way of dashing into the room and pushing one another for the alleged best seat. Since I often lead several classes of up to fifty students through the halls, this method has proven totally stress-free for me and other classes are not disturbed.

Astrid M., secondary school

Stop without speaking a word

In music and typewriting/word processing I have to go into a room with the students. I expect the students to be quiet. Of course, sometimes not all the students do this. If this is the case, I stop and do not even turn around. The students will become quiet again, and we can move on. If the pupils are sometimes excited, then it can also happen that I stop two or three times on the way to the music room. But that is okay, because this happens without words.

I still remember how you said at one of the first seminars I attended that it is unnecessary to talk about the misconduct, in this case chatting, after the students are already calm. That's when I realized how much unnecessary energy we expend.

Martin N., Secondary School

Students become pantomime artists

Often the children chatted on the way to the gym and while changing clothes. So we arranged that as soon as we cross the threshold of the classroom we may only talk to each other in pantomime. This also applies to the teacher! I showed the children what I meant by pantomime. They laughed, but when the threshold of the classroom was crossed, they were silent and they gradually became talented pantomimes.

Monika S., elementary school

What else you can do to keep it quiet:

- The teacher walks behind the class. This way you always have an overview!
- Have a school competition: Which is the quietest class?
- Kids take an imaginary key and lock their lips. The teacher "collects" the keys and puts them in her pocket. Once they get there she redistributes the keys.
- After everyone is lined up, the teacher holds up her left hand and puts the index finger of her right hand over her lips. This is the signal for: *"I am ready to go. Not another word."*
- *"Zip your lips."* (students pretend to have a zipper on their mouth and zip it shut)
- Drama games for elementary school: *"We are Indians and sneaking through the hall on tiptoes. Who sneaks the quietest?"* or *"We're all fish now!", "We're all angels and float through the hall."* Put an imaginary fish or a word in your mouth. He/she is not let out until the whole class is in the gym or in the classroom.
- Learn a whispering poem while walking through the hall.
- Give a counting order while walking: How many steps to the gym? Count floor tiles, hold your breath and count how many steps you can walk until you need to breathe again. How many normal breaths do you need to take to get to the music room?
- Sprinkle the rows with imaginary "quiet spray" before leaving the room.

19

Organizing tips

Administrative Tips

It is said that a teacher spends more than fifty percent of her time on classroom management and administrative tasks such as collecting homework, keeping lists, changing seating arrangements, writing notes to parents, disciplining students, etc. I'm sure you know exactly what a headache all of this administrative work is!

These tasks not only take away precious teaching time, but they also often get on our nerves.

You surely know situations such as these:

> **Imagine...**
> You enter the classroom and get your students' attention. Everyone is quiet. You are about to begin. And suddenly there's a bunch of kids clustering around you:
>
> "Here's my excuse from yesterday."
> "I forgot my money for the field trip."
> "Did you bring the worksheet from last week?"
>
> By the time you have taken care of all these things, the class will be restless again and chatting. You will have to get their attention again.

There is a better way: Delegate! Delegate! Delegate!

First of all, let the students do as much of the administrative work as possible. It'll save you time as well as your nerves. And the students are learning self-responsibility.

Just think about it: What kind of administrative work in your class could you give the students? Here are a few examples:

Pupils can take attendance

The students sitting in front of the teacher's desk enter the absent students' names or those who are late on a calendar at the teacher's desk. The students are meticulous! *("Heinz is 7 minutes and 32 seconds late.")* You are not distracted and can immediately attend to the class. You decide yourself when to enter this information into the class register.

Collectors and Distributors

We hand over administrative tasks, such as collecting notebooks or signed sheets of paper, to students who place them on the teacher's desk by the beginning of the next lesson. These can be set as classroom jobs which can be changed weekly or monthly.

Distributor

We have three students who pass out papers, books, etc. Each one is responsible for one row. If there is any fooling around while they are passing things out, I wordlessly take the papers or books out of this student's hand and pass it on to another student. When I am substituting in another class, I am the one who hands out materials!

Christoph M., elementary school

Subject boxes or files

Once, when I cleared out my office at home, I gave the class a lot of stackable plastic boxes. My colleague, Franz, and I had many lessons together at the bilingual middle school. We labelled each box with the name of one of our subjects. We inserted all the leftover documents and worksheets into these boxes. This way the children who were missing on the day in question could take the worksheets themselves, and we did not have to carry them around with us for days on end until the child came back to school.

Mailboxes

We had a hanging file register and designated one file for each child. Messages, homework exercises, and worksheets for the pupils who were absent, were filed there. You can also designate a student as a postman. The postman distributes whatever needs to be handed out to the files.

Class offices

In my 4th grade the students took on various activities. Here are some examples:

- **Homework file**
  I have a large paper poster in class with an English homework list. Two students were responsible for collecting the homework and entering who had done the homework and who hadn't. They kept track and whoever had already done fifteen assignments won the prize of one extra hour in the computer room.

- **Excuses**
  I have a cardboard box with four drawers - one of these drawers is called "excuse notes". This is where students should put their excuses. If they need to be reminded, I take the drawer out and hold it up.

- **Important dates**
  We have an extra whiteboard hanging next to the doors of the classroom. I let the pupils put all of the important dates - hiking days, fieldtrips, tests, etc. - on this board.

- **Books and games**
  The "Book Box" is managed by the pupils. They collect the books, sort them by subject and keep the box in order. The same applies to the games cupboard.

- **The class buffet**
  The pupils organize the buffet themselves. They make a list of who brings what. The teacher should keep an eye on this making sure everyone is equally involved. We have had some very fruitful discussion about this in our social learning lessons.

- **Seating arrangements**
  Other rituals are the seating plans and the division of classroom jobs. These are changed at regular intervals.

  The seating plan is set up either by the pupils themselves, the teacher or by various and varying criteria: The students' names are, for example, drawn or other criteria such as zodiac signs, the color of socks, cards with numbers, the first letter of students' names are used.

Eva K., secondary school

Keeping things in order

Scene:

Martin's schoolbag is a mess. The teacher has told him to empty the schoolbag and repack it. He is now sitting on the floor, with the contents of his school bag stacked on his left hand side. He picks up the first sheet of paper from the stack, looks at it and puts it down to his right. Then he takes the notebook, which is on the top of the left pile, looks at it briefly and puts it on the new pile on the right. Then he takes another sheet of paper from the left stack and puts it on the right stack. Then there is another book and so on until the entire left hand stack is piled up – in the reverse order - on his right hand side. And then he picks up the right stack and carefully puts it back into the schoolbag.

When I watch a scene like this, what does it tell me?

Plain and simple: He has no idea how to pack a schoolbag.

The Martins and Martinas in our classrooms are often overwhelmed. We tell them to keep things in order - and they don't know what that means or how to do it. Didn't he learn that at home? Didn't he pay attention? The reason doesn't matter. To succeed, we must start where the student is at the moment. We have to teach him that - again, a structure - in a way he understands.

For example, you could make "keeping order" the theme of circle talk. "Why is it good to keep your school things in order? What are the advantages? What tips can we give each other to keep our school supplies tidier?"

And then, as discussed, we determine the structure or approach with the students.

We:

1. identify the problem,
2. consider a detailed solution and define the instructions step by step,
3. discuss the necessity with the students,
4. seek advice from students and integrate it into the process if possible,
5. model the new structure for the students, and then we practice it with them,
6. praise them if it works,
7. If after a while it doesn't work one hundred percent, we will practice it again and possibly make changes to the existing structure.

Some ideas

How do we do that?

I show the pupils how this is done using a school bag or backpack (it is important to take a positive example. Taking a messy school bag as an example would be an embarrassment to a student).

All loose papers are removed. Then I divide them up into three stacks:

- Papers that are to be filed in a notebook,
- Papers that are kept elsewhere and
- Papers I can throw away.

I put the papers that belong in a notebook in that notebook. I put papers that belong somewhere else where they belong. And - most importantly - the papers that should be thrown away as well as all the other junk, go straight into the trash!

Andreas M., secondary school

What do I need and what don't I need

My students empty their school bags once a week. We discuss what they need in their bag and what they don't. We do the same with their lockers.

Daniela G., secondary school

The "Organized Table Drawing"

It has become clear to me that my idea of a tidy desktop differs very much from the idea of some of my students. I have solved this problem by making an "organized table drawing" as a big poster. On it are, for example,

- two stacks - one stack of books and one stack of notebooks – these are kept on the shelf underneath the desktop.
- the pencil case is at the top right of the table for right-handed pupils, for left-handed pupils it is on the left,
- there are two sharpened pencils, an eraser etc. in the pencil case,
- important worksheets are in a pile,
- the water bottle, filled and closed, is at the top right of the table,
- there's nothing on the floor and trash is in the trash can,
- the school bag is hanging on the hook on the front of the table.

I hung this poster on the bulletin board and discussed it with the children. Now my pupils have tidy desks. If a desk is not tidy, all I have to do is point to the poster. Great!

Susanne R., elementary school

Photographs - How should it look?

Before school starts in autumn, I am on the move with my camera in the classroom. For example, I organize the games cupboard exactly as it should look. Then I photograph the inside of the cupboard, print it out and hang the picture on the inside of the cupboard door. So everyone knows exactly where what belongs.

I do the same with a student's desk. I set everything on the desk and on the shelf beneath the desk to be exactly as it should look. Every child gets this photo pasted on the table in small format. Sometimes we use adhesive tape to stick an outline of the notebooks, the pencil case etc. on the table. Every time a pupil is convinced:
"I can do it now without the tape," she may remove it.

Anna S., elementary school

Visual classification system

I use this system for the individual objects the students use on a daily basis:

- we have red folders for the German notebooks and books,
- we have green folders for the math notebooks and books,
- we have blue folders for the English books and magazines,
- we also need a folder in the appropriate color for each of these subjects to keep worksheets.
- The other subjects are also color coded. For example, History is yellow, Physics is violet, etc.

I have been using this system since I started teaching, and it works very well! It makes packing the school bag or backpack much easier for the students too.

When I write the homework on the board, I write it in the respective color. In addition, I always write the homework in the upper right corner of the board!

At the beginning it takes a lot of time to check all of this, but as time goes by, it gets easier. It is well worth this bit of additional work and time in the beginning. I have also had a lot of positive feedback on this system from parents.

Daniela G., secondary school

Worksheets without names

Have you ever gotten worksheets, tests, etc. with no name on them? (This is actually a purely rhetorical question. Has there ever been a teacher who hasn't experienced this???)

So, as we discussed in previous chapters, after we have identified the challenge, we need to develop a structure. Here is a suggestion:

Discuss with the students why it is necessary to write their name on a test. "Just imagine you wrote an A on the test. But, because I don't know who this test belongs to, I cannot give you this good mark!

Hang up a poster with the exact words of WHAT to put in the headline (name, date, etc.) and WHERE the headline should be on the worksheet.

> *"Watch carefully as I do this now. I'm doing it exactly as it says on the poster. Here is the title. It's at the top in the middle. Now I leave out one line, and now watch what I write now exactly! ... the date. First comes the month – May - then the day - 20th - and then the year. What year is it? (I purposely write this question twice)*
>
> *Oh, no! Look! I made a mistake!! Do I throw the paper away now?*
> *No! Of course not! I'll erase the mistake."*

Then the students practice it. Several times.

Tidying up

In every lesson or every day the time comes when it is necessary to clean up. Since you have already practiced non-verbal anchoring techniques, you will certainly and hopefully no longer say: "*And now we'll clean up together!* Here are a few anchors you could use:

- an acoustic signal, e.g. a gong, a singing bowl or a music anchor,
- symbol cards showing dustpan and a broom.
- an hourglass,
- pass the trash can through the class,
- hold up the picture of a trash monster

The Pink Panther music

Play the Pink Panther music (which takes just under three minutes). By the end of the music, the students should have tidied up, packed their school bags, put the chairs up on the tables and put the school bags on their backs - without talking. It works! It used to take at least twice as long, and I had to admonish the students more often. Those days are past. Last year, some students even sang along while cleaning up!

Margit W., secondary school

"I have to go to the bathroom"

We all have experienced this too. You are telling the students an exciting story or explaining something very important, and a hand shoots up. You ask: *"Yes, Martin?"*, and he asks: *"Can I go to the toilet?"* The tension and the thread of the story are gone - and you start all over again.

These are disturbances we can expect. And disturbances that we expect can - fortunately - be proactively eliminated.

Let's stick with the *"I have to go to the bathroom" example for* now:

Smurf and Smurfine traffic light

Students may go to the toilet without asking. There are some ground rules:

- Only ONE student is allowed to go at a time,
- but NEVER while I'm explaining an important topic to the class.

To keep this under control, we have introduced a "Smurfine" and a "Smurf" sign that hang on the classroom door. One side is red, the other is green. When a kid goes to the bathroom, he turns the figure to show the red side. If the figure is red, you have to wait. When he returns to the room, he turns the figure around that the green side shows.

Carola F., elementary school

"W" for WC

A student who has to go to the toilet puts up his hand with the three middle fingers of one hand forming a "W". Teacher nods a "yes" or "no".

Gabi S., elementary school

"Toilet List"

I put a "toilet list" next to the door. On one side of the list are the girls' names, on the other the boys' names. Below each name are two clothespins for girls and boys. If someone has to go to the toilet, he takes one of the clips and attaches it next to his name. When the child returns, he removes the clip next to his name and rehangs it on the clothespin position. This way the teacher knows at a glance who is in the toilet.

Monika S., elementary school

Toilet traffic light

20

Greetings

Greeting is an important social skill. It establishes contact between two people and provides a positive basis and opening for communication. Furthermore, a greeting conveys the feeling that one is perceived and appreciated.

Many years ago I held several courses in a former East Bloc country. I really liked the country and especially the warmth of the people there. I stayed in a very well-known former communist hotel. The hotel was in order. But not really keeping pace with modern times. Like in the old communist days, there were about three times as many employees as were needed. Sometimes I had the feeling that there were more hotel employees than guests! That would have been fine, but the guest, as in earlier times, was not noticed at all. For example, I went to the wonderful breakfast buffet and had to wind my way between about ten employees standing at the restaurant door. I greeted everyone in a friendly way - and not a single person reacted. It was as if I was air. And after having made this daily passage as an invisible woman for a whole week, I started pinching my hand and asking myself if I even existed!

At the university where I studied in America, we were told during the first week of orientation: *"Our college is a friendly one. If we walk on the campus or meet anyone in the building, we say hello because it makes everyone feel better."* We did and it was true.

And then I came to Austria, where the people greeted each other even more than there! I will never forget how my Austrian husband and I left our home one day. Someone just came in through the front gate, and my husband greeted him. Afterwards he said to me: *"You didn't greet him."* I replied, *"Why should I greet him? I don't know him."* And then he explained to me that it was customary here to greet every person you meet inside an apartment building. This was new to me, but I adapted - and I really like the custom. You greet not only in the stairwell, but also when you enter and leave the waiting room at the doctor's office or upon entering or leaving shops, etc. However, this tradition has been neglected a bit recently, and many teachers want to teach our students that greeting others is part of good manners.

When I was teaching in the middle school, we included various activities that would be helpful for our students when they left school and entered the job market. One of these activities was the greeting. First I wrote the following sentence on the board:

Greeting makes friends!

The students discussed this statement first with their neighbor and then in the large group. Then I wrote the subtitle of the lesson:

How do we greet someone?

We sat down in the chair circle, I then told them: *"Our aim today is to give a friendly handshake around the circle. I'll show you how it's done!"*

I give the students a model. I show them step by step how to shake hands with someone: which movements, which words, which gestures and facial expressions are needed. The students observed my colleague and me, we discussed it, and then we practiced it until it became perfect.

Step one:
"I would like to give Peter, who is sitting next to me, a friendly handshake.
Watch us carefully as we do this."
I greet Peter with a friendly smile
and a warm handshake.

Step two:
*"What did you notice? What exactly did I do? What is it that makes this a **friendly** handshake?"*

The students are responding:

- "You turned to Peter."
- "You made eye contact."
- "Both of you smiled."
- "You took his right hand and shook it."
- You said, "Good morning, Peter."

- "You shook his hand."
- "You shook it firmly, but not too hard," etc.

Write these steps on the board so that the students can transfer them to their notebooks.

Step 3:
"Let us now take a closer look at the process.
I want to be sure that the handshake is firm, but I don't want it to hurt either.
Take a good look at Peter and me again.
Now I do this with Susi (I turn to the other side where Susi is sitting). And now please do the same with your neighbor.
How was that? Did we forget anything?
Who can show us this now? What did you notice and see?"

Step four:
"And now let's send the perfect handshake around the circle."

While the students practice greeting, I give feedback on whether they are doing it right.

It is important that these greetings are practiced over and over again so that they become automated.

Other topics for follow-up lessons would be:

- How do I introduce one person to another?
- How do I show my conversation partner that I am listening?
- What are good phone manners?
- How do we behave when we have visitors in the classroom?
- Sayings like, *"A smile is the shortest distance between two people,"* or *"A smile is my style."* can be discussed.

Some ideas

The fourth grade greets the first grade

On the first day of school the fourth graders can welcome the new first grade children (and their parents) and then accompany them to the right classroom. This is good for everyone - the first graders feel more comfortable, the fourth graders can practice their social skills, and the parents will be very impressed!

Welcome song in several languages
From the book: "Motion hits from Moscow to Morocco" with CD, Wolfgang Hering, Ökotopia Verlag, Münster.

Elfie H., Elementary school, Vienna

Welcome and farewell anchor

To greet and say goodbye at the beginning and end of the lesson, I chose the place in the classroom a few steps away from the classroom door leading into the classroom. The students stand up. No one moves, nobody has their hands in their pockets or is talking to their neighbor.

When I say hello, I say "Good morning", and I always say goodbye with "Have a nice day!" They respond with, "We wish you the same", or they repeat the greeting.

Almost all my students greet me when we meet in the corridors. I think that's wonderful!

Elfie K., middle school

Greeting without words

Music is playing in the background. The pupils walk crisscross through the room and greet each other nonverbally – using eye contact, handshakes, smiles - and then verbally with good wishes for the day.

"Good morning! ", "Welcome! And have a seat!"

The students stand up and the teacher welcomes each student personally making **eye contact**. After a student is greeted as we learned and with a smile, he or she sits down. Be very calm. No speaking. Take your time.

Personal welcome at the door

Stand by the door and greet each student when he or she comes through the door. Make sure your posture is open, you are smiling and make eye contact.

Three handshakes

Welcome the students at the beginning of the lesson. Each student proceeds to greet three other students with a handshake and then sits down quietly.

A smile

Send a smile silently from one student to another around the room.

Sending a handshake

Stand in a circle with closed eyes. Hold hands. The teacher presses the hand of her neighbor to the right or the left. When it returns to her, everybody open their eyes and say *"Good morning!"*

Suggestopedic Text: Kevin Cool

This is a suggestopedic text or role play you can use for social learning.

Kevin Cool Reaches Level 5

or

Greeting works wonders!

by Karoline Skledar and Barbara Prettenhofer

Kevin Cool is very excited today because it's his birthday. Finally he is getting his much longed for computer game of the newest generation as a present.

With this game he can play interactively, compete with others on the World Wide Web and enter his results into a ranking list.

The equipment includes video glasses, surround sound headphones, sensor-controlled gloves and shoes with vibration feedback.

Kevin puts on the equipment with enthusiasm and starts the game full of expectation. Everything darkens, the game begins.

But suddenly, there's a loud bang...

...and a girl appears in a bright light.

Lucy:

Hello, player! I am Lucy Level.
Welcome to my world.
Four exciting levels await you.
Will you pass them?
Each level prepares you for the next one.
So remember well what you learn
in the individual levels.
The faster and more strategically you
play, the more points you can score to
reach the top of the leaderboard.

Kevin: *You bet!*
Let's go!

The scene on the screen goes dark and a beautiful old fortress appears. The entire castle appears impregnable - only through a large, heavy iron gate is access possible. In front of the gate stands a grim-looking and heavily armed guard.

Lucy: *Your first task is to get into the castle!*
Good luck!

Lucy disappears with a loud bang.

Kevin: *Oh no, this is not going to be easy...*
High, thick walls, a mighty gate,
a grim guard...
What am I going to do?

Climb up? - too high.
Fight? - too dangerous.
Give up? - certainly not!
Maybe there is a code word?

Kevin carefully approaches the guard and thinks of some words.

Kevin: *Open sesame!*
007!

But nothing happens. Suddenly an idea comes to him!

Kevin: *Good day!*

Suddenly the guard turns to him, greets him back, and the gate opens. Kevin enters, and Lucy appears at his side again.

Lucy: *You've passed the level of greeting*
Remember the code word.
Maybe, it will come in handy!
Good luck with Level 1.

LEVEL 1
Level of the Greeting

Look out!
Your life energy is almost used up!

Lucy disappears, and Kevin enters the courtyard.
Suddenly he smells the wonderful scent of food.
He follows the smell and finally ends up in the kitchen.
There is a cook who is preparing a feast.

Kevin: *I need life force.*
Can I get that from you?

But nothing happens.
Kevin reaches for the food, but it disappears before his eyes.

He remembers the previous level.

LEVEL 1
Level of the Greeting

LEVEL 2
Level of Request

Kevin: *Good day!*
I need life force!

The cook greets him back, but nothing else happens.

Kevin: *Good day!*
I need life energy, PLEASE!

The cook greets him again, smiles and gives him a delicious meal.

Lucy appears at his side again.

Lucy. *You have now managed the Level of Request.*
Make your way to the dungeon.
There's an innocent man there waiting for your help.

Together with Lucy he makes his way to the dungeon.
Lucy disappears again.

LEVEL 1
Level of the Greeting

LEVEL 2
Level of Request

LEVEL 3
Level of eye contact

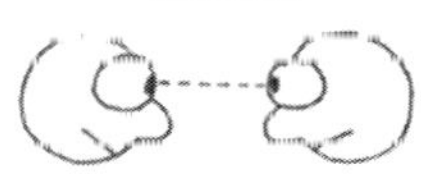

A thick iron grid blocks the way to the cell block. Again a big, grim guard is watching the entrance. In his hand he holds a large bunch of keys. Kevin remembers the first two levels and says:

Kevin: *Good day!*
Could you please unlock the cell?

Nothing happens. What's missing?!?!

Suddenly the eyes of the guard start to sparkle slightly.

Kevin smiles, looks the guard in the eyes and says:

Kevin: *Good day!*
Could you please unlock the cell?

The guard looks him in the eyes, smiles, greets him back and unlocks the cell with a big key. The innocently imprisoned boy is set free.

In return Kevin gets a piece of chewing gum as a present.
Immediately Kevin starts to chew.

Lucy Level appears again.

Lucy: *Way to go!*
The level of eye contact is also passed.
There are only two more tasks ahead of you.
The next level leads us to the throne room.
There you will meet the royal family.
They can tell you the secret path to your destination!

In the throne room the royal family is gathered around a large table. All eyes are on Kevin. Kevin nervously chews his chewing gum, yet he remembers the previous code words, looks the king in the eye and says

Kevin: *Hello,*
could you please show me the way to my destination?

The king looks at him but does not react. Kevin starts to think what else he can do. He chews his gum thoughtfully. From the corner of his eye he sees that the king is looking towards the wastepaper basket.

Kevin has an idea!

He spits the gum into the wastepaper basket, looks the king in the eye and starts again...

Kevin: *Hello,*
could you please show me the way to my destination?

The king nods in a friendly way, greets him and shows him the secret path behind the curtain. Behind the curtain Kevin sees a steep spiral staircase. The stairs lead up higher and higher, and finally he enters a small room with a large balcony.

Kevin steps onto the balcony and suddenly he hears thunderous applause. Down in the castle courtyard thousands of people - including Lucy Level - cheer Kevin and congratulate him on winning the game.

LEVEL 1
Level of the greeting

LEVEL 2
Level of request

LEVEL 3
Level of eye contact

LEVEL 4
Spit out chewing gum

21

The respectful classroom

"We treat each other with respect! "

One of the complaints I hear most from teachers around the world is the frequency of swearing and disrespectful behavior in the classroom. Only in one country has it been different until now - Thailand.

A friend, Jasmin, who is a teacher from Liechtenstein, worked in Thailand for a year or so with an Organization called, Youth Connect (http://www. youthconnectthailand.org/). Youth Connect is located in Mae Sot, a Thai city on the border to Burma and works among other things with Thai schools and teachers, who prepare Burmese refugee children for working life in Thailand. Some years ago my son Derrick and I visited Jasmin, her colleagues and several school classes there. A great experience! Among other things, I noticed that all the children were fully involved in the lessons and that there were apparently no behavioral problems. When I asked one of the teachers if they had no discipline problems, he replied: *"No. We are not acquainted with such problems. Here respect is the highest commandment. We also have a 'respect hierarchy'. At the highest level is the king. In the second place are the monks. And in third place are the teachers."*

It would be nice if it were the same with us! In addition to that, with increasing age in Thailand, one also gets more and more respect!

I am convinced that treating each other with respect - we with our students and they with us and their classmates - is a key to a self-disciplining classroom. And a better world.

They often don't understand what we mean.

My son Derrick used to teach in an alternative school. There were a number of students there who had behavioral challenges. When he got home the first day after school, he called me and said, *"You can't imagine how the students talk to each other. So disrespectful! But this is going to change now!"*

The next day he took a white sheet and paints to school. The students painted the sheet similar to the picture above and hung it on the wall. He put a waiter's bell on the teacher's desk.

A class rule that's found in many classrooms is *"We treat each* other with *respect."* But what is respectful? I know what it means, and so do you. But many of our students have no idea what the word "respectful" means. We get upset about the way they talk to each other. But often our students talk like that at home too. Our challenge is to teach our students the meaning of the word "respectful" first. Only when they know what it is can they be like that.

That's why Derrick arranged with his class that he would ring the waiter's bell every time something disrespectful was said or done. When this happened, everyone stood up, including him, pointed to the poster and said, *"100% respect!"* That's exactly what they did, even if somebody said something disrespectful about themselves like *"I'm so stupid!"* Stand up, point and say *"100% respect!"* Students must also learn to respect themselves. You have to respect yourself before you can respect others.

The clou was that by using this technique the students learned which statements were disrespectful. Within days the situation improved and soon the process was no longer necessary. Of course there were occasional slips, but sometimes simply when the bell rang it was enough to restore the respectful behavior.

NEVER allow a student to speak to you disrespectfully

No student/human being has the right to talk to you disrespectfully. It is your responsibility to draw the line and insist on respectful interaction. You get respect by giving respect, and also by demanding respect!

React immediately if a student says something disrespectful to you. Do not engage in a power struggle or discussion. Stop talking immediately, step aside, freeze, and look at the student with a serious and withering look. Wait a moment – pausing is the most powerful non-verbal tool you can use - and then say just one sentence, such as *"I always treat you with respect, and I expect the same from you."* Then you say **nothing more**. Otherwise the almost hypnotic state will break down.

Remain frozen in your posture and keep eye contact for a moment. Then break eye contact, take a step back to your starting position, loosen your posture again and act as if nothing had happened.

If you use this procedure, which is a variation of the discipline anchor (see chapter 22), practice few times at home in front of the mirror. It must be (almost overly) dramatic and precise. It important that you do not get involved in a conversation. If a debriefing is necessary, do it later an in private.

Never allow humiliation or degradation of other students in the classroom. Treat the students as if they were adults and let them know that you expect the same behavior from them. If the boundaries are clear and you act as an example, the class will become your reflection. And everyone will profit.

Also the frequent use of swear words destroys the respectful atmosphere we want to create in the classroom. Often the students do not even know what these swear words mean and they do not understand that they are offensive.

Some ideas

Flush the swear words away

The students in my class often insulted each other with swear words. One day my colleague brought some toilet paper rolls into the classroom. She put them on the teacher's desk and said, "Today we are going to talk about name-calling."

We had a class discussion about swear words during circle time. "What are curse words used for? Which ones hurt you the most?" etc.

The students were then given a piece of toilet paper. Each student wrote down all the swear words he used or no longer wanted to hear. Finally the paper was crumpled up and flushed down the toilet. If someone slipped up and used a swear word, everyone shouted: "Toilet paper!"

Justine K., middle school

The "No Swear Word Zone"

At the beginning of the school year I told the students we were declaring our classroom to be a "No Swear Word Zone". Whoever goes through the door to this room leaves all the curse words outside the door. We deliberately brought every swear word to the door. If they absolutely wanted to scold and swear at someone they could but they had to do it in front of the door outside the classroom.

Some colleagues asked what I did with students who turned this rule into a game and were constantly running out of the room. With time this wears off. Especially because the other children don't want it and they tell them so. In the meantime, the students have discovered harmless alternative words such as crap or even funny replacements where everyone has to laugh and then the anger is forgotten.

Martina S., religion teacher

P.S. By the way I have also been sent to the door!

A Suggestopedic Story: Recess

Many of my colleagues at the bilingual middle school I taught at in Vienna have done the Suggestopedia training courses with me. Two of these colleagues wrote a suggestopedic text about recess and kids using swear words. They wrote this story with swear words and then replaced all the swear words that the pupils normally use with each other with the corresponding form of the fantasy word *"Quapp"*.

The day of the drama performance came. We announced to the class, *"Now we're going to tell you a story."* As always with these stories, the students were happy to see a play being performed by their teachers - but when we read the title and the first line:

"RECESS!
Similarities with living persons are IMPORTANT and not accidental!"

they grinned sheepishly. They knew exactly who was meant - namely themselves! What would happen next?

We teachers acted the drama out for the class. They were sitting on the edge of their chairs! Then we did various activities and games to make them aware of how unpleasant swearing can be to others.

And it worked! There was much less swearing in class. Occasionally we had to review what we had done and introduced new activities to remind the students of what they had learned. But the first and most important step was taken care of with the text my colleagues wrote. The pupils learned some very important social lessons and we saved our ears!

(I wanted to include the story for you here but then realized that the translation from German to English didn't make sense. Swear words vary from one country to another and the text would lose a lot in translation! But feel free to develop your own story according to the guidelines above)

22

The discipline anchor

(See You Tube: https://www.youtube.com/watch?v=vKjzknWxLUo&t=173s)

We don't like to discipline misbehaving students - but sometimes we have no choice. We have worked proactively. We have tried to nip negative behavior in the bud. But on some days it just doesn't work. It is for these situations that we have the discipline anchor.

The discipline anchor

About ten years ago I presented a workshop entitled "Respectful, non-verbal disciplining" at a teachers' congress near Buenos Aires in Argentina. As is customary at such congresses, each speaker had two minutes at the opening to introduce themselves and their own workshop, so that the participants could think about which workshops they wanted to participate in during the congress. I included a demonstration of the disciplining anchor in this short presentation.

I stood on the stage to the right and welcomed the teachers present - there were several hundred participants. I held my body relaxed and said: *"I am really happy to be here with such a lively group in Buenos Aires..."*

The group was truly extremely lively. Although it was only the opening and they didn't even know each other yet, they all were laughing, talking and even making enthusiastic waves across the room together! By now I know - and I appreciate it very much! -that South American teachers are simply bubbling over with the joy of life. But back then I was totally surprised and thought: *"Great! But if the teachers are so lively, what are the students like? I think these people need me!"*

I stopped there and continued to talk: *"We all became teachers because we like working with young people and we want to teach, but sometimes..."*

Now I stopped talking in the middle of the sentence, my body froze, and I looked around the room with a serious look and then slowly walked to a point on the left side of the stage. Arriving there, I stood in a frozen posture, let my gaze wander through the room and then said in a very serious and monotonous voice: *"...but sometimes...in school...it is necessary to discipline...".*

You could have heard a pin drop. They were all holding their breath and speechlessly staring at me.

After a few seconds I moved back to the first point on the right side of the stage, loosened my posture and continued with my normal voice and a smile: *"... and that is the topic of my workshop. I hope lots of you will attend!"*

As they were still sitting there in shock, I was afraid that I had flown to Buenos Aires for nothing and that nobody would come to my workshop! My fear was unfounded: I even had to repeat the workshop several times so that all the teachers who were interested could participate.

Since then, I have demonstrated this disciplining anchor hundreds of times. Each time it has the same effect. Everybody becomes quiet as a mouse, holds their breath and waits tensely for my next words. The teachers are enthusiastic - and they become even more enthusiastic after they have successfully tried out the technique in their own classrooms.

The discipline anchor is a structure that works almost like magic. Those of you who have read my book "Nonverbal Classroom Management" or have taken courses with us already know it well. This anchor or structure is simply a "must" for those who are not acquainted with it yet. Therefore I hope that those who already know it will consider this chapter as a welcome review.

Self-discipline is the goal

First of all, I would like to emphasize that the discipline anchor is very effective, but it is only a relief measure, a kind of first aid that we use when the house is on fire. Our ultimate goal is to educate our students to be self-disciplined. If we succeed in this, we can fortunately leave our disciplining policeman roles behind us!

We have taken precautionary action

- by using influence rather than power,
- by establishing rapport,
- by setting clear rules and guidelines,
- by taking pro-active measures and
- by means of a pre-warning or "yellow light",

Nevertheless situations can arise from time to time where we have to discipline. We have no choice. It is our task and our duty to ensure a smooth, orderly and safe daily routine in the classroom. If a student becomes disruptive, we must move from our usual sphere of influence to that of power.

In such situations the disciplining anchor is a gift from heaven!
Below is a list and explanation of all the steps of the anchor, but first it is important that we look at the difference between disciplining a student and guiding or counseling him toward a change in his behavior.

Discipline or guidance

Between these two concepts there is a world of difference.

I use **discipline** when there is a disruption in class. My goal is to eliminate this disturbance as quickly as possible and without words, to establish order in the classroom so that the lesson can continue.

> The goal of disciplining is:
> Amnesty (peace) and amnesia (forgetting)

When I discipline a student, I speak as little as possible. I do not announce any consequences. Bringing about a long-term change in a student's behavior is not my goal. I am respectful - but I act for the good of the group and not the individual.

A **guidance or counseling session**, on the other hand, lasts longer and takes place - if possible - under four different conditions. Here it is about the student's behavior, the intention behind this behavior and the consequences this behavior have within the classroom and for the student himself.

> The aim of such a meeting
> is finding solutions and changing behavior in the long term.

This is about continuous and constant changes and improvements. A period of time has elapsed between the event leading up to the disciplining itself and this meeting. The student and you have gained distance, the emotions have cooled and you can both take a more objective view.

More on this in the next chapter.

The discipline anchor - step by step

> 1. Choose a discipline anchor in the room BEFORE you need it

For me this place is in the front of the room, on the side near the sink and wastepaper basket. The class rules are hanging on the wall nearby.

> 2. Set this anchor with negative content BEFORE you
> actually need it

Go to the spot you have chosen and say something negative there, like: *"Unfortunately we can't go on the field trip today because it's raining cats and dogs."* The words you say are not important. The statement should only contain some negative content.

Now the negative anchor spot has been established. Whenever there is a need to discipline, you do it right there on that spot. It is very important that you do not teach on this spot. Otherwise you run the risk that your teaching material will be "contaminated" with negative feelings.

The scene:

The class is interested and actively involved.
You notice that Susi and Magdalena are chatting.

2. Be as proactive as possible.
As an early warning, give a "yellow light" or warning before using the anchor.

You have already taken pro-active measures with Susi and Magdalena, and you have issued a warning.

3. Distinguish between large and small discipline matters.

Although chatting usually falls under the category of smaller digressions, you have already warned Susi and Magdalena and given them a yellow light. In addition, a similar situation occurred yesterday. You decide that discipline is now necessary.

4. Do not look at them for the time being!

Otherwise the danger is too great that you will say something while standing or sitting where you normally teach. That would cause you to contaminate your teaching spot. Your teaching anchors should ALWAYS be associated with positive and motivating feelings.

5. Stop talking. Even if in mid-sentence. Put down everything related to teaching.

6. For the anchor to work, it must be done
SLOWLY and DRAMATICALLY.

Otherwise it loses its effect. It should be noticeable to all students that something unusual and out of the ordinary is about to happen.

You stop speaking in mid-sentence.
You put down your papers.
You put the chalk down.
You turn off the LCD projector.

By now, at the latest, the students who are paying attention will realize that something is going on. They may look at you expectantly.

It is important that you leave everything that has to do with teaching at your teaching spot. Otherwise these items may be contaminated while disciplining.

You turn and...

7. You walk in the direction of the discipline anchor. On the way...

8. ...make sure that you are breathing properly...

9. ...and that you are dissociated.

10. When you arrive at the anchor, you freeze in the following posture.
    - You stand up straight.
    - Your weight is evenly distributed on both feet
    - The tips of your toes are pointing forward,
    - Your chin is slightly tilted down.

11. Let your eyes wander through the room and make eye contact with all students.

12. Now make eye contact with Susi and Magdalena.

13. Say ONE sentence at most.

Don't talk too much

Otherwise the almost hypnotic tension is broken. And then it can happen that Susi or Magdalena will give you an answer. Or - even worse - that other students will interfere in the process. Soon the whole class will be talking!

It makes absolutely no sense for you to speak in this situation.
Everyone - both the student who is being disciplined and the rest of the class – are so surprised that they pause for breath. When a person holds his breath, he does not hear what you are saying.

Do not turn disciplining into a teaching moment.

The discussion comes later. Right now, you just want to be able to stop the interruption and get on with your teaching. This is not the right moment. Even if you are calm and dissociated, the student is probably in an agitated state. If the student is upset, he will not hear what you are saying.

Do not announce any consequences

While disciplining it is, in my opinion, the wrong time to announce the consequences. Even if you are dissociated, the student isn't. And discussing consequences in an emotional moment can only lead to further problems or at least to inner rebellion on the part of the student.

The consequences should have a direct connection to the offence. That means they should help the student learn from the experience not to do the same nonsense again. You can't do that when he's upset.

After you have finished using the discipline anchor and order in the classroom has been restored wait until the students are, for example, doing seatwork. Then go to the disciplined student and say quietly:

> *"Susi, you know that what you did was not right. And you know there will be consequences. I want the consequences to be meaningful. You should learn something from them. I'll think about this and we can sit down tomorrow at 3 pm to discuss it. If you want, you can think about it too and make your own suggestions."*

So Susi has time to change from the emotional state to a logical one.

The most senseless punishment you can give is one that has to do with your subject matter. Once again, there is the danger of contamination here! For example, if I say to Susi: *"For tomorrow you can copy five pages in English"*, Susi sits at home and while she is writing she thinks: *"I hate English! I hate English!"* Then it's no wonder if she's not motivated in English class. So - don't punish her with your own material! And, please, not with your colleagues' material either!!

My colleagues and I have prepared a questionnaire for such disciplinary cases. Instead of some form of punishment, we give the student this questionnaire to fill in and then use it as a basis for the counselling interview. The questions and the counselling interview are covered in the next chapter.

14. Break eye contact.

15. Loosen your posture and breathe deeply.

The class will breathe with you - and the group rapport and feeling of community is restored.

16. Leave the discipline anchor and go back towards the teaching place.
Take at least two more breaths on the way.

17. Once you have arrived back at your teaching spot,
change your posture and breathe deeply.

Your physiology determines your inner state. This means that if you maintain the frozen posture you had at the disciplining anchor while now standing on your teaching anchor, you will transfer this disciplining inner state to the teaching spot.

In addition, the class reflects your inner state. If you are still frozen, not breathing fluidly and radiating the negative state you had on the discipline anchor, the students will also assume it. In this state there is no learning - and your material is contaminated.

The goal of any disciplining measure is:

18. Amnesia (forgetting) and Amnesty (peace)

The peaceful state that prevailed before the disciplinary measures were taken is restored. The lesson can go on - as if nothing had happened at all.

Therefore it is very, very important that you adopt a relaxed posture during the rest of the lesson and that your breathing is fluid.

19. The next time you make eye contact with the disciplined student, smile kindly
at him. The student himself is ok. His behavior wasn't.

That's the non-verbal signal: You're okay. I'm not angry with you personally, but your behavior was not okay. The student will certainly react positively. And you will probably even be able to see the relief in his non-verbal posture when he realizes that you still like him.

The next time

After you have used this anchor a few times, the students know what to expect when you are on your way to this anchor or even turn in that direction. Each time you will have to say less. It may even happen that the students themselves whisper to the disruptive student or make him aware that he is misbehaving. If he stops before you get there, you can save yourself from disciplining!

Some ideas

Like a miracle

If it should happen that I am annoyed about something or at a pupil, I stop at the waste paper basket, next to which there is a cabinet. I just stand here and demonstratively clear my throat. And like a miracle it becomes quiet as a mouse.

Even if the incident should be right at the beginning of the lesson when getting the class's attention or if there was a disturbance during the break, I only have to clear my throat and freeze my movement. Then I can be sure that it will be quiet in no time.

Corinna S., Vocational School

Wow!

Today I had to use my discipline anchor for the first time. It worked perfectly. I was almost tempted to say, "Wow!!" The children were quiet and looked at me with big eyes. I've never experienced anything like it before.

A statement by one of the students last week surprised me. Thomas said to me: "Sonja, today you didn't scold us at all, and it was really peaceful and calm. Will it stay that way now?"

This statement has particularly strengthened my belief that this is the right way to teach. Thank you!

Sonja L., elementary school

Teacher, you're standing in the wrong place!

... My anchors are working well. The waste paper basket is next to my discipline anchor. Last week I forgot and scolded a pupil from a different spot. The kids said, "No, Mrs. Schmid, you have to go to the waste paper basket!"

Christine S., elementary school

I just switch sides and look serious

If there is a disturbance, it is usually enough to simply step on my discipline anchor or take a step in that direction - my body freezes, my face gets serious and without saying a word the students know what is going on.

It is quite interesting to observe that when I stand on the discipline anchor, the faces of the children change. They become very serious. When I go back to the other side of the room, their faces light up immediately.

Lisi R., elementary school

I was afraid of making a fool of myself.

I had an eleventh grade class in mathematics. There was a clear gap in terms of achievement: about a third of the class was talented, interested in mathematics, technology and science and willing to work. The middle third was average and the last consisted of kids who were repeating the grade or were poorly motivated. As was to be expected, the class was at times undisciplined and restless.

You taught us about the discipline anchor in the training course, but it seemed so dramatic and I didn't want to make a fool of myself in front of the class.

But the situation in this class was becoming so unpleasant that one evening I practiced the discipline anchor steps at home in front of the mirror and used them at the next opportunity. I slowly and dramatically put the book, compass and protractor on my desk, looked around the class and slowly walked to my discipline anchor. The class was in a state of shock and it worked. Standing on my discipline anchor I said in a very serious voice, "That is enough." and the atmosphere changed.

I didn't have to use the anchor a second time. Since that day all I need to do is to put down my tools and wait until it's quiet again.

Ilse S., high school

Traffic lights

Each child received a complete "traffic light", i.e. a green, a yellow and a red card.

At the beginning of the day, the three cards, with the green card on top, were in a stack in front of each pupil. I explained that if a class rule was broken, the green card would move to the bottom of the stack and the yellow card would be visible. If there is another violation, the yellow card would move to the bottom and the red card would be visible. At the end of the lesson we would discuss our behavior on that day and think about solutions. The children were very enthusiastic about this process. Now I don't have to admonish them anymore, I just have to change the color of their traffic light.

Monika S., elementary school

The boom-boom bomb

The BOOM-BOOM-BOMB, is a drawing of a bomb with a long fuse on the board. The fuse gets a bit shorter with every disturbance. I seldom have to shorten the fuse and I usually have an absolutely calm class (This tactic works from the very small ones to the high school students!!) Should the bomb explode, the following applies: the entire class community is liable for the disturbers. The students love this activity. When I come into my classes, the bomb is already drawn on the board, with a looooooong fuse...

I passed this idea on to some colleagues. A fellow teacher, who was indeed struggling a lot with the pupils and shed bitter tears almost every day, tried the bomb. For the first time, she came out of the classroom smiling. Meanwhile the students draw the bomb on the board in preparation before the teacher comes into the room.

Another, very amusing variation: The Road to Mistelbach (or some other town near where you are teaching.) I, or the students, draw a street on the board. Starting point is our classroom, end point is the border to the town we have chosen. I've fitted a small car with a magnet, and every time there's a class disturbance, the car moves a little further. If something goes very well, the car turns, jumps up and down and drives back a little bit. The students (even the older ones) love it.

And the very best thing is that I don't have to scold or talk at all! I stand smiling at the board and just wipe away a chalkmark or push the toy car around. The class itself does the rest. The atmosphere is relaxed and in no way tense.

Michaela G., Religion

23

The coaching session

Distinguish between disciplining and coaching

It is very important that the two actions, the disciplining and - if necessary - the later coaching session are not combined.

The purpose of disciplining is "amnesty and amnesia".
This means that if there is a disturbance during the lessons, it is my aim to eliminate this disturbance as quickly as possible and without excitement, so that peace can reign again in the classroom and the lessons can continue undisturbed. This should happen as unobtrusively as possible so that the disturbance is forgotten – at least for the moment.

If I discipline, as explained in the last section, no consequences for the misbehavior should be announced at this time. Even if I have succeeded in remaining dissociated, i.e. objective, the student's inner state is quite excited. And when he is excited, he does not hear a single word I say to him. So why should I talk? Both parties need time to gain perspective so that the consequences are objective and related to the offence.

Instead of immediately pronouncing a punishment or giving a sermon, my colleagues and I give the disruptive student a questionnaire to fill out before the coaching session. He could do this at home. But another possibility is to set up a few desks in the hallways near the classroom where his emotions can cool down and he can gain some distance while filling out the questionnaire. We then use his answers to these questions as a basis for the subsequent session.

There are three questions on the questionnaire:

1. What happened?

When answering, the student may only use "I messages". No accusations or blaming of others.

You will be amazed at the answers you get to this question! We think it is clear to the students what they have done wrong. We have told them repeatedly! But you will see from the answers that they often have no idea what they are being punished for. Obviously the student has to understand what he did wrong before we can expect him to change his behavior.

2. What effect did my behavior have on my classmates and the teacher?

Causing disturbances at school is selfish behavior. The student is so busy with himself and with what HE personally wants that he forgets all the people around him and their needs. When he stops to think of the effects on his classmate and his teacher, he gets a different perspective and is lured out of his egoistic thinking.

3. What will I do in the future so that this kind of thing does not happen again?

This is a very important question. Here too, we sometimes set the bar too high. We simply assume that our students know how to behave in the way we expect. Very often this is not the case. Usually the pupil didn't do it wrong on purpose – it is simply the only way he knows how to react. And even if they now understand what they did wrong, we need to give them alternative courses of action for the future.

One of the ways we can help here is with the coaching session. We can suggest alternatives ways of acting and reacting. We can use brainstorming, replay the situation as a role play or present a new way of reacting to the same situation in the future in a guided fantasy.

The coaching session doesn’t take long and there are a lot of advantages involved. One of the main benefits is that the relationship between student and teacher is strengthened through this session. The student experiences supportive attention from the teacher and their respect for one another is enhanced.

Some ideas

Some time ago I was at a seminar in Tyrol. There were several courses taking place in the seminar house, and during the break at the buffet I met a teacher again by chance, who had been in my course about ten years ago. She told me:

> Your seminar totally changed my teaching. I still use a lot of the techniques we learned in my teaching and I am very happy with the results. But the most important thing I learned in your class was the fact that the lively, kinesthetic students simply don't understand what they are doing wrong. Now I look at them with different eyes. And that's why I enjoy and get along with them much better now.
>
> Anna M., grammar school

Questionnaire

At our school there is a penalty point system to help teachers to impose appropriate sanctions for various misdemeanors e.g. "coming late" = one penalty point, resistance to instructions = five points, etc. When a student has 20 points the parents are notified, for 40 points a teacher-parent-student-director discussion takes place and so on.

At the beginning I made excessive use of this system until I realized that I was actually harming myself and the class atmosphere by using it. It leads to teacher-student conflict.

I now use the three questions "What happened?", "What effects did my behavior have on my classmates and on the teacher", "What can I do differently in the future...", rather than giving penalty points and have had much better experiences with them. The students react positively and, with only a few exceptions, answer the questions. This has changed my standing within the class from a position of power to one of influence. Influence works so much better than power struggles! Thank you!

Christian G., high school

Table Leg Number 4:

Setting limits - giving support!

When a child is born, it is oriented exclusively to its own needs. In this way, he or she attains security and trust. Soon, however, the time comes when the child must learn that other p have needs which differ from their own. In order to achieve a balance between one's own and those of others requires empathy towards others as well as limits.

Limits give our students stability. They result in a harmonious and respectful as well as po atmosphere in a classroom where learning succeeds.

Our topics in this chapter are the creation of a "win-win" atmosphere, where teachers and stu treat each other with respect. This is brought about by setting clear boundaries and limi promoting a sense of self-responsibility and self-discipline among our students and by av power struggles in the classroom.

24

The power of influence: Everyone is a winner!

Let's start again with a story:

The wind and the sun

The wind and the sun had an argument about which of them would succeed in getting the lonely wanderer to take off his coat.

The wind blew and stormed, and the poor man pulled his coat ever tighter around his body.

Then it was the sun's turn. Lovingly she sent out her rays, and soon the man opened the top button of his coat, and a short time later he took off his coat.

We get to choose:
Wind or sun? Power or influence?

The sun had it much easier.
The traveler offered no resistance and immediately removed his coat

This is clearly a win-win situation.
And this is the situation we want to create in the classroom.

What is a win-win classroom?

In a "win-win" situation there are only winners and no losers.
Both sides are strong, but neither dominates.
We work together and not against each other.
We unite our strengths to find a common positive solution.

In a "win-win" classroom, the needs of everyone involved - both teachers and students - are met. Competition is eliminated. As a result, learning barriers disappear and the class works as a team toward common goals. Respectful, clear and specific boundaries are established. Within these boundaries there are autonomous choices that contribute to the students' sense of self-responsibility. Each individual is unique and contributes to the success of the class community with his or her own strengths, and each student has the opportunity to be successful. Every single person - both the students and the teacher - is responsible for their own behavior and also for the achievement of the jointly defined group goals. The students are satisfied and so is the teacher. Everyone is a winner.

Be pro-active and not reactive!

The school regulations and disciplinary measures that prevail in almost all schools are reactive. They consist of a list of unwanted and forbidden forms of behavior and a matching list of consequences that become increasingly negative the more often the rules are violated. Teachers become policemen and students are treated as criminals. This model is based on fear of the negative consequences and is the opposite of a pro-active, preventative approach, which requires self-disciplining behavior on the part of the students.

Discipline is reactive

The student does something negative, and the teacher has no choice but to react to it in order to eliminate the disturbance and restore the smooth running of the teaching process. The moment I have to discipline, I move from my sphere of influence to power. I am on the defensive. Sometimes that works. At least for the moment - But it does not enhance your charisma or aura of positive natural authority, which is the basis of positive classroom management.

Self-discipline is preventative and therefore proactive

The student who is self-disciplined shows a high level of emotional intelligence. He can take responsibility for his own actions. He is in control of his emotions and reactions and he is able to make his own decisions within the agreed limits. Learning self-discipline, i.e. taking responsibility for oneself and one's actions, is one of the most valuable gifts we can give our students.

Influence rather than power

Sometimes we have no choice but to use power.
It is our duty to lead the class efficiently. We must set limits to ensure the safety of our students and create a positive learning environment. If the gentle method of influence does not work, we have no choice but to move into the sphere of power.

For the students and for ourselves it is a great advantage to recognize possible problems before they arise and to nip them in the bud. When I use influence in the classroom, I work proactively and have the class under control. Problems are solved before they arise. The students become responsible and autonomous. I gain positive, natural authority and I can pass on some of the responsibility to the students. Therefore, in any area of classroom management, influence is always preferable to power.

What is the difference?

When I use power, I, and I alone, decide what to do. My counterpart or the others have no say in the matter. There is only one course of action and I determine what it will be. My reality is the only true one, and the others have to adapt.

When I use influence, I offer different choices. I set a common goal together with the class. Various routes are shown, but the choice of which path is chosen is left to the group. The teacher steers silently and unobtrusively in the background. She offers perspective and acceptable suggestions, while the freedom of choice remains with the students.

When I lead my students, leaving the decisions to them, they become independent and learn self-discipline. If I give them controlled freedom of decision, I avoid power struggles. Students love the feeling of being autonomous. They offer less resistance because, as we all learned in physics class...

Pressure generates counter-pressure

If I want Billy to change seats in the classroom and say, *"Billy, sit over there now!"* there are two ways Billy can respond to this challenge.

It may be that - let's take the positive variant first - Billy says:
"Yes, Mrs. Nitsche!" and he quietly takes the items on his desk and moves to the other seat. Of course, when this happens, I remain superficially calm. But inside I rejoice while thinking to myself, *"Hallelujah! Billy voluntarily changed seats, and now I don't need to do anything else here!"*

But it can also happen that Billy looks at me and says calmly, *"No, Mrs. Nitsche, I want to stay here."* And he stays put. If this happens, I must move into the sphere of power because his refusal jeopardizes my aura of positive, natural authority.

The basic question is: *"What did I do to contribute to this situation?"*

The answer: I have made a request for which there are only two answers: either *"Yes"* or *"No"*. If Billy is rebellious - and this is often the case with the age groups we deal with - he will answer with *"No"*. Billy feels, consciously or unconsciously, pressured by the challenge. He takes my request as an ultimatum and automatically resists.

There are two types of resistance:
When Billy clearly and unambiguously says *"no"*, he is actively resisting.
This form of resistance is relatively easy to deal with. A clear *"no"* is tangible.
I ask him, for example. *"Why are you saying 'no'?"* and the basis for a coaching session has been established.

The second type is passive resistance. We are confronted daily with this form of resistance in the classroom: *"I didn't do it!"*, *"I didn't understand the homework"*, etc. This form of resistance, which is vague and not so easily defined, is more difficult to counter.

And how do I get him to cooperate?

Fortunately, there are many roads leading to Rome, and there are several peaceful ways to get Billy to cooperate. Depending on the respective situation and my personal preference I can, for example:

- Ask him politely to change seats rather than giving him an order. A *"please"* or a *"thank you"* can work wonders.
- Explain to him why he should change seats,
- Make him aware of the advantages of the new seat,
- Have the other students change seats and let him sit where he is!
- Ask him for an alternative idea or solution,
- Give him a serious or astonished look,
- Wait in silence for him to get up and change seats,
- Decide if it is even worth your while getting into a power struggle with him,
- Have the neighbor, he was bothering or chatting with, move to a different seat.
- Use humor,
- Wordlessly give him a yellow card,
- Invite him verbally and nonverbally to take the new seat,
- Ask him to please come and help you with something,
- Smile at him while politely and firmly asking him to move,
- Offer him friendly, active "jump-start" help. Carry some of his things there for him.
- Give him a choice: *"You can sit here or there. Which seat do you prefer?"*
- Give the seat change a time-limit. e. g: *"Let's try it for two lessons."*
- pay attention to your choice of words: *"You may sit there"* instead of *"You must..."*
- Ask another student to switch places with him,
- Make eye contact, wag your pointer finger back and forth and shake your head *"No"*,
- Switch to another activity to distract his attention from the problem,
- Reduce the tension for the moment: *"Neither of us has anything to gain by arguing with each other now. Let's leave it for the moment. We can talk about it later."*

And so on and so forth. There are infinite possibilities. Your imagination should know no limits. Some ideas will fit, some won't. The art is to choose the right pro-active measure to suit the situation and the student!

And if it doesn't work...?

I hear you asking, *"What if it goes wrong and I have to discipline a student?"* Despite all our efforts, it will occasionally happen that I have to step out of the sphere of influence and into the sphere of power where disciplining will be necessary.

However, there are some general and very important guidelines that should be followed to avoid getting into a dangerous power struggle.

Never embarrass the student

The most important rule:
Only admonish and discipline a student in private. If you discipline a student in front of the class, he will be embarrassed This creates immediate resistance as he must save face in front of his peers. A small thing can very quickly become a big problem

Louanne Johnson, whose teacher story is featured in the film "Dangerous Minds", told in a webinar from Behavior Needs http://www.behaviourneeds.com/ how she took a disruptive high school student into the hallway:

> I told him: *"There are three possibilities: "You can change your behavior and go back into the classroom." "Or you can stand out here for a while and think it all through." Or you can go to the principal. That decision is your responsibility and I'm not going to make it for you. It's my job to help you become a successful person and a student, but you have to decide if that is what you want to be."*
>
> I went back into the classroom and he stayed there for a while. Before he re-entered the classroom, I insisted that he shake my hand and give me his word of honor that he would not disturb my lessons again. I told him: *"If you want, you can sit in the back of the classroom, do nothing and fail, but under no circumstances should you interfere with others, who want to learn, or hinder me in my work."*
>
> If he disturbed anyone again, I'd walk past him and quietly say, *"You gave me your word of honor."* Not once did a student fail to keep that promise. But it had to be his personal decision and not mine.

If necessary, use the discipline anchor. Stay calm and do not let yourself be drawn into a conversation. After the disturbance is past, continue with the lesson as if nothing had happened. As soon as the opportunity arises - e.g. when the students are busy with seatwork - speak to him privately: *"We both know, Billy, that what you did just now was not right. There will be consequences. But I want to take my time before we discuss the consequences, so that they are fair and considered. We could either talk after school today or tomorrow before school starts. Think about the time that's best for you and tell me at the end of the lesson."*

Stay calm and neutral

Accusations, insults and preaching are always out of place. In any kind of conflict situation, an emotional reaction on your part has the same effect as pouring gasoline on fire If we expect emotional intelligence from our students, we must of course be able to control our own emotions.

Allow the student time to cool down

Even if you have kept calm while performing the anchor, the student is likely to be worked up and excited after having been disciplined. In order to achieve a lasting effect and above all to choose consequences that are suited to the offence, it is essential that this is done without emotions. Therefore we need to give the student (and ourselves) time to calm down.

Especially the non-verbal messages contribute to the atmosphere of the conversation. Your gestures, movements, facial expressions and your voice express your support and lead the student from an emotional to a logical state. Speak softly, slowly and correctly. Speaking loudly or ranting is confrontational and undermines your aura of positive natural authority. Students find it difficult to respect a teacher who jumps up and down in front of the class like a little Rumpelstiltskin. In addition, when you act and speak emotionally, you give control of the situation to the student. He becomes your reflection and will also responds loudly. Maybe he gets angry and ignores you. Or maybe he thinks, *"What else can I do to make her angry?"* and the negative behavior is intensified.

A time-out spot

A good opportunity to cool down is provided with a "time-out" area. We have all experienced it: The student who gets emotional in a conflict with you or with classmates and gets totally out of control. Daniel Goleman describes in his book "Emotional Intelligence" that self-control is an important characteristic of emotional maturity in such situations. It is important that we help our students recognize the moment when they need to say *"Stop!"* and withdraw until they have their emotions under control.

If this happens in the classroom, they need a place where the pupil concerned can withdraw – immediately and without having to ask for permission. Perhaps you would like to discuss something with an upset student in a quiet moment and come to an agreement.

It is usually sufficient if the student is allowed to leave the classroom for a short time and stands in front of the door until he/she has calmed down. A teacher told me that while clearing out the garage she saved an old parasol and rather than throw it away, she brought it to school. There she put it up in a corner of her primary school class. Whenever a student felt that he had to step out for a short time for emotional reasons, there was always room behind the umbrella. Another middle school teacher bought a canopy bed net and draped it from the ceiling around a chair in the back of the classroom. After she and the class had talked about emotional outbursts, they agreed that if someone felt he was going to explode, he could sit down in that seat and stay there until he was calmed down enough to return to his seat (the class was very surprised when the first person to take the seat was their teacher!)

A change of location can work wonders!

Change the location, change the emotion.

Some of my colleagues and I each have a small green folder for emotionally charged situations. For example, if I noticed that Billy is upset and in danger of getting emotionally out of control, I would call him to my desk and ask him to bring my green folder to Mrs. Miller in room 227. I would write a note in the folder, for example: *"Greetings from Pearl."* Billy then went on his way with the folder, and when my colleague saw the green folder, she knew that Billy needed some time and space to calm down. She kept him with her for a while and also gave him some task to do. That way he experienced a change of location and also a little time to calm his emotions. When he then came back to my classroom, he had calmed down enough that I could talk to him reasonably either at that moment or a little later.

> **Time-out table**
> We set up this table in the hall near the door to our classroom at the beginning of the year. If it gets loud or is simply too much for a pupil, he can if he wants to go out and sit at this table without asking first. After two or three minutes I go outside and ask briefly what is going on or if it is better now.
>
> Corina K., elementary school

Let the student have the last word

Our students very often have strong auditory tendencies. They like to talk and when it comes to discussion, auditory people ALWAYS want to have the last word. If the teacher is also auditory, this can lead to problems and an escalation of the discussion!

Let's listen to this:

Auditory teacher: *Susi and Magdalene!*
Will you please stop talking!

Susi: *We didn't say anything!*

Auditory teacher: *What do you mean, you didn't say anything?!*
I see you and hear you talking!

Magdalena: *She started it!*

Auditory teacher: *Magdalena, I'm not blind!*
And I'm not deaf either!

Billy: (sitting on the other side of the room)
Yes, that's right, Mrs. N., I saw it!
Magdalena really didn't say anything.

And so on and so forth.
Auditory students and auditory teachers. This tends to lead to an escalation. And soon the whole class will be talking! Or Susi and Magdalena say something cheeky. Then the teacher has no choice but to discipline them.

The solution?

> **Let the student have the last word - at the very beginning, before the situation escalates.**

Instead of allowing such a scene, it is better to let the auditory student have the last word at the very beginning of the interaction. It could sound like this:

Teacher:	*Susy and Magdalene!* *Will you please stop talking!*
Susy:	*We didn't say anything!*

The teacher is silent. She stretches out a hand towards Magdalena and Susi and looks away at the same time as she continues the lesson.

So Susi is satisfied - she has had the last word.
And the teacher can continue with the lesson undisturbed.

Offer choices

Students love choices - and they are allergic to ultimatums and commands. The only time a student deliberately misbehaves is when he or she is involved in a power struggle. Therefore, statements like *"Do it now!"* or *"Because I said so!"* should be avoided at all costs. Look for compromises, alternatives and choices. If students are allowed to make their own decisions, they will feel autonomous and thus become responsible.

In a classroom power struggle, there are no winners, only losers. Resistance disappears and personal responsibility grows when we give choices.

Some ideas

- Give two or three specific choices: *"Do we want to discuss this after class this afternoon or tomorrow before school? Think it over, and then tell me what you prefer." The* important thing is that you're happy with all the choices, no matter which one he chooses!
- Tell them that homework is no longer compulsory. For every homework assignment turned in the student will get a point. *"There will be 35 homework sessions per semester. 32 to 35 points is an "A", 28 to 32 points is a „B".*
- Make one of for example five test grades a bonus grade. "*There will be five tests this semester. Four of the five grades will count. Each student may choose one grade that will not count toward the final grade."*
- Distribute one "free card" per student. They may use their card during the semester to skip a compulsory task (except for tests).

Show understanding

Let the students feel that you are aware of both their duties and their needs. Treat your students with respect and consideration. Talk to them as you would talk to others in your circle of friends. Show understanding and empathy: *"I understand that you do not want to do this now. But it must be done. Is there anything I can do to make it easier for you?"*

Always differentiate between behavior and person

If a student does something he is not supposed to do, he is not a bad person. He just did something wrong at the wrong time. We know that, but sometimes our students don't understand. They often think that if we get angry or rebuke them, we don't like them anymore. Therefore, as soon as it is appropriate, you should smile at the student or give some sign that you still like him.

With a smile you can say: *"Just because I like you, I still can't allow such behavior in our classroom." "Are we getting along well again?"* or *"Fortunately we've got that sorted out now!"* Or, even better, just smile and say nothing. You will notice the relieved look on the pupil's face! Show them that you like them as a human being and not just as a student.

What's past is past!

Back when I started teaching, I sometimes had difficulty getting the attention of the class at the beginning of the lesson. Unfortunately at that time, I was not yet aware of these techniques, nevertheless I also "ritualized" the beginning of my lesson. First I walked into the room. I stood on the podium as was customary at that time. Not a single student noticed me. They laughed, talked to each other, continued eating their snacks and playing games. To get their attention, I slammed the class book loudly on the teacher's desk. Out of sheer surprise, they jumped a few centimeters into the air - and I had their attention.

The second part of my repertoire at that time was that I then scolded them in general for about two minutes. I didn't single anyone out – just with the entire class: *"Everytime I come in here ..."*. I then stopped scolding and returned to normal.

When I told this story many years later in a seminar in Tyrol, a seasoned teacher asked me: *"But Pearl, why did you scold them? They were already quiet. You should have praised them."* And how right he was! His words represented a major turning point in my career - and they also helped me a lot in my private life!

Many of us have the tendency to scold the students or others AFTER their negative behavior has ended. We believe we need to give a lecture so that the misbehavior no longer occurs. The problem is that our counterpart often closes his ears. And the next day, the exact same thing happens again. The situation worsens, because by scolding we reinforce the negative instead of the positive behavior.

What's past is past!
And if I praise the students for the right behavior or for correcting the wrong behavior, the chance is much greater that the positive behavior will happen again!

Praise the behavior you want to see in the classroom!

I tested this technique almost every day in my second stage of school teaching at the middle school. The results were excellent! Justified praise works wonders! You can see it in the faces and postures of the students. They literally grow a few centimeters when praised. And when they are scolded, they close their ears, figuratively and in reality!

Set high expectations

When I was employed at the bilingual middle school, another school, a high school, borrowed me as a native speaker once a week for a few years. I taught there a few hours a week in a charming, eager to learn class. Every lesson with these children was a pleasure for me.

At the end of the third school year I learned that I would return to teaching exclusively at my home school in the coming school year. Therefore I said goodbye to the children in this class on the last day of school. I told them how much I had enjoyed being a teacher in their class and that I would really miss them in the coming school year. The expressions on their faces ranged from totally surprised to almost shocked. When I asked them for an explanation, they said: *"But you are the only one who says something like that. Everyone else just tells us how naughty we are."*

Now I was surprised! Later I asked my colleagues and they told me that this class was, in their opinion, "the worst class in the school. And they reminded them of this almost daily". But why were they so good then in my lessons?

It suddenly became clear to me. If we tell the students that they're naughty, that is exactly what they will be. If we show them that we notice when they are good and praise them for it, we reinforce this positive behavior and they are indeed good. It is often our attitude that makes the difference. It has a direct influence on the behavior of the students and acts as a self-fulfilling prophecy!

Expect positive behavior

When my own children were teenagers and went out at night, I often said, *"Please be back by midnight."* A limit was set. But what I avoided saying was, for example, *"Please be back by midnight. And if you're not, this and that and that and that will happen..."* For me personally this sounds like a challenge to be late. It also expresses my expectation that they might be late. I am suggesting negative behavior.

Expect the positive. Express these expectations to the students. And see what happens. As a student once told me: *"Don't worry, Mrs. Nitsche. We won't disappoint you."*

Roman teaches at a Viennese secondary school and he wrote the following to me in an email:

Here are a few of my experiences where I implemented some of the techniques you taught us in your seminars.

- When a student needs to be admonished, I first look at him "knowingly", followed by a friendly smile. I stand on my discipline anchor while doing this.

  It's utterly amazing how well this works! The student already knows what he did wrong, and the smile is enough. He then smiles back at me - and stops the unwanted behavior. The matter is settled! It's not necessary to say a word!

- Using the techniques you taught us, I speak much more quietly than I used to. Student feedback:"Mr. D., you've been much calmer lately and so kind. We like that!"

- I also perceive myself as more relaxed and positive. Luckily, I can't smile and feel bad at the same time!

- I now have a completely different perspective concerning provocative students. I I have come to realize that no student intentionally annoys a teacher. I no longer get annoyed and therefore have much less stress. The long day at school has become less exhausting.

- If a student needs to be admonished, I stand close to him and speak very quietly so that the others do not hear what I am saying. This helps students to save face in front of their peers and they react promptly with no resistance.

- I often offer behavioral alternatives, for example: "You can stay in class and behave as I expect you to or you can sit in the hallway and come back when you've calmed down." The result: The student starts to think - rather than overreact.

25

Set boundaries - Provide Security!

One complaint that I often hear is that children often come to school without having experienced any limits in their upbringing. Parents today are sometimes stressed and insecure. They often feel very helpless because they do not dare to set limits for their children. We live in a consumer world and many parents are afraid of losing the love of their children if they cannot fulfil the wishes of their offspring. They are in competition with other parents who give their children more pocket money and toys. Or they do not want to repeat their own childhood experiences with rigid and inappropriate limits for their own children. Out of uncertainty about what is right and what is not right, parents often lose the necessary clarity and avoid setting limits where they would be appropriate.

As a result, not only the parents, but also the teachers, who now have to cope with these children at school, feel overwhelmed. Both have a task: parents must learn to get a feeling for what is right, to trust their own competency and then to act responsibly. We teachers are confronted with the reality of teaching some children who have not experienced limits and it is our task to cope with it. Blame and complaints about the poor upbringing of many of our students are partly justified. But complaining about it gets us nowhere. Here - as with so many situations in our everyday lives - it is important to first define the problem and then work on it in a solution-oriented manner.

Limits instead of rules

We are used to - and this is a good thing - setting up class rules at the beginning of a school year. In most schools there are also school rules, and very often, be it class rules or school regulations, the consequences for exceeding the rules are very clearly stated. In most cases, the more rules a school has, the more behavioral problems there are. We become policemen.

I would like to propose here that we keep the concept of "rules", but that we give them a new name: "limits". Now you may well ask yourself: "Limits*? Rules? Isn't that the same thing?"* And I would have to answer, *"Yes, it is. Only the perspective is different. And very often that perspective is what determines whether the measures work or not."*

Pro-active limits provide new perspectives

Boundaries are proactive because they inform students how far they can go until a positive advantage is withdrawn. As discussed earlier, pro-active measures are ALWAYS better than re-active ones. To be pro-active, we need to look at the concept of discipline from a new perspective. This is not about punitive behavior measures that focus on what students have done wrong, but about preventive measures that aim at maintaining a positive environment while avoiding conflicts and disturbances.

When I work proactively, I teach my students self-discipline. Disciplining a student who has done something wrong is a temporary solution and brings only short-term relief. If my students, however, are practiced in disciplining themselves, future disruptions are prevented. By teaching students to practice self-discipline they have learned a valuable life skill. And my role as a teacher has changed. I am no longer in the role of a "policewoman", but I am a guide and am showing the students the way to success.

Rules emphasize the negative. Limits emphasize the positive.

A rule is a ban. It tells me what I cannot do. If the rule is broken, there are negative consequences. The student does something that is not correct and I react punitively.

A limit, however, is a proactive measure. Here the emphasis is on the positive factors and events at school. "WIIFM" or, as I said before, *"What's in it for me?"* This concept, which stems from the advertising world, is the basis for all motivation. My students and I decide and list what we appreciate in the classroom. What do they and I want to experience every day so that our class is enjoyable? Once we decide what we want the classroom experience to be, we draw the "boundaries" around this. The advantages remain as long as the boundaries are respected. If they are exceeded, the benefit is immediately – at least for a short while - retracted.

A rule emphasizes the negative that happens to me if I violate it.
A limit emphasizes the positive which I can maintain as long as I respect the limits.

I present it to my students like this:

> *"Imagine our classroom is like a big football field. On this field are all the benefits and privileges we enjoy every day. When we are here on the field, it is good for all of us. All around the field are the boundaries. We have to respect these boundaries so that we can continue to enjoy the positive aspects. Everything that happens here on the field is allowed. But if anyone crosses the boundaries of the field, the benefits are immediately - at least for the short term - cancelled."*

An example of a rule would be:

"If you don't put the puzzle pieces away properly, I'll take the puzzle out of the play corner."

An example of a border:

"If you put the puzzle pieces in order, we can leave the puzzle in the play corner."

The difference is subtle - but powerful!
The emphasis is changed from negative to positive. This is an important difference. The students and not the teacher are responsible. The decision is left up to the students. At the same time, the teacher still has everything under control, because he has chosen the limits within which the pupils can choose.

Another example:

You want to read a story to your class, but the students are too loud at the moment. Say in a calm and neutral voice: *"I want to read an exciting story. But we can only do that if it is as quiet as a mouse. At the moment it is too loud. My offer to read you the story is valid for twenty seconds."*

Look at the clock and wait calmly. Try to look expressionless and do not repeat your words.

If it gets quiet, praise them and start reading. They've earned it.
If it doesn't get quiet, just close the book wordlessly and put it aside. Stay neutral. Don't say anything more than, *"Well, it didn't work out today, but I'm sure it'll be better tomorrow."* And immediately begin another activity.

Or:
You and your colleagues are on ski trip in the mountains with your students. The advantage is the ski course. The limit is absolutely no alcohol consumption. If the limit is exceeded, the student is sent home.

Or:
The students visit the library. Martin discovers an adventure book and spends the whole lesson reading it. He wants to borrow the book. The advantage is that each student can borrow three books from the library. Martin has three other library books at home. Therefore he must return at least one book before he can borrow the desired adventure book.

Or:
Susi always monopolizes class discussions. The other pupils don't have much of a chance to get a word in edgewise. At the next discussion give Susi five matches/coins/paper clips. For every contribution she makes, she hands in one item. When her items are gone, she is not allowed to continue to contribute to the discussion. The advantage is to be allowed to participate in discussions. The limit is the five "speaking objects" she has at her disposal.

Or:
The advantage: the students can choose where they sit in the classroom.
The limit: If they disturb the lessons by chatting with their neighbor, the teacher will move their seat.

Or:
If a homework assignment is not submitted, there is a one-day grace period. If the student turns the homework in without being reminded by the teacher, it will be accepted. If this limit is exceeded, the homework will not be evaluated.

The most important thing is to stay calm. No accusations, no ranting, no threats. Don't get involved in any discussions. The students have made the decision, and the responsibility is theirs. You have given them the choice. The students, not you, are responsible. There is no anger and no guilt.

It is also very important to stress that things could be different tomorrow or sometime soon. If I take away a benefit forever, I take away any motivation to do things differently in the future!

Limits provide a sense of security

Limits are like traffic lights. They show students how far they can go and when to stop. If they don't stop at the red light, they lose their license for a while! Just like in normal life. Borders are pro-active structures, they are signals or rituals. They create a feeling of security and safety, qualities that our children often lack nowadays. Of course, your students will sometimes test the boundaries - that's normal. But they will appreciate the structure and the possibility to make autonomous decisions.

What are the characteristics of a good limit?

- **A limit provides clarity:** it clearly states what the students are supposed to do and the benefits of doing so are made clear.

- **A limit represents a "win-win" situation:** Adhering to the limit is to everyone's advantage. We are all winners, and there are no losers.

- **A limit is pro-active:** A boundary should nip a problem - **BEFORE** it actually becomes a problem - in the bud.

- **A limit is expressed in positive terms:** It emphasizes the benefits that everyone can enjoy by respecting the limit.

- **If a limit is not respected, the benefit is withdrawn IMMEDIATELY - for a limited period of time:** After a limit is set, it is important that it is observed without exception. Avoid warnings. They are a waste of time. When we issue warnings, we take away the power of the limit. We take back the responsibility on ourselves rather than passing it on to the students!

Limits are respectful. They are based on mutual consideration. They do not seem threatening. They provide emotional security in the classroom. They enable positive and negative consequences in a peaceful environment. Students appreciate them, and teachers do too.

How do you set limits?

I usually let the students set up their own class rules or boundaries, under my guidance of course. This contributes a lot to a feeling of autonomy and fulfils the students' basic need: to be self-determined and autonomous. We then write the rules on a poster and everyone signs it.

A second variation that I sometimes use is that I myself specify the three basic rules:

1. Respect yourself.
2. Respect others.
3. Respect the school and all that it contains.

These are actually all the rules and boundaries you need.

The essential point is that students understand the word "respect". As discussed above, many of our students come from families or environments where respectful interaction is not common. Therefore, the first thing we need to do is teach them the meaning of this word. We can use techniques such as Derrick's poster that says "100% respect"; we can make a poster on the subject of "respect in the classroom"; we can role-play small scenes that show respectful behavior; we can have discussions about it. And, very importantly, we can identify alternative, respectful forms of action. Instead of focusing on something they are not supposed to do, we show them what we expect them to do.

Tomorrow is another day!

This is a very important statement and crucial for the success of setting limits rather than rules! "Tomorrow is another day!" Thus it is always possible to start anew. The focus is on the behavior and not on the person itself. And the door to improvement is always open.

Borders are like the opening hours of a supermarket.
You want to go shopping and are standing in front of the supermarket at 6 a.m. sharp. But the store is open between 7 a.m. and 7 p.m. During this time you can shop and have your choice among all the great products inside the store. If you arrive earlier than 7 a.m. or later than 7p.m., however, the store is closed. You will not receive anything. That's the deal. No one is going to scold you. You will not be punished. The store is closed.

And what time will you be there tomorrow?
Probably between 7:00 a.m. and 7:00 p.m.
This is the beauty of setting limits: Tomorrow is a new day!

Some ideas

Playing football in class

In my first year as the homeroom teacher of a middle school class, I was looking for a way to have the 13 year old boys in my class get more movement during recess. In our school we had two "big" morning breaks. During one of them the kids were allowed to go to the roof terrace, play games and let off steam. However, this was only possible in good weather. During the second break nothing concrete was planned.

Autumn and winter were long and wet, so a solution was urgently needed. I suggested to the students that we build a small soccer field in the classroom. We marked the goals with masking tape and to make room for the game, two tables had to be moved out of the way. As in every soccer match, there were rules, of course. And at the end of the break everything had to be cleared away quickly. If these limits were not respected, there was no football match for a week. The arrangement worked well and the children were enthusiastic and much more balanced than before.

Sonja S., secondary school

Student Participation

The students participate in most decisions: e.g. where to go on the hiking day, which class rules they would like to have, what is important to them in a good class community. We then do the following activity, in which they can move, talk to each other and evaluate their ideas.

Each student writes the rule that is most important to her on her card. I turn on music and they move through the classroom with a pencil and the card. When the music stops, each student looks for a partner and they read out their sentences to each other. Discuss why they find this rule to be important. They write down a score of 1 to 3 for each rule. Then they continue on their way.

After a number of rounds, each person adds up the points on their card.

Finally, the card with the highest score is determined and the remaining cards are taped to the board in the order of points. We use these points to set up a list of rules for our class in the coming school year.

Andrea W., middle school

Role plays

Role playing games offer a very effective way of setting class boundaries and rules. Role plays enable pupils to see a situation from different perspectives. That makes it easier to come up with solutions and alternative courses of action. Although the problem itself is not new, the game enables the students to look at it objectively with different eyes from a new perspective.

How do we keep our materials in order? What do we do if there is an accident during recess? What should we do if there is bullying in class? What can you do if you want to play a game, but nobody has invited you to play along?

A class should have a maximum of six rules or boundaries. Otherwise, the boundaries become confusing and unclear. And don't expect everyone to understand all the boundaries at once. Don't do it all in one day. Choose one item per day. Discuss this with the pupils and work on this boundary in detail. Look at it from as many different perspectives as possible.

When you have presented all the rules, you can form small teams that secretly choose one example from the poster. They should think up two short skits: one skit should show how it should be and the other how it should NOT be. The others then have to guess which rule has been chosen. Or the teacher can give a mini-role play demonstration showing how NOT to line up in a row of two, for example. Make it all dramatic and funny. The students will never forget it.

Or do a short and fun quiz about the class rules, for example:
What materials should you bring to class every day?

a) A cheese sandwich, a comic book and a cell phone
b) A hairbrush, lipstick and a mirror
c) A fountain pen, the English book and your homework.
d) Your hamster and a bar of chocolate

Have the students make a poster:

Design a poster on class rules

Together we set up class rules for the drawing lesson. I then wrote them on the board and the pupils had to design posters demonstrating these rules. All the rules had to be written on the board, they could be shown in pictures or words, and the poster should not cause any negative feelings.

In the next lesson I hung up all the drawings so that the names of the students were not visible. Each drawing was numbered and the students had to choose their favorite by the number. The group whose drawing got the most points was the winner and they got a small prize. In this way, they creatively learned the rules.

Claudia S., middle school

And what about the consequences?

If you set limits instead of rules, the answer to this question is very simple: The consequence: The advantage is withdrawn for a short time. The consequences are carried out consistently (there is a reason why these two words, "consequence" and "consistent" are so similar!) and without any excitement.

Very important: the consequence is not simply pulled out of thin air. There should be a direct connection between the offence and the consequence.

- If a student forgets her crayons, she cannot paint a picture in color.
- If a student disturbs others, he must sit somewhere else.

The student is responsible for the behavior she displays. She is rewarded for positive behavior with the advantages the classroom provides and if she does not respect the limits, she is "punished" with the short-term withdrawal of these advantages.

Effective consequences

- have a **connection** with the rule that was broken,
- are **predictable** for the student,
- are **fair** and **proportionate to the rule that was broken,**
- **are not directed against the child, but against his actions**,
- **never** come **without warning** and are **limited in time,**
- are only used **after everyone has had the opportunity to "to cool down."**

You can learn a lot from a mistake. That's also what the consequences are there for. But this only works if the consequences are announced without anger and excitement, but with empathy. The dignity of the student is respected and is unconditional. That is one hundred percent respect.

The table top

The "win-win" classroom

The Win Win Classroom

Now the foundation has been laid: the carpet and four firm legs. And the moment has come when we can set the tabletop, which is labeled with the words "Win-Win" classroom, on it. Now the classroom management runs by itself. Self-discipline has replaced discipline measures. This is a classroom where students and teachers can learn and work together in a harmonious and respectful environment.

On the following pages you can read reports by teachers who have succeeded in placing the win-win tabletop on the stable frame we have constructed.

Hello, Pearl,

...my classroom is very different today than it was before we met. I don't need to discipline anymore. The atmosphere is calm. The students respond very well to non-verbal communication techniques, and I am using anchors with a great deal of success. The students are aware when things get too turbulent or too loud. It is no longer necessary for me to admonish them. They take over the responsibility and regulate the atmosphere in the classroom themselves.

Dissociating has helped me a lot. Now I can dissociate in precarious situations and thus keep a clear overview. I used to take things much too personally. Today it is different. I am much more objective, which is good for the students and for me too.

My teaching has changed in that I talk much less than I did before. I don't need to talk so much because now the students listen to me. Everything has become much clearer and the quality of my teaching has improved.

Anita S., secondary school

Dear Pearl,

...in retrospect, I look back on the first eight years as a teacher as my teaching ice age! I was alone in the classroom, had no knowledge for dealing with pubescent children. My colleagues were constantly at war with one another. We had very few teaching aids. There was no music room etc.

My life changed.
First of all, I changed schools.
And then I met you and learned about your techniques.

The first time I saw you in front of the seminar group it was as if a big light went on in my head. I immediately recognized myself in you! When I spoke, the palms of my hands pointed upwards, my head was slightly tilted to the side. My whole being resonated rhythmically in your flood of words! Yes, your words spoke to me. I knew a bit about body language from other seminars I had attended, but I had never put two and two together to realize its relevance to my everyday life.

For example, the difference between an inviting voice, which invites others to participate and a decisive voice, used to gain the class's attention or to discipline. I had been using these voices unconsciously for years. But now they became valuable tools I could use on a conscious level.

A new life began for me. A happier one! From now on, your messages resounded in my ears. They were my daily companions. The more internalized they became, the more pleasurable teaching and school became for me and my students!

Group rapport
Fortunately, I have been teaching "only" music at my school for a number of years now. In my classes I can use, practice and consolidate the skills I have acquired from the seminars on a daily basis.

My musical "warm ups" at the beginning of the lessons create wonderful group rapport! Singing and playing instruments within the group offer countless possibilities for fun-filled cooperation. As we discussed in the seminar - the class becomes a team.

Attention anchor

Usually the children are charged and full of energy after singing a song. In order to get their attention again, I use my attention anchors. I silently point with one hand to the smiley face hanging on the wall. Or I simple wait in a very calm way while standing on the spot I call my attention anchor.

Discipline anchor

Occasionally - fortunately this is happening less and less - I use the discipline anchor: There I put everything I'm holding down, move in the direction of the discipline anchor. My palms are facing the floor, my posture is stiff, and I slowly look around the classroom. The result is absolute calm. The acting part is very important here! At first it was a problem for me to then go back to teaching with joy and singing as if nothing had happened. But it works better each time!

Keep the teaching material "clean"!

This was an eye-opener for me. I am very careful with this. No more copying song lyrics as punishment. Never again! Your words are always in my ears: "If a student has to copy a lesson, he becomes resentful and it could happen that he then rejects music class. Music is so important to me and I want it to be that way for my students too!

Dear Pearl, keep up the good work. I cannot put into words how grateful I am for all these insights and for this knowledge! Thank you so very much.

Pia S., music teacher in a secondary school

Dear Pearl and Derrick,

...sometime, a few years ago, I met you, Pearl, at a big event for the introduction to "Nonverbal Classroom Management". I wrote down several easy to implement tips, tried them out at school and shortly afterwards I enthusiastically attended my first seminars with you.

At that time I had just taken over a terrible 4th grade class (today I know, thanks to you, that there is no such thing!) and I was desperate. I started using your techniques. I used music to calm myself and my class down. I worked with anchors and strategies. The tips helped me a lot and slowly my attitude toward the children began to change. By Christmas I suddenly realized I had grown very fond of the class I used to dread and they had grown fond of me!

As a rookie teacher, I did not feel comfortable when meeting with the children's parents. However, in the course of your seminars, I slowly began to recognize the hidden messages behind what they were saying. I learned to hold back and not to react intuitively. I did my best to understand the parents and their concerns.

Nowadays I am no longer afraid of parent meetings. Actually I find them quite beneficial. That doesn't mean that I love all the parents I speak to. There is still one mother I find it very difficult to get along with. But then I simply imagine "The little Pearl" that you gave us. She is always sitting on my left shoulder and whispers good tips to me in difficult situations! It's amazing how well that works. I am no longer personally offended. I was even able to end a conversation with this mother with a big smile!

Yes, the smile. This is the biggest secret I learned in your seminars, and I have made it into my life motto! It's incredible what a simple smile can do! I try to always enter the classroom with a smile on my face and to smile at each child as they are leaving the room. And I hope you can imagine what a pleasant atmosphere we have in the class! If I am angry, I do show it. But even then only briefly. I always make it clear that I am angry because of a situation and never with the child.

The children love guided fantasy as well as the suggestopedic stories on your website. These stories are my personal hobbyhorse. Last school year we worked on the stories about the German articles, the text on traffic education, Friedensreich Hundertwasser and my own about the artist Franz Marc. (www.pearls-of-learning.com)

... but the most important thing I learned in the many seminars I attended with you was actually that my whole inner attitude changed from a negative to a positive one! I have much more confidence in myself than before. Yes, I now even believe I can work with "children with social and emotional needs" and I am attending a university course on this very subject. Thank you.

Verena W., elementary school and integration teacher

The important afterword

We started with a story, and I would like to end this book with a story as well:

The Fly

I am writing this book in Thailand, where I am currently on a "writing vacation". I have rented a small house here, and since it is a hot day today, I am working in the living room right now. I look out over the sea and the boats that are anchored there. It's a peaceful scene. But only a few meters away from me, I hear the desperate sound of a fight between life and death. A fly is trying with all its strength and energy to fly through the glass pane of my window. Its efforts are in vain.

The hum of the wings tells me the fly's strategy: "Try harder." But it doesn't work.

The fly tries harder and harder, but its desperate attempts offer no hope for survival. It doesn't have a chance. No matter how hard it tries, it won't be able to break through the glass. But it keeps trying and trying, and it won't give up.

The fly is doomed to failure. It will die there on the windowsill.

The tragic irony is that only a few meters away, the door is open. Five seconds of flying, and the little creature could reach the outside world that it is so desperately seeking. Only a fraction of the effort it is now using would be necessary to solve the problem and achieve freedom.

It's the same with us:
The opportunity to become free is there. We just have to take it.

New perspectives offer solutions

Why doesn't the fly try another way? Why does it insist that this idea, combined with more effort, offers the only chance of success? Why doesn't it try something else for once?

Obviously the fly believes that this is the only solution. It only sees this one way out. But more effort or trying more often or harder will not necessarily bring more success.

It's quite simple:
If I do the same thing over and over again, I will get exactly the same results over and over again. In order for me to do something new, I must first look at the situation from a different perspective.

We don't have to try so hard. We can go home at the end of the school day with more energy than we had in the morning when the first bell rang. Let us not take on the role of policemen who have to enforce order and discipline, but let us act as companions who give our students the tools for a happy and responsible life. Let us not try to fly through the glass, but rather experience new perspectives. Another perspective sometimes works wonders.

If you now look at the school, your students and teaching with different eyes, this book, one of my life works, has been a success.

This is my wish for you and for our children.

Contact information

I hope you enjoyed this book and got some good ideas for enriching your lessons!

If you want to send me comments, suggestions, new ideas or anchors, I would be very happy about an e-mail.

Our books are available from Amazon and in bookstores.

If you would like more information about our institute and the **courses we offer**, please visit my website:

www.pearls-of-learning.com
or write to
pearl.nitsche@chello.at

We have a fan page on **Facebook**: "pearls of learning", where I post every second to third day. Some of the posting are in English and some in German. If you are on Facebook and you like the page, we would be happy if you click o "Like". If you are not on Facebook, you can still visit the page at

www.facebook.com/pearls.of.learning

look at.

There are also some excellent short films about our techniques on **YouTube,** search criterion: Pearl Nitsche.

And of course, the best thing would be to meet you personally in a seminar (or to see you again)!